EH50 E7 LANG
34/23

Literacy and Orality

To
'Goosh' Andrzejewski

*in grateful appreciation of his continuing contribution to the field of literacy and
orality, and his warm and generous help to his fellow workers*

Literacy and Orality

*Studies in the
Technology of Communication*

Ruth Finnegan

Basil Blackwell

Copyright © Ruth Finnegan, 1988

First published 1988

Basil Blackwell Ltd
108 Cowley Road, Oxford, OX4 1JF, UK

Basil Blackwell Inc.
432 Park Avenue South, Suite 1503
New York, NY 10016, USA

British Library Cataloguing in Publication Data

Finnegan, Ruth
Literacy and orality: studies in the
technology of communication.
1. Communication
I. Title
001.51   P90

ISBN 0–631–15626–7

Library of Congress Cataloging in Publication Data

Finnegan, Ruth H.
Literacy and orality: studies in the technology of communication/
Ruth Finnegan
    p.   cm.
Some essays published previously.
Bibliography: p.
Includes index.
    1. Communication.   2. Literacy.   3. Oral tradition.   I. Title.
PN91.F49   1986   302.2'2—dc19   07-29960

ISBN 0–831–15626–7: $49.95 (U.S.)

Typeset in 10 on 12 pt Ehrhardt
by Opus, Oxford
Printed in Great Britain

Contents

Preface

This volume is a collection of papers written between 1969 and 1984 on various themes to do with literacy and orality. It focuses on specific aspects and debates relating to this complex subject, in particular on arguments about the significance of oral and written forms of communication for human culture and thought (do they bring about a great divide in human development between 'oral' and 'literate' stages of society?), and on the relevance of studies of their cognitive, literary and artistic significance for these controversies. The papers are diverse in their origins and coverage, but represent a relatively consistent (if developing) standpoint and philosophy. I have tried to make this approach more explicit and set it in the context of the wider literature and of the current debates about information technology in the newly written Introduction.

The original versions of the papers appeared as follows: chapter 2 as 'Communication and Technology' in an Open University teaching text (Social Science Foundation Course D101, Unit 8), Open University Press, Milton Keynes, 1975 (minimally revised and with the removal of the direct teaching and self-test material); chapter 3 as 'Attitudes to speech and language among the Limba of Sierra Leone' in *Odu* n.s., 2, 1969, Institute of African Studies, University of Ile-Ife, Nigeria; chapter 4 as 'Literacy versus non-literacy; the Great Divide?' in R. Horton and R. Finnegan (eds), *Modes of Thought*, Faber, 1973; chapter 5 as a paper at the Convegno Internazionale, 'Oralità: cultura, letteratura, discorso', Urbino, 1980 (later published as 'Oral composition and oral literature in the Pacific' in B. Gentili and G. Paione (eds), *Oralità*, Edizioni dell' Ateneo, Rome, 1985); chapter 6 as 'Oral literature and writing in the South Pacific' in Norman Simms (ed.), *Oral and traditional literature, Pacific Quarterly Moana*, 7, 2, 2 (Outrigger Publishers, Hamilton, New Zealand); chapter 7 as a paper at the International Council for Traditional Music Conference on 'The Oral and the Literate in Music', the 3rd ICTM Colloquium, Tokyo, 1984 (later published as 'The relations between composition and performance: three alternative modes' in Tokumaru Yoshihiko and Yamaguti Osamu (eds), *The Oral and the Literate in Music*,

Academia Music, Tokyo, 1986); chapter 8 as a paper on 'Orality and literacy: some problems of definition and research' at the International Conference on Transmission in Oral and Written Traditions, Australian National University, Canberra, 1981 (previously unpublished).

I have not rewritten the papers for this volume, apart from the occasional minimal updating of references to help readers to locate more recent work, and brief introductions relating them to the argument running through this book. They therefore appear much as they did when they were first written and thus, with the exception of chapter 8 (revised rather than totally recast), they in the main reflect the debates of the time when they were first composed. The Introduction puts them in the framework of more recent research and controversy, in particular relating my discussion of the traditional technologies of speech and writing to contemporary debates about new electronic forms of information processing.

Acknowledgements

I have amassed so many intellectual debts over the years that I will not even attempt to list them here, with the sole exception of that to my husband, David Murray, who even more than others lived with the development of the thoughts here, and shared some of the fieldwork. Many others have inspired and helped me over the years, including some with whose conclusions I sometimes argue. Those to whom I am most indebted for both agreements and disagreements will recognize their names and their contributions here; I hope they will not be too unforgiving when I have perhaps not quite got things right. Also, though much of this volume is about not exaggerating the importance of the *medium* of communication, I have to admit to Jo Doherty, Mandy Bright and Margaret Allott that their processing of my ragged writing into smooth linear type really did represent quite a transformation.

The author and publishers are grateful to the following for permission to reproduce material previously published elsewhere: The Open University for the use of 'Communication and technology' (D101, unit 8) in chapter 2; the Institute of African Studies, University of Ife, for chapter 3; Faber and Faber Ltd for chapter 4; Edizioni dell' Ateneo for chapter 5; *Pacific Quarterly Moana* for chapter 6; Tokumaru Yosihiko and Yamaguti Osamu, Nippon dentô ongaku kaigi and Academia Music Ltd, Tokyo, for chapter 7.

Ruth Finnegan
The Open University

1

Introduction

These essays focus on a subject that has long interested those concerned to understand human culture: communication and its implications for human thought and action in a comparative and historical framework. The topic raises fundamental issues about the nature of our experience and development as human beings, and the constitution of human society, thought and artistry. The present collection of essays offers some reflections on these questions. It builds particularly on recent work in social anthropology and history, together with some report on the results of firsthand field research, but is presented in a non-specialist framework in the belief that this is a subject of intrinsic interest to scholars across a wide range of disciplines.

It is also a subject that touches on a series of highly topical issues in the world today. The so-called 'information technology revolution' or 'communications revolution' based on computers plus telecommunications has become a taken-for-granted part of our contemporary vocabulary. At the same time there is continuing and contentious debate about its possible consequences for our lives today. How will developments in information technology affect political participation, for example, economic development, the quality of life or human communication? Will 'IT' revolutionize current forms of organization and democratic participation, or will it merely reinforce existing power divisions? Are we entering a new age with new modes of thinking, new concepts of the self, new notions of what it is to be a 'human being'? Do the changes in communication technology determine our future or do we have any choice?

These and similar issues are all too often debated as if they were totally new and unprecedented. Every age, perhaps, likes to think it has its own imminent 'revolution', and its own sense of engagement in cataclysmic changes, whether for good or ill. But now is not the first time in history that there have been arguably far-reaching changes in the technology of communication. Indeed many of the current questions recall the strikingly similar debates about earlier forms of communication. It is often not realized that work by social anthropologists and social historians on the implications of the introduction or maintenance of 'earlier' technologies like oral communication, writing or print can both illuminate current changes and their (debatable) interpretation, and also provide a wider comparative and historical perspective for their assessment. Current debate does not have to reinvent the wheel, but could proceed more intelligently by building on this earlier theoretical and empirical scholarly work.

The present collection of essays provides some background and contribution to these questions from work in the context of orality and literacy, forms on which there is by now an extensive body of literature and vigorous ongoing debate. This is sometimes brushed aside as merely part of an 'outdated' past, but is of direct relevance to issues about information technology today.

'Orality' and 'literacy' as information technologies

I must first make some brief comment on the terms 'orality' and 'literacy' and how I am (and am not) approaching them. My aim is not to try to produce a comprehensive verbal definition of what – as will appear – are inescapably complex phenomena. Indeed, part of the difficulty of many of the generalizations associated with these concepts is that simplified terms are used to try to encapsulate inevitably complex and varying processes, and many different aspects and institutions are only too easily lumped together under these simple-sounding labels (for some accounts of their complexity and variety see, e.g. Tannen, 1982, 1984; Levine, 1986; Harris, 1986; Street, 1984; Whiteman, 1981; Graff, 1981a). This collection of essays is thus merely intended to throw light on specific aspects rather than pretending to the impossible task of a definitive account of orality and literacy in general. What I do want to make clear at this point, however, is why, contrary to some views, I believe that the study of these traditional forms of communication are both of interest in themselves and relevant for current discussion about the modern 'information technology revolution'.

The currently popular term 'information technology' is often assumed to be a self-evident and well-established concept in the English language. In fact it is quite recent in its present meaning referring to the convergence of computing and telecommunications made possible by striking advances in microelectronics.[1] Differing definitions abound, but one which would probably be broadly accepted by both IT specialists and the conventional

---

1 For example it is not mentioned as such in many of the standard 1970s dictionaries, including the authoritative Supplement to the *Oxford English Dictionary* (1976).

wisdom is given in the authoritative *Macmillan Dictionary of Information Technology:* 'The acquisition, processing, storage and dissemination of vocal, pictorial, textual and numerical information by a microelectronics-based combination of computing and telecommunications' (Longley and Shain, 1985, p. 164). This sums up many common views, and in its focus on the microelectronics base fits well with the technological developments and applications which have become accepted over the last generation or so (explained in publications such as Forester, 1980, 1985; Megarry, 1985; Zorkoczy, 1985).

However we can also step back a little from recent events to focus on the first part of this definition: the *process* of information handling. Indeed the term 'information technology' is also used (e.g. Burns, 1984, pp. 13ff; Zorkoczy, 1985, p. 3) in the wider meaning of *any* technological system for processing information, irrespective of the exact means for doing this. In other words, it can refer to any system created to deal with representing, collecting, storing, recording, processing or communicating information in any form through man-made means. In this wider sense, some form or another of information technology is found in every known society. There are drum and smoke signals, alphabetic and non-alphabetic writing and notation, calculating and mnemonic devices (from abacus to counting systems to visual art used to support human memory), techniques for copying and duplicating, filing systems, telephones, wireless and gramophones, television, postal services and, not least, the man-made system of human language. Information has also been processed through a series of different media down the ages: movements of the human body, clay, stone, shells, papyrus, wood, animal skin, canvas, paper, strings, airways activated by human beings (as in musical instruments or whistling signal systems), the human voice, wires, radio waves, disks or silicon chips. In this wider context, electronics-based 'modern IT' is only one set of examples among the many different technological systems and media used at various points throughout human history for the storing, representing, manipulating and transmitting of information.

Taking this sense in a wider comparative and historical perspective reminds us that earlier forms of information processing too have been interpreted as bringing about previously unimagined changes in the means of storing, transmitting or manipulating information. The development of writing was one, so was printing, then the invention and spread of telegraphy and telephony in the nineteenth century. In each case, far-reaching social effects have been claimed, some optimist (like greater personal freedom), some pessimist (greater bureaucratic control), in strikingly similar vein to parallel prognoses about modern IT. Indeed it has become almost a cliché to class all three as 'revolutions' in communications of the same kind as the contemporary 'IT revolution'. 'The "writing revolution"', as Roy Harris expresses it in his illuminating analysis in *The Origin of Writing*, 'was the first of the great communication revolutions in the history of mankind. The next came several thousand years later, followed after a much shorter interval by the development of telegraphy and telephony' (1986, p. 24). Ithiel de Sola Pool sums up a widely accepted view:

Starting in the middle of the nineteenth century a revolution in communications began with the telegraph, later expanded by the telephone, then radio and television. By using electronic signals instead of visible marks on a surface, it became possible to transmit messages instantaneously to a distance and to do that not only for written words, but also for representations of voice and graphics, too. That was a revolution in information processing as significant as the two previous great revolutions in that field: the invention of writing, millennia ago, and the invention, 500 years ago, of a way to produce written messages in multiple copies. (Pool in Dizard, 1985, p. xi)

The current 'revolution' in new IT is nowadays dissected in book after book and there has also been some analysis of the implications of the nineteenth-century telecommunications systems out of which it has in part developed (e.g. Pool 1977, 1983a). This volume, by contrast, concentrates on the earlier forms of literacy and orality, forms which, I would contend, can also be classed as information technologies.

Literacy in the form of both writing and printing will no doubt be readily accepted as a recognizable, albeit earlier, example of information technology – man-made means for processing information – in the broad sense of that term. 'Orality', however, may strike the reader as a much less obvious case. But I would argue that oral communication must also be included in any consideration of information technology in a comparative and historical perspective. When the implications of writing or of print are being assessed, the implicit or explicit contrast is always precisely with that other information-processing system of oral communication. Most analyses of writing as a form of information technology are thus parasitic on an implied opposition to oral communication, posited as a complementary or opposed information system. So, if only as a counterpoint to 'literacy', some account of the arguably complementary characteristics and role of 'orality' becomes necessary.

There is a more positive point too. Oral communication looks at first sight unproblematic and 'natural'. But, like literacy or, indeed, computer technology, its use too rests on social and cultural conventions and on a man-made system of communication – in this case the remarkable system of human speech. It is, certainly, a technology that we take for granted, just as human beings always do with *established* systems which seem too natural and self-evidently human to need any explanation, in sharp contrast to the newer (and thus apparently 'intrusive' and 'unnatural') technologies. Nowadays these threatening and 'unhuman' information-processing systems seem to lie in electronic-based technologies – in particular 'artificial intelligence' or computer-mediated communication. But in earlier times the threat was seen as coming from the external technology of writing – a view expressed in Plato's *Phaedrus* (274–5) – then later in the mechanization of print. The threat of the new and 'unnatural' continues, but by now, of course, writing and – even more – vocal communication through the conventions of human speech look 'natural' and so non-'technological'. But, in a parallel way to more recently developed information-handling systems, they too are socially created products of human ingenuity and development.

'Orality' and 'literacy' then are taken in this collection of essays to be earlier – though still important – forms of information technology which are as worth investigating as those recent ones which are now more in the public eye. They raise as many issues for the quality and development of human culture. Indeed, as I indicated earlier, the debates surrounding the implications of these traditional systems of communication may have something to tell us about more recent developments.

There are two main ways in which scholarly work on these earlier forms can throw light on current issues. First, there are the arguments over what their implications actually have been for human beings and for social and cultural development more generally. Second, and closely related to these, there are the more general and theoretical debates about how to approach and analyse both the technologies themselves and their wider implications.

Effects of literacy and orality?

First, then, do we know what have been the effects of literacy (either as writing or as printing)? And what general conclusions have been established by earlier writers that might throw light on current developments?

The essays in this volume centre on these questions. Literacy and, in particular, print have often been seen as bringing a whole host of effects – in fact in some views held responsible for just about all the 'goods' of modern western civilization. These range from economic development or political modernization to 'rationality', abstract thought, sophisticated literary expression, individual self-consciousness, or the growth of science (many of these, incidentally, familiar enough topics in recent speculations about 'modern IT' too). Indeed such effects are often taken as so self-evident as to need no demonstration. Roy Harris sums them up as follows in his exposition of the supposedly non-contentious background to his analysis of writing:

The writing revolution was not merely of political and economic significance. The autonomous text was naturally suited to become the basis not only of law but of education and literature. Anthropologists and sociologists nowadays recognise no more fundamental distinction than that which separates literate from preliterate cultures, and the differences are manifest in countless details of social organisation and institutions. More speculatively, it has been claimed [Ong, 1982] that writing profoundly affected the way people came to think and to argue: that it brought in its wake a restructuring of human mental processes. (Harris, 1986, p. 24)

But how true are these claims? There is now a large literature on these topics, in which, as will be clear in the later discussion, there is much less agreement about these postulated effects of changes in communication technologies than might seem from the confident assertions of some writers, including those who would like to draw lessions for modern IT.

These questions about the effects of literacy are explored in the following chapters. Chapters 2 and 8 discuss them in relatively general terms, while chapters 3–7 take up specific aspects in particular cultures, mostly on the basis of fieldwork or firsthand experience. Chapter 3, for example, examines the hypothesis that people without a tradition of literacy are therefore necessarily without the 'typically literate' capacity (as it is often seen) of abstract detached thought, using the case of a rural West African people, the Limba of Sierra Leone, while chapter 4 extends this to a discussion of the nature of literary expression in oral contexts. Similarly chapter 5 assesses the assumption that 'oral societies' all tend to have basically similar non-literate forms of poetic expression which are then radically changed with literacy, through an examination of oral literature in the South Pacific.

It would be inappropriate to anticipate this detailed discussion here, but some comments can put it in the context of the wider literature on the implications of literacy and orality. Much of this has concentrated on the effects of literacy (rather than orality), and has either explicitly or by implication taken the line that it is possible to detect *general* – or at least widely applicable – patterns in the results of literacy for society and for human development (e.g. Ong, 1982; Goody, 1977; McLuhan, 1962, 1967, 1970). Most often these results are seen as basically beneficial for human society, and discussed therefore in such terms as 'progress', 'development' or 'modernization'. A pessimistic tone is rarer. There are occasional comments on the effects of literacy in reinforcing or extending inequalities (e.g. Street, 1986; Postman, 1973); more often even the critical assessments consist more in a kind of romantic nostalgia, in 'the world we have lost' tone. But even there the general flavour is that such losses were worth the sacrifice and that our own fate lies upwards and onwards through literacy and perhaps, yet further, through modern electronics systems.

Other writers would challenge, or at least bypass, this generalizing and in the main optimist approach. They stress instead the specific historical circumstances in which literacy or orality have variously been deployed, and the *different* ways the various media of communication are used in different cultures and different historical periods, depending as much on culture and historical specificity as on the technology as such. The uses, and thus effects, of literacy may be diverse rather than single. In the same vein of a suspicion of generalized conclusions, specific and more limited implications of writing or of print are examined in particular contexts, rather than a search mounted for some overall package. Such studies in depth (e.g. Clanchy, 1979; Cressy, 1980; Street, 1984; Shuman, 1986; Meggitt, 1968; Furet and Ozouf, 1982; Opland, 1983; Bauman and Sherzer, 1974) give a much more complex picture of the actual uses of writing, print and oral communication, and of the interactions between them. Their evidence and approach lead to a radical questioning of many previously accepted generalizations about literacy and orality and their respective consequences.

The essays collected here fall within this second tradition. They could of course be criticized for being too cautious about proposing general theories. And I certainly do continue to react against the (in my view) often non-empirically based speculations and generalizations in some earlier works. Many of these, even when illustrated with specific (usually ethnocentric) examples, show little awareness of the complexity of human culture or of firsthand contact with oral communication processes. But this critique of unbased or premature generalization does not mean that one must retreat to the extreme position favoured by some anthropologists and historians that we can *only* study specifics and that every culture and every situation must be seen as unique. General questions are still worth asking – indeed this is why the technologies of orality, literacy and modern IT are being considered together here – even if the answers turn out to be more complex, and perhaps less favourable to ourselves, than we would ideally like. Perhaps we cannot find simple general laws about orality and literacy. The alternative is not necessarily empty relativism. A critique of unfounded and hasty generalization can help us to a greater understanding both of ourselves (including our own often ethnocentric preconceptions) and of some common syndromes in human culture – widely found patterns, that is, (rather than laws) of human usage, interaction and expression.

To do this, however, one has to begin with a more open mind about human action than is implied by the commonly assumed notion that the *technology* of writing, or print, or computers comes first and brings about inevitable effects. This brings me to the second main point in this introductory chapter: the debates over the analysis of technology and its relation to human culture. This is a wide-ranging question which cannot be followed up in detail here, but it is necessary to make some comment on its significance for the analysis of orality and literacy, and its relevance for approaches to modern IT.

How important is technology?

Many of the generalized accounts of the 'impact' of literacy rest on the implicit assumption that once literacy – or indeed modern IT – is acquired, certain results follow. The implicit or explicit technological determinism that underlies such approaches makes the consequent generalizations seem plausible. For if the *technology* is the same (whether writing, print or networked computers) then the social and cultural results will be the same too.

The immensely influential writings of Marshall McLuhan epitomize this approach. For McLuhan the reality behind the revolutions of human history lies in the technology of communication. He speaks, for example, of the 'psychic and social consequences' of typography that 'suddenly shifted previous boundaries and patterns of culture' (1967, p. 182). And this is how he sums up his *Understanding Media*:

Thousands of years ago man, the nomadic food gatherer, had taken up positional, or relative sedentary, tasks. He began to specialize. The development of writing and printing were major stages of that process. They were supremely specialist in separating the roles of knowledge from the roles of action . . . But with electricity and automation, the technology of fragmented processes suddenly fused with the human dialogue and the need for over-all consideration of human unity. Men are suddenly nomadic gatherers of knowledge, nomadic as never before, informed as never before, free from fragmentary specialism as never before – but also involved in the total social process as never before; since with electricity we extend our central nervous system globally, instantly interrelating every human experience. (McLuhan, 1967, pp. 381–2)

A similar preoccupation with the far-reaching effects of the technology of communication lies behind many of the generalizations about orality and literacy, where the fact that a culture – or even a group or an individual composer – is either oral or literate is taken to bring many other social or mental characteristics. Many besides Havelock have seen the invention and use of writing as a kind of 'thunder-clap in human history' (a term he applies to the alphabetization of Homer), 'an intrusion into culture, with results that proved irreversible' (in Havelock and Hershbell, 1978, p. 3). Ong puts it even more strongly when he contrasts his conception of the traditionalist, acoustic, participatory, concrete, communal and natural world of orality with the new world of writing ... and what functionally literate human beings really are: beings whose thought processes do not grow out of simple natural powers but out of these powers as structured, directly or indirectly, by the technology of writing. Without writing, the literate mind would not and could not think as it does, not only when engaged in writing, but normally even when it is composing its thoughts in oral form. More than any other single invention, writing has transformed human consciousness. (Ong, 1982, p. 78)

Print, as he develops his argument further, thereafter 'both reinforces and transforms the effects of writing on thought and expression' (1982, p. 117). In all, he concludes there are 'basic differences ... between the ways of managing knowledge and verbalization in primary oral cultures (cultures with no knowledge at all of writing) and in cultures deeply affected by the use of writing ... The shift from orality to literacy and on to electronic processing engages social, economic, political, religious and other structures' (Ong, 1982 pp. 1, 3). Even Jack Goody, whose writings have been so powerful in alerting us to the complexity and significance of communication, who speaks from a more sophisticated and informed knowledge of non-industrial experience and who is cautious both about single-cause theories and the extreme formulations of binary divides in human experience, sometimes implicitly reinforces this technology-based interpretation. He is concerned both with 'the major differences that writing can make to the organization of social action' (1987, p. 171, cf. pp. xi, xiii, 185) and with its effects on 'cognitive processes' (1977, p. ix and *passim*; cf. 1987, p. xiii), in the general context of an interest in 'the contrast between the written and the oral' (1987, p. vii). As he expresses it, in words that would be accepted by most writers in this tradition, 'Writing puts a distance between a man and his verbal acts. He can now examine what he says in a more objective manner' (1977, p. 150). This, he argues, has further consequences: 'the shift from the science of the concrete to that of the abstract ... cannot be understood except in terms of basic changes in the nature of human communication' (1977, pp. 150–1).

This position is followed up and assessed in later chapters, but here it is worth remarking that exactly the same ideas are found in much of the conventional wisdom about modern information technology. For this too is commonly seen as bringing in its train a series of consequences for our lives, and ones about which, once the technology is developed, we have little or no choice. The idea that the *technology* is what determines our future comes through clearly in such statements as the following typical assessments, only two among the many current expressions of this position:

Ineluctably the advent of microprocessors and information technology will have the most profound and far-reaching consequences ... the view that we are witnessing a truly profound and pervasive change in our society is now so widely held and the evidence for it is so unequivocal that it seems justifiable to speak of the 'microelectronics revolution'. (Maddison, 1983, pp. 13–14)

Information technology will impinge on all areas of life . . . It will radically change society just as technological developments in the 19th century changed society from being predominantly agricultural to being predominantly industrial. (Sommerville, 1983, p. 2)

This view, then, sees the technology as the crucial factor, as bringing with it a series of social consequences at every level. It affects 'Society' as a whole, industry, organizations, social interaction, mental processes, and even our own views of ourselves as human beings. All *we* can do, at least in the more extreme versions of this approach, is to facilitate and absorb the impact of this developing technology – perhaps at best making some endeavour to ease its way and smooth out some of the less desirable effects of the necessary transition.

This is the technology-led theory of social change in which the technology is viewed as autonomous, that is as itself self-standing and independent of social shaping and as more or less inescapably determining social forms and relationships. This is a model which is not just academic but also directly affects policy recommendations and practice, often with the implication that the 'information technology revolution' is coming anyway so we had better be there complying with it. It is typical of many publicly funded projects, for example the expensive government-backed Alvey Programme set up to encourage technological development on the assumption that this in itself will improve the British economy – but with virtually no attention to such social factors as markets, distribution, organizational contexts or diverse human choices. Similarly, in the words of one official statement, 'The advent of the paperless office, which not so long ago seemed a very distant possibility, is now becoming a close reality. It is vitally important that we do not fall behind our competitors in the IT field' (Kenneth Baker, Foreword to Jarrett, 1982). Countless memos round organizations advocate 'new technology'. They only go on as an afterthought (if at all) to consider for what, for whom, or how, or (even less often) to question who is making the choices and in whose interests.

In this model, then, what is seen as coming first is the technology, and social conditions follow. Similarly 'human factors', if they enter in at all, are thought of as secondary and arising from the technology. The view is: get the technology right and then think of any consequent human problems. The information technology revolution is coming on us and what we have to do is to prepare as best we can for it.

There is also the less strong view sometimes known as 'soft technological determinism' (Pool, 1983b, p. 5). This allows some space for human choices to modify technology's impact – as in 'Techology . . . shapes the structure of the battle, but not every outcome' (Pool, 1983b, p. 251) – but still regards the technology as coming first. Technology still has its impact on us with relatively little room for the impress of social and political institutions or of decisions by individuals or interest groups.

These approaches to recent information technology are thus all of a piece with parallel assumptions about the earlier communications technologies of oral media, writing and print. The common factors that inform them is their implicit (sometimes explicit, technological determinism. In this model what essentially counts is not the social, political or cultural institutions, but the underlying and determining technology.

As will become clear in the later chapters, many scholars now dispute this model. In part this is because the detailed findings of historians, anthropologists, sociologists and others suggest that human development is more complex than can be subsumed under the one simple key of the form of communication. The implications of print, for example, have been found to work out differently in different historical circumstances, and to be shaped as much by the power relations in a particular society or by the particular groups which use and control it as by the technology itself (see, e.g. Graff, 1981b, 1982; Street, 1986; Smith, 1979; Levine, 1986; Cook-Gumperz 1986; and chapters 2 and 8 in this volume). Some would now say the same of more recent technology too: 'The information society,' in one view, 'is emerging as a result of the interaction of scientific, technological, economic, social and cultural forces and is not a mere mechanistically determined product of technology' (King, 1984, p. 1); or, more cynically,

It has not . . . been some inert and mute technology called telematics that has carried us over the threshold of an information age. The reality is that business users demanding advanced telematics services have mustered policy makers' support effectually, so as to enhance their private control over not merely information technology – but our economy and society as a whole. (Schiller, 1982, p. xv)

In this approach, social, not technological, factors are paramount. Nor is the 'information technology revolution' a pre-determined inevitability, for, as Burns sums up his account of the implications of 'new information technology',

Ultimately, the way that the world we live in will look in the 21st century will be determined by the collective, accumulated choices of ourselves as individuals, and the directions taken by the corporate bodies whose actions determine the general shape of our society. (Burns, 1984, p. 234)

It will be clear from such statements that the different assessments of the implications of information technologies also go beyond the question of detailed empirical evidence to that of the theoretical models and methodology being invoked. What is being queried is not just this or that 'result' of various information technologies in the past or present, but the whole idea that such technologies can be taken as self-standing or regarded as of themselves having 'consequences'. 'Technologies', after all, do not discover themselves, do not get developed apart from society, nor themselves make decisions – they are brought about by people, acting within particular institutional frameworks. As one recent analyst put it, 'Technologies are not autonomous ... [so] one cannot properly speak of technologies as having impacts' (Slack, 1984, p. 102).

This challenge to the causal 'impact' model will be familiar from the detailed analyses of earlier information technologies by historians and anthropologists, in terms both of their empirical findings and their more sophisticated approach to the complexity of causal relations in a social context. The same well-tried approach of looking not just at the technical element but also at people's ideas and choices, power relations, institutional arrangements, and actual usage in specific contexts, has now to be painfully rediscovered for the case of more recent information technology.

Clearly there are constraints and opportunities in any specific technology as it becomes established in a particular culture and there is a strong argument for paying attention to these. Similarly the argument that the form of communication technology is one important factor among others in human organization and development is worth taking seriously (an argument followed up in chapter 2 here). But, in the last analysis, to see orality or literacy (or by extension computers) as themselves the sole or major determinant on human choices or social arrangements, is, I believe, misguided. The essays in this volume can thus be read as conducting a running argument with both the empirical and the methodological implications of technological determinism.

Technology and the Great Divide theories

There is a further corollary of these theoretical debates. This relates to the common notion of some fundamental divide between two basically different types of society (or of human experience); these two types are referred to as 'oral' (or sometimes 'primitive') and 'literate' (or 'civilized') respectively. The background and nature of these binary theories is discussed later (especially in chapter 8), but there are two relevant points worth noting now.

First, it is often not recognized that what underpins such theories is that same implicit technological determinism that has just been discussed. If changes in the forms of information technology bring about radical social changes, then there are indeed likely to be fundamental divisions between those societies (or individuals) that basically rely on oral communication, and those that use writing or, later, print (with yet another category formed by the coming 'information age' of telecommunications-cum-computers). Much of the plausibility of the 'Great Divide' theories has rested on the often unconscious assumption that what the essential shaping of society comes from is its communication technology. But once technological determinism is rejected or queried, then questions immediately arise about the validity of these influential classifications of human development into two major types: the oral/primitive as against the literate/civilized.

Second, as touched on earlier and as will become clear in the later chapters, much of the apparent evidence which in the past seemed to provide support for the technology-based Great Divide theories has in recent years come to be re-assessed by anthropologists, folklorists and others. Marshall McLuhan's communication-technology theory, for example, partly took off from the widely accepted and at one time apparently definitive conclusions of Milman Parry and Albert Lord. They had argued that there were special 'oral' processes of literary creation which were opposed to, and mutually exclusive with, literate procedures, explained in Lord's brilliant and enormously influential *The Singer of Tales*. This work formed one of the inspirations for McLuhan's *Gutenberg Galaxy: The Making of Typographic Man*. As he puts it in the Prologue:

The present volume is in many respects complementary to *The Singer of Tales* by Albert B Lord . . . *The Gutenberg Galaxy* is intended to trace the ways in which the *forms* of experience of mental outlook and expression have been modified, first by the phonetic alphabet and then by printing. The enterprise which Milman Parry undertook with reference to the contrasted *forms* of oral and written poetry is here extended to the *forms* of thought and the organization of experience in society and politics. (McLuhan, 1962, p. 1)

But, as described later (especially in chapter 5), Parry's and Lord's general theories are now in question as *universal* guides to the nature of oral and literate processes, and even more in the conclusions drawn by some of their followers about the nature of oral and literate societies generally. The same caution needs to be exercised for many other assertions about oral and literate cultures respectively. Many of these claims are only touched on lightly in this volume but it is worth emphasizing that the conclusions from research, not only about the supposed 'primitive mentality' associated with orality, but also about, for example, concepts of individualism and the self, conflict and scepticism, or detached and abstract thought in non-literate cultures now look different from what they did a generation or so ago.

The result is that once-confident assertions about the supposed differentiating features of oral and literate cultures are now exposed as

decidedly shaky. The traditional information technologies of orality and
literacy respectively have not, after all, been proved to bring definitive
consequences for human society and experience nor to give support to a
technologically based great divide between the oral and the literate

2

Communication and technology

This chapter centres on the question of how far the technology of communication conditions social change. It starts out by stating the persuasive arguments, put forward by McLuhan, Innis, Goody and others, for saying that the communication technologies of writing, print or telecommunications have crucially influenced human and social development. This strong technological deterministic thesis is then briefly queried and qualified on grounds which are illustrated further in later chapters and taken up for more detailed discussion in the final chapter.

Communication and human language

Communication is an essential element in human society. In its various forms, it is the basis on which the varying cultures and civilizations of the world have rested.

A statement like this is easy to make – and probably most people would find nothing to quarrel with in it. But its precise implications are not so easy to grasp. In particular questions can be raised about the significance of forms of communication for the study of society. This discussion explores some of these questions.[1]

A word should, first of all, be said about language. This is usually taken to be the fundamental and characteristically human form of communication. Perhaps one needs to qualify this statement by pointing to the significance of *non*-verbal forms of communication like gesture or facial expression and the attribution of 'language' to certain animals in at least some sense of the word – but by and large this general assessment is widely accepted. It has

1 This was written in the early 1970s and much relevant work has appeared since (e.g. Goody, 1977, 1987; Ong, 1982; Clanchy, 1979; Street, 1984; Parry, 1985; Tedlock, 1977, 1983; Levine, 1986). These recent publications have reinforced rather than undermined my basic approach here, however, and I have engaged only in very minimal updating. Further reference to some of this more recent work is given in ch. 8.

frequently been asserted that language is basic to human society – from Aristotle's comment in the fourth century BC that one of the essential characteristics of humans as social beings is their 'power of reasoned speech' (Aristotle [1962], p. 28) to Sapir's insistence in this century that the existence of a developed language 'is a prerequisite to the development of a culture as a whole' (Sapir, 1960, p. 1). It was once believed that some human cultures had not reached the stage of having a proper language at all and communicated in gestures, or else that their languages were so rudimentary as to have only a few score of words in their vocabulary and no system of grammar. But it is now fully accepted that every known human culture possesses language in the fullest sense. As one eminent linguist sums it up:

There is no more striking general fact about language than its universality . . . We know of no people that is not possessed of a fully developed language. The lowliest South African Bushman speaks in the forms of a rich symbolic system that is in essence perfectly comparable to the speech of the cultivated Frenchman. (Sapir, 1949, p. 22)

This is worth being clear about, for otherwise the universality and fundamental importance of language for human society may be overlooked. In fact verbal communication through humanly developed language is common to all societies and can be seen as the universal background against which all other forms of communication take place.

Because communication is so fundamental we tend to take it for granted and not to reflect overmuch on the various forms it takes. But a closer analysis of communication patterns – and particularly the various technological channels through which communication can flow – suggests that it may have far greater influence over our social and economic life, even perhaps our mental make-up, than one might at first suppose. As discussed below, some social scientists and others argue that the differing technologies of communication are *the* crucial factors in the development of differing types of society and underlie, even determine, our modern form of life and likely future development – and all this without most of us even being aware of the influence of these powerful forces on our actions. The main body of this chapter will be devoted to explaining and illustrating how the differing media of communication can be viewed as constituting the fundamental factor in our human and social development.

Communication, it can be argued, is a sphere where the *technology* involved may have an immense significance for the society in which it occurs, and perhaps radically affect the concurrent forms of social and economic organization. Writing, printing or electronic media all have, arguably, differing implications for the society in which they occur. So too has the absence of such media, when the sole reliance is on face to face verbal communication without writing. Indeed some go as far as to argue that the whole process of industrialization, the present state of industrial society, and future social development would have been impossible without certain technological developments in the forms of communication, and that the technology of communication must therefore be seen as an essential condition for modern industrial society.

This may sound like a far-fetched claim. But there is apparently much evidence to support it, drawn from many different disciplines. This chapter first goes through some of this evidence (first for writing; then print; then telecommunications); and then, in its final section, gives some reconsideration and qualification to this claim that communication technology is indeed crucial for social, economic and political development.

Writing

Take, first, the implications of the change from reliance on the *spoken*[2] word alone to that on the medium of *writing*. The invention of writing can be treated as part of the history of technological development (e.g. in Singer et al., 1954, 1958). Whether it is on clay, stone, papyrus, parchment or any other of the numerous materials used, the invention and use of writing gives rise to a whole new range of possibilities in the organization of society and articulation of human aspirations.

The most obvious property of writing is that it gives *permanence* to verbal expression. Words can be transmitted through space and over time in permanent and unchanging form.

The possibility of communication through space in written, and thus fixed, form opens up many opportunities. Precise communication at a distance is now feasible instead of reliance on face to face communication, and this can have far-reaching effects for social and political organization. It is true that one must not exaggerate this: even in oral (or largely oral) cultures messages can be carried over vast distances by word of mouth, there are special drum or whistle languages through which verbal expression can be transmitted in amplified form over several miles (Finnegan, 1970, ch. 17), and signal systems have often been developed. Also, it must be remembered that communication through writing, divorced from the richness of face to face interaction, can have its limitations. Nevertheless it remains true that it was, and is, only with the invention and use of writing that reliable verbal communication of lengthy and complex statements becomes systematically possible over a distance.

---

2 'Spoken' in this context is to be taken as *including* (rather than contrasting with) sung or chanted verbal communication. The contrast is with *written* forms.

It was this that may have made possible the emergence of large empires in early antiquity. Writing on clay tablets was, for instance, one of the features of the Mesopotamian urban civilization, and it has been claimed that the early monarchies of Egypt and Persia, the Roman empire and the city-states were 'essentially products of writing' (Innis, 1964, p. 10). This is not just something that applies to the dawn of history. The Roman Empire into which Christ was born, the long-lived and far-flung civilization of China extending over several million square miles, the medieval European kingdoms, the bureaucratic Fulani kingdoms of nineteenth-century West Africa with their reliance on Muslim learning – all depended in one way or another on communication in writing.

Similarly, consider the extensive states and federations of the contemporary industrial world. It would be impossible to imagine such large areas as the USSR, USA or India functioning as political and economic units without reliance on writing for communicating at a distance through space. Even in smaller groupings, like France or the United Kingdom, the use of writing is an essential link in connecting the different areas into one unit despite distances which make reliance on face to face communication alone impossible.

Even though writing is now augmented by the use of other communication media, a moment's reflection brings home how essential the medium of writing still remains even in the most 'modern' of contemporary states. To take just a few examples at random, consider the crucial role of writing for the kinds of activities we tend to take for granted in modern society: publishing and implementing laws; issue of passports, driving licences or international vaccination certificates; circulation of newspapers and books; publicity and information leaflets; Open University and other distance teaching; postal service; medical prescriptions; country-wide examination systems; civil service and regular administrative functions.

A further effect of the use of writing as a medium for communication at a distance is a rather more subtle one. This is the divorce between audience and speaker, reader and author. One case where this applies most strikingly is literature. Where, as with oral (i.e. unwritten) literature, communication depends on personal performance, on audience response and on the *direct* personal interaction between author and public, the effect is likely to be rather different from that of *written* literature which facilitates the opportunity for the independent and withdrawn author, and for abstract meditation divorced from the pressures of an immediate audience or from the immediate need for *action*. This consequence is not very easy to document or measure exactly, but is often alluded to in the common assumption that the adoption of writing led to the possibility of greater impersonality and, perhaps, rationality in human affairs – a theme that recurs fairly often in the analysis of the nature of industrial society.

Permanence over *time* is an equally important aspect of writing. The written word can remain the same not only over days or months, but from one generation to the next, and even over centuries or millennia.[3] It can serve as a kind of 'transpersonal memory' by which 'men were given an artificially extended and verifiable memory of objects and events not present to sight or recollection' (Innis, 1972, p. 10). This simple fact – one which we take for granted – has a surprising range of consequences.

In the first place, this facility too aids the development of large-scale organizations and states. A complex state would be nearly impossible to administer without the existence of permanent records. Payment of taxes, criminal records, the publication and implementation of laws, financial accounting, the organization of large-scale institutions (a state, a university, a hospital, a commercial company) – all of these depend in one way or another on having a permanent record: and the most common and straightforward medium for this is *writing*. The power of religious and political leaders too can be enhanced through the provision of a written record of their origins and justification. One can instance the hieroglyphic writing so permanently engraved on stone in the early Egyptian kingdoms; the genealogy of the British royal family preserved over many centuries; or the sacred books of so many of the world religions, all of which claim to provide a written record from the far past.

But perhaps the main point under this head is the possibility writing gives for the creation of bureaucratic organization, whether at a state level or in the sense of large corporations and firms within the state. This is something which, though incipient in literate communities even in pre-industrial times, is often said to be peculiarly typical of modern industrial society. Indeed one of the main characteristics of modern bureaucratic organization has been said to be precisely the conducting of official business through written documents (Weber, 1964, p. 332). It is a salutary thought that even so sophisticated and complex an organization as, say, the British welfare state, the Soviet government, ICI or Shell all depend ultimately on the simple technological fact of the discovery and adoption of writing.

The whole idea of scientific history, and perhaps of abstract reasoning, also seems to depend on the invention of writing. The very existence of a fixed record imposes a distance between the events themselves and their description. Written history can develop as something detached from immediate day to day pressures, verifiable both *after* the event and, if necessary, despite current political alignments. A contrast may be helpful

3 Certain fixed mnemonic devices *have* also been developed independent of writing – the systematic use, for instance, of knots or notched sticks – but these have in general neither the scope nor the complexity made possible by writing.

here. When the description of the past depends on recollection and on what is said to be handed down 'by tradition', as in an oral culture, the account is liable to be directly susceptible to present-day fashions and the current allocation of power. As we all know, we tend to 'remember' events and narratives in accordance with our own preconceptions and expectations – to *interpret* them in fact. Interpretations of the past which, perhaps quite innocently, fall in with current power relationships are to be found everywhere – it is the pretender who wins in the end who is added to the official genealogies as the 'true' king, while his opponent and the loser is then assumed to have been unjustified in his claims. There are many cases of this kind of 'recollection' and unconscious manipulation of the past in oral cultures.

One striking instance of the moulding of oral tradition to suit present realities comes from the Gonja people in northern Ghana. The local myth of origin was recorded by an observer at the beginning of the century. It recounted how the founder of the Gonja kingdom came down from the north in the old old days with his seven sons and established himself as king. When he died the seven sons inherited the kingdom in turn and their respective descendants ruled over the seven parts of the kingdom. These seven parts corresponded to the seven official divisions at the time the story was first recorded. Later, however, two of these seven divisions disappeared for administrative reasons, so the Gonja kingdom now consisted of just five parts. When the myth was recorded again (sixty years after the first time), the mythical founder was only credited with *five* sons! (Goody and Watt, 1968, p. 33). An oral – unlike a written – account can easily be bent to fit present political realities, and (failing an outside written record) there is no documentary evidence by which it could be proved to have changed.

Another example comes from the mainly non-literate Tiv people of northern Nigeria. Their main form of 'historical' record was genealogies, which they traced back through fourteen or seventeen generations. Yet there was constant dispute about these, and the deciding factor about which version was accepted seemed to be the current situation. One law case for instance involved a question of genealogies, for whether or not a certain man (X) received compensation turned on the exact position of one of his ancestors, Amena. The elders disagreed on whether Amena was one man, two men, or even perhaps a woman! It was first decided that he was not a woman, but the issue still remained: if he was one man, then X was not due compensation; if two, then he was. In the event, X could not be compensated in any case, because none of the relevant property happened to be currently available. Two days later, however – and this is the point – the elders all agreed that Amena was only one person *on the grounds that* the compensation had not been paid. The orally transmitted genealogy was thus not at all a fixed permanent record but a changeable account, changing according to the current availability of property and result of a law case (Bohannan, 1952).

Now of course this sort of reinterpretation according to the current situation goes on in every kind of society, literate or oral, and dignifying a discipline by the name of 'history' is no guarantee of objectivity. But where there is a permanent and unchangeable record *in writing*, there is, by that very fact, at least the possibility of a detailed and self-conscious check on the truth of historical accounts. For the first time, as it were, people can become aware of verifiable sources detached from the immediate time and place with which they are concerned. The past can become something objective and analysable, rather than a transmutation or reflection just of the present. Sceptical and searching analysis of the past becomes possible, and with this, as Goody and Watt sum it up, 'scepticism about received ideas about the universe as a whole' (Goody and Watt, 1968, pp. 67–8).

One of the effects of the writing down of English law in the twelfth to thirteenth centuries was that 'for the first time uniform written rules were applied to day to day legal prodecures ... A bureaucracy grew up in the thirteenth century whose writings reached every bailiff and local official and hence potentially every village in England' (Clanchy, 1970, p. 173). It became possible to compare different accounts of the past objectively, to some extent irrespective of contemporary claims: self-interested appeals to 'immemorial custom' could be decisively contradicted when there were *written* records, in a way not possible in a purely oral situation. Thus it seems that increased objectivity and uniformity in legal practice too can be attributed to the 'decisive change-over from oral to written modes' in English law in the twelfth and thirteenth centuries (Clanchy, 1970, pp. 172–3). Similarly in twentieth-century Africa the claim to be descended from the 'traditional rulers' (and thus qualified for chiefship) could be made by a large number of candidates in the period when such claims could rest on unwritten (hence uncheckable and malleable) 'tradition'. But once the records of such genealogies were committed to writing, there became less room for manoeuvre and inconsistencies with the written account became noticeable. Here again writing – the existence of a permanent and unchanging record over time – became the condition for the sort of consistency and predictability that we associate with rationality and bureaucracy.

It may seem that an awareness of the past and the opportunity for objective history is a somewhat trivial point, relevant perhaps for constructing arts syllabuses but scarcely for the wider understanding of industrial society. But it can also be held that the kind of sceptical and detached approach made possible by the emergence of objective written history may be one of the prerequisites for modern industrial society. It is, perhaps, one essential basis for the whole development of scientific thinking. Certainly it makes for much more systematic analysis and investigation. Even at the simplest level

It is easier to perceive contradictions in writing than it is in speech, partly because one can formalize the statements in a syllogistic manner and partly because writing arrests the flow of oral converse so that one can compare side by side utterances which have been made at different times and at different places. (Goody, 1973, p. 7)

'Rationality,' furthermore – which is closely connected with the kind of objectivity and analytic detachment envisaged here – is often taken to be an essential condition for the development of bureaucratically organized society. One of the aspects of a 'rational' approach is an attempt to detect and eliminate inconsistencies: to take a long view, one not submerged by the detailed pressures of the immediate moment. Here again a written record becomes invaluable.

A number of writers have seen the essential characteristic of industrial society in the west as consisting of the kind of rationality and bureaucracy discussed here. Max Weber, for instance, stressed the 'formal rationality' of modern western institutions both political and economic. He explains this as their dependence on 'rationally established norms by enactments, decrees, and regulations' (Weber, 1946, pp. 298–9) with one aspect of modern capitalism being 'a calculable legal system and administration in terms of formal rules' (Weber, 1962, p. 25). What is apparently so fundamental a characteristic of modern industrial society can thus be interpreted as ultimately dependent on a technological invention in the sphere of communication: that of writing.

The existence of writing also leads further to the possibility of the *accumulation* of information over time. Even a single individual can gather more information if he keeps notes, and this gain is vastly multiplied when the accumulation is extended beyond what one person or one generation can encompass. The knowledge and experience of different periods and different cultures can be recorded in written form, to which others from quite different backgrounds can have access. This has far-reaching implications for the practical and intellectual development of any society. The whole development of western science and technology, the emergence of highly specialized experts, the existence of higher education as we know it – all of these would be inconceivable without the accumulation of knowledge made possible by writing.

The technology of *writing* is relevant both for the transmission of accumulated knowledge from one generation to another and also for contact between different cultures. The spread of religions like Islam, Christianity or Hinduism has been made possible by writing. These are all 'religions of the book', dependent on literacy and on the existence and circulation of 'a virtually indestructible document belonging to one of the great world (i.e. literate) religions' (Goody, 1968, p. 5). A universalistic rather than locally-oriented outlook becomes possible. The same applies to the transmission of other types of knowledge between different cultures and periods. It is true that the mere existence of a written record does not necessarily imply that it will be actually *used* – but at least the opportunity is there and has often been taken up. Writing made possible the transmission and rediscovery of the accumulated wisdom of the classical world at the Renaissance, the various religious revivals based on an appeal to the original 'true faith', or the transmission of the rich Chinese culture in Japan in the eighth century. In this way the experience accumulated by literate people through the centuries and throughout the world can in principle become available through the medium of writing – and even if in practice only a fraction of this wealth of information has been actually tapped, it is obvious that, with writing, the accumulation and exploitation of the world's information resources can be infinitely greater than when these depend just on transmission through word of mouth with reliance on personal memory alone.[4] There are clear implications here, it seems, for technological development, for increasing information and control, and for material progress generally.

Economic development too can be linked with writing. Written records make systematic accounting possible as well as the whole complex of sophisticated mathematical procedures. With the use of writing, international trade with orders placed in writing becomes feasible. While money itself does not necessarily depend on writing, nevertheless writing seems to facilitate the use of a standard currency system over large areas – like, for instance, the paper money printed in China from the tenth century AD (Carter, 1925, ch. 11). Economic and social development today is widely regarded as dependent on the ability to read and write. This is constantly stressed, for instance, in UNESCO publications: literacy is essential 'to raise productivity and welfare in the underdeveloped world' (UNESCO, 1970, p. 10; see also Cipolla, 1969, ch. 4). Other development experts consider that around 40 per cent of adult literacy is probably the essential threshold for economic development (Anderson in Anderson and Bowman, 1966, p. 347) and 'literacy . . . is essential to industrialization' (Cherry, 1971, p. 25). Some go so far as to see the continuing existence of adult illiteracy in the developing world as a 'millstone round the neck of progress' (Jeffries, 1967,

---

4 It is worth noting too that the average lifetime has tended to be lower in the past, and in underdeveloped countries generally – precisely those in fact which tend to be non-literate – than in the modern (literate) industrialized nations.

p. 160). In this view writing is an essential prerequisite for economic development and industrialization, not just in earlier European history but also in developing countries today.

This might seem enough. But there are yet other possible consequences of the use of writing as a communication medium. There is not space to elaborate them here – and some are highly controversial – but I shall list them briefly. (A number link with aspects discussed earlier.)

Some writers have suggested that writing is, in addition, a precondition for democracy and freedom. Some hope it will lead to increased 'peace and understanding' as literacy spreads across the modern world (Jeffries, 1967, p. 14) and Lenin was clear that 'an illiterate people cannot build a communist state . . . an illiterate person is outside the sphere of politics.'

Related to this is the suggestion that true individualism is only possible with the use of writing (e.g. Carothers 1959, McLuhan, 1967, pp. 88–92). Similarly writing can play a part in encouraging free and sceptical thought and dissent, and this in turn can be seen to link with the claimed increase in 'rationality' said to follow the reliance on writing. Other suggested consequences are the increase in urban living – 'it is the advent of writing that sets into motion the urban revolution' (McLuhan, 1970, p. 81) – and a greater division of labour due to the accumulation and specialization of information made possible by writing.

With the widespread reliance upon the written word too it is possible that local culture may become more heterogeneous than in a fully oral culture, through the intrusion of foreign elements piecemeal through written records. At a more subtle level the form of communication may become slightly different. Some writers also hold that the emotional involvement in language and reliance on the magical power of words (once believed to be typical of non-literate cultures) gives way to a scientific and objective use of language, paralleling a general turning away from myth to history, superstition to science. At the same time, the emphasis is turned – in McLuhan's famous terminology – from involvement in an oral or acoustic mode of knowing and apprehending to a visual one: writing (for the eye) becomes the focus, rather than the spoken word (for the ear). Finally, while some suggest nostalgically that we have lost as much as we have gained from the changeover from oral to visual, most writers on the subject take it for granted that the spread of writing (with all its consequences) inevitably spells progress.

Writing is something we take for granted, so much so that we do not usually bother to consider its implications or even notice its existence. Yet the emergence of this single, apparently small, technological development – the invention and adoption of writing as a medium of communication – has been regarded as the essential prerequisite for many, perhaps most, of the basic features which we hold characteristic of modern industrial society. Comments about writing in earlier history or ancient empires may, at first sight, seem very remote from today. But since they serve to highlight certain effects of writing which are still with us today, they can give a wider historical and comparative perspective to our understanding of present-day industrial society.

In short, life as we know it now would apparently be impossible without writing. It could not have developed as it has without writing, and, what is more, the developing nations of the contemporary world may have no chance of achieving economic development without a similar reliance on the medium of the written word. In this sense, then, a technological invention can indeed serve as the motive force – or, at least, as the essential precondition – for certain types of social change.

Some go further and say that even the physical medium itself has inescapable results for society and for the very content of what is communicated. This is the truth that underlies the much-quoted aphorism of Marshall McLuhan: 'The medium is the message.' Something further must be said briefly about this aspect.

The 'medium' can be taken in the wide sense as referring to writing as opposed both to speaking and to telegraphic and electronic media: the possible implications of the medium in this sense have already been explored. But one can also look at the effects of the medium in the narrower sense of the actual *material* used.

We are accustomed to think of paper as the obvious medium for the written word. But in fact many other materials have been used: clay, stone (which we still use for inscriptions in certain circumstances), bamboo, leaves, silk, papyrus, parchment. H. A. Innis has pointed out the enormous effect of these various materials on social and political organization. The baked clay and stone of certain early empires were durable over *time*, but (particularly stone) less suitable for transmission over *space*, and their use tended to go along with a monopoly by priests and rulers over the use of writing and written knowledge. Papyrus, on the other hand, was more fragile and short-lived, but did solve the problem of communication over *space*. The bureaucratic development of the Roman Empire with its effective administration depended on papyrus; but at the same time, this medium encouraged monopoly of power by a bureaucracy, as well as having the disadvantage of not enduring well over time (Innis 1964, especially p. 47). But papyrus was not easily available to all; it was produced in one limited area in Egypt. With the spread of Islam at around the eighth century, exports of papyrus to east and west were cut off and parchment became the main material in the west and the basis of the book form known as the codex. This in turn had important implications for political development and the control of power. To quote Innis:

The durability of parchment and the convenience of the codex for reference made it particularly suitable for the large books typical of scriptures and legal works. In turn the difficulties of copying a large book limited the numbers produced. Small libraries with a small number of large books could be established over large areas. Since the material of a civilization dominated by the papyrus roll had to be recopied into the parchment codex a thorough system of censorship was involved. Pagan writing was neglected and Christian writing emphasized . . . The bar on secular learning gave a preponderance to theological studies and made Rome dominant. The monopoly of knowledge centring around parchment emphasized religion at the expense of law. (Innis, 1964, pp. 48–9)

It is clear from this kind of analysis how wide the consequences of the apparently trivial matter of the actual *material* used for writing can be for the whole power structure, interests and organization of a vast area. The same point could be made of paper which, with its adoption in the west, led to seemingly revolutionary results for society (of that more later, under the head of printing).

Before leaving this topic one further point should be mentioned. Writing was not the only medium through which knowledge was widely communicated in the past. There is not room here to consider communication through *visual* means (pictures, carvings, icons, etc.) but it must not be forgotten that this aspect played a very important part, perhaps particularly significant when the mass of the people have been illiterate. [The illustrations of religious paintings, woodcuts and carvings in the original publication of this paper cannot be reproduced here, but some striking examples can be found in Scribner's analysis (1981) of the use of woodcuts for both communication and propaganda in the Reformation.]

This general discussion of writing as a medium, together with its various materials, leads on to the topic of *printing*. To some this is merely a particular form of writing not necessarily demanding an elaborate discussion of its own. To others, however, the invention and spread of printing (particularly in the west) represents a new stage in the developing technology of communication, and one which had great, even revolutionary, effects on society at large. It is desirable, therefore, to pay some attention to print as a medium for communication.

Print

Before discussing the social implications of printing, it is necessary to say something about its nature and invention. This is a more important and more complex matter than may at first appear.

In the west we are accustomed to reckon the invention of printing as the date when movable type was first used by Johann Gutenberg to print books in the fifteenth century. In the far east, by contrast, the invention of printing is commonly dated to the period when *block* printing was invented (eighth century) and then used for book printing (ninth century); in that context the development of movable type was merely an unimportant later addition from the eleventh century onwards (see Carter, 1925, p. 23 and *passim*). The reason for this difference between the far east and the west lies in the graphic form involved. The Chinese script is based on a large number of ideograms each of manageable size and recurring only from time to time; it was thus relatively easy to reproduce in wood block form so that it became feasible in China to print large numbers of books long before this was possible in the west. The basic unit of the alphabetic script, on the other hand, is the single letter: too small to carve easily, constantly recurring in differing combinations, and extremely elusive to handle. This meant that the block-printing method was, for *alphabetic* (unlike ideographic) scripts, too laborious in time and effort to compete with the established practice of copying by hand. It was only with the invention of *movable type*, used in a fount, that printing on a large scale with infinite repeatability became a practical and economic proposition in the west. It is striking that so apparently simple a thing as the actual form of the script should have such far-reaching effects on the relative possibilities and dates of printing in the far east as against the west (Carter, 1925, especially pp. 23ff; Scholderer, 1963, pp. 7ff).

Quite apart from the mechanics of printing itself, a further crucial factor is the *material* used. Pursuing this aspect may seem at first sight to lead us into the details of technology and away from the study of the social implications of communication media. But in fact it seems that an essential prerequisite both for the full development of printing and for the wide circulation of printed products was the existence of a cheap, light and easily available material: paper. The stock material in the west until then had been parchment: suitable for the lengthy process of copying by hand and practical enough for catering for small numbers of readers but not easily produced in the amounts required for large-scale printing, and far too expensive for printing large editions of books. It has been calculated, for instance, that *each* copy of the early bibles printed would have needed the skins of three hundred sheep (Carter, 1925, p. 153). The invention of paper (apparently by the Chinese eunuch Ts'sai Lun in AD 105) and then its widespread use underlay the extensive production and circulation of printed books in China and the far east generally. The use and manufacture of paper gradually spread westward: manufactured in Samarkand by 751, Baghdad by 793, Egypt by 900, then Spain in the twelfth century, Germany in the fourteenth, England in the fifteenth, Philadelphia in the seventeenth ... (Carter, 1925) It was only with this advent of paper that printing on a large scale became in effect feasible. Some would even go so far as to say that it was the adoption of paper in Europe rather than the invention of printing that was the really crucial factor, for once the material was available, the means to exploit it were bound to be developed.

At any rate, whichever should be accorded priority, it was from the coordination of these two developments – movable type and paper – that the rapid multiplication of books on a large scale, their extensive distribution and the accessibility to a large range of the population became possible for the first time, with all the social consequences likely to flow from this. Once again, it could be argued that the technology was the key factor which made this possible.

The consequences of the reliance on print as a medium perhaps do not differ in principle from those already suggested for writing. But these consequences tend to be magnified a hundredfold in that the distribution of, and access to, writing now became so much greater.

It is easy to forget in discussing the effects of literacy that for most of the world's history those making direct use of writing have been a small minority. There was frequently a monopoly or near-monopoly over the use of writing held, say, by priests and rulers in early Egypt, by the mandarins in China,[5] and to some extent by the Christian Church in medieval Europe. Many of the suggested advantages of literacy (increased 'rationality', for instance, or individual freedom) were often just not available to the majority of the population. Further, the written works were not in practice accessible to all, but often limited to the educated few or to those living in urban centres or belonging to certain institutions. In fact, it has been strongly argued that, despite the theoretical existence of writing in medieval Europe, this was limited to certain groups, so that it was still in many respects an 'oral culture'. It 'retained massive oral–aural commitments' (Ong, 1974, p. 97), the written word was read *aloud*, literary works were commonly composed for *oral* performance and thus circulated among the population by word of mouth (Crosby, 1936), and education even in the universities was largely through *spoken* lectures and 'disputations' (Ong, 1974, p. 97).

The use of print meant that access to writing could be extended much more widely. Not that the existence of print in *itself* guarantees widespread literacy in the absence of a far-reaching educational system (witness the high illiteracy rates in many developing countries even today). Even large absolute numbers of printed books can still go along with the limitation of control over writing to a small minority, particularly when the script is an ideographic one, as in China. But it does at least provide the *opportunity*,

5 Though literacy in traditional China was not *entirely* confined to the scholarly elite (Gough, 1968, pp. 71–2).

hard to envisage without printing, for the widespread and rapid distribution of the information, attitudes and economic benefits already mentioned as the likely consequences of writing. 'Printing ... allows individuals to withdraw, to contemplate and meditate outside of communal activities. Print thus encourages privatization, the lonely scholar, and the development of private, individual points of view' (Carey, 1967, p. 19 on McLuhan).

The political and administrative consequences are sometimes claimed to be equally striking. Widespread access to print gives the possibility of control and political activity in a way that is usually assumed not to be easily open to non-literate peoples. Lenin's dictum about an illiterate person being 'outside the sphere of politics' has been widely quoted and followed: 'the first thing he needs is to be taught the alphabet.' Nationalism, too, can be seen as a consequence of print. The national language starts to be widely circulated in fixed and visible form, and maps give a kind of visual appreciation of the nation. Political unification through language groupings became possible as 'printing turned each vernacular into an extensive mass medium' (McLuhan, 1967, p. 189).

These kinds of effects are intensified by the increasing literacy due to print so that the differences between a society in which only a few people read and write and the typical industrial society of today with nearly universal literacy are so extreme as perhaps to amount to a qualitative and not merely quantitative distinction. Certainly two 'revolutions' over the last few centuries in Europe have both been seen as connected with printing and widespread literacy: the Reformation which revolutionized the religious scene of Europe and relied on people's universal access to 'the book' (the Bible); and the 'Industrial Revolution' which from an economic and technological viewpoint is usually taken as the main formative influence underlying modern industrial society. Cipolla sees the increasing literacy that came with print as a precondition:

Had literacy remained the well-guarded monopoly of a few mandarins, European society could hardly have developed in the way that it did. The Industrial Revolution was not the product of one or two high priests of science; it was the outcome of the daily down-to-earth experiment and tinkering on the part of a number of literate craftsmen and amateur scientists (Cipolla, 1969, pp. 101–2).

Print can thus be seen as forming the basis for economic revolution, and perhaps also for political and religious revolution. In addition some writers, especially McLuhan (e.g. 1962, 1967), have regarded it as leading to a revolution in our whole way of apprehending the universe – we move from an auditory mode of knowing and perceiving to a situation in which the most commonly accepted mode is a *visual* one. Man becomes 'typographic man' – aloof, detached, specialized and cut off (or so McLuhan would hold) from the psychic and emotional unity possible in a more 'oral' culture.

Even if only *some* of these consequences attributed to the printed word actually held good, it is still striking that so much that we think of as characteristic of the modern world – economic, social, religious, political – is built on the foundation provided by print as a medium of communication, supported by the material of paper. Once again it appears that the technological basis of our social forms is far more crucial for our social and economic development that we would normally suppose.

Telecommunications

What some would regard as the final stage in the development of the technology of communications came with the discovery and expansion of telecommunications in the nineteenth and twentieth centuries. Telecommunication is, literally, communication-at-a-distance and is generally taken to cover such things as telegraphy, telephones, radio, television, teleprinters, tape recorders and gramophones. The development of computers has tended to go alongside the expansion of telecommunications and to some extent to coincide with it, since computer information is also often transmitted at a distance. The general type of medium relied on is often broadly described as electronic, while the type of human characteristic of our modern age is sometimes characterized as 'electronic man'.

The invention and development of telecommunications date from the nineteenth century, and these media continue to extend and change today with recent developments such as video-tape cassettes, cable television, communications networks, and many more. (For some brief accounts see, e.g., Cherry, 1971; Megarry, 1985; Zorkoczy, 1985; Forester, 1985.)

The most important single property of these media is the *speed* with which information can be transmitted. Indeed they are generally for all intents and purposes instantaneous. Distance is conquered, so to speak, and we can see or hear far-off events *as they take place*. Through television (and satellite) we can see a hold-up attempt in another country at the very moment of taking place, listen to a relative's reaction in another continent as he hears of his daughter's engagement on the telephone, sit in our own home and observe sporting events live from the other side of the world, or watch astronauts as they bounce on the moon or repair their craft in space. Even when the *instantaneous* quality of modern telecommunications is not exploited the general speed of communication can be vastly greater than in earlier centuries. *The Times* was already innovative in 1837 when it organized a pigeon post from Paris to Boulogne, cutting the time to four hours from the courier's fourteen hours (Scupham, 1970, p. 168). But now reporters can report from all quarters of the globe, and have their stories recorded with next to no delay to the message in transit. And the newspapers themselves can be simultaneously printed in several centres and distributed within hours by the modern transport system – itself a significant factor in the modern speed of communication. In an analogous (though perhaps not identical) way the speed of modern computers in processing and feeding out information adds to the general speed of communications today; and computerized information can be transmitted by modern telecommunications channels in the same sort of way as the transmission of voice or vision.

The extension and increasing use of telecommunications has, it seems, a number of consequences for social and economic organization and, perhaps, for man's mental processes also.

In the first place it has been said that space has been 'dissolved'. One does not want to exaggerate this so-called 'conquest of distance', but it is true that there is a sense in which distance now matters less. You do not need to live near your relatives in order to stay in close contact. Whether they are on the far side of the town, the other end of the country, or even in a distant continent, you can still keep in immediate touch by telephone. You can learn what is happening at the other side of the world and can experience, at least vicariously, the interests and customs of other groups.

This 'conquest' of space obviously has certain consequences. One suggestion is, for instance, that now we can communicate so effectively at a distance there will no longer be the same need to live close together in the future, and that the trend towards living in large urban concentrations will be reversed. Already it is possible for head offices of large firms, which need to be in hourly communication with branches all over the country, to be sited outside the main urban centres. Some analysts see this as likely to be one of the most significant trends for the future development of society. 'The city,' writes McLuhan, 'is obsolete' (1970, p. 12) and, according to another analysis, we shall see

the reversal of a historic trend which has proceeded with scarcely a break for 5,000 years. The traditional role of the city as a meeting-place is coming to an end; Megalopolis may soon go the way of the dinosaurs it now resembles in so many respects. This century may see the beginnings of a slow but irresistible dispersion and decentralization of mankind. (Clarke, 1968, p. 38)

How far these trends can really be predicted for the future is not clear, however. There is little hard evidence, for example, that the dispersion into small village communities envisaged by some theorists (*The Blueprint for Survival* (Goldsmith et al. 1972), for instance), is very likely. Telecommunications has been with us some time and yet the overall trends towards urbanization seem, if anything, to have been intensified. So the exact extent and incidence of any physical dispersion due to closer telecommunications links is not as yet clearly established.

What is clearer is the general effect of telecommunications in reducing isolation and ignorance about foreign or far-off ways. It would be too extreme to suggest that we are fast approaching the stage of having one universal world culture purveyed by mass media like television, but it is true that many barriers caused by isolation from other people's cultures have been broken down. In Great Britain, for instance, there is now vastly more knowledge throughout the country of the different sub-cultures within the nation – the various accents and dialects, ways of life remote from our firsthand experience, and groups of which we have no firsthand acquaintance – and some of this increased understanding must be put down to the broadcast media of radio and television. It has been claimed too that class barriers have been lowered through the existence of modern communications, at least in the sense that differing class cultures are both known and brought closer to each other through the media. As one writer puts it:

Space in the modern world progressively disappears as a differentiating factor. As space becomes more continuous, regional variations in culture and social structure become ground down . . . The rise of a worldwide urban civilization built upon the speed and extensiveness of travel and electronic media have progressively diminished – though they have come nowhere near eliminating – spatial, transnational variation in culture and social structure. (Carey, 1967, p. 30)

This tendency is presumably reinforced by the fact that, however unequally goods are still distributed throughout the economy, modern telecommunications media like television, radio and to some extent telephones nevertheless *are* distributed widely (if unevenly) throughout most industrial societies. In Britain, for instance, the radio is sometimes claimed as 'the first expensive modern durable to be purchased generally by the working class' (Breach and Hartwell, 1972, p. 148) and the diffusion of both telephones and television is now numbered in millions. This is very different from the case where direct access to the communication media – as with the medieval scribal tradition – was confined to a relatively small literate group.

Something similar applies in a worldwide context. Literacy and the spread of books is often said to have encouraged nationalism. Television, radio and telegraphic communication can break through these barriers, especially where at least some of these media have such widespread distribution. Transistor radios are listened to even in the remotest of regions: the Somali nomadic herdsmen in the semi-desert wastes of northern Somalia, for instance, regard radio sets as part of the normal luggage to be added to their camel saddle-pack (Andrzejewski, 1963, p. 24). With the widespread media of communication many hope that greater international understanding will be possible. One writer puts it in extreme terms, in the context of the increased 'conquest of space' through the technique of satellite-aided electronic media:

[This may] help to enforce good behaviour and co-operation even upon reluctant parties . . . The inexorable force of astronomical facts will destroy the political fantasies which have so long fragmented our planet. When all major artistic productions, entertainments, political and news events can be received simultaneously by the whole world, the parochialism and xenophobia of the past will be unable to survive. (Clarke, 1968, p. 38)

This assessment that the modern development of telecommunications could lead to increased unity is shared by many writers, several of whom regard the change in communication technology over the last century as being as revolutionary in its results as the introduction of the technologies of writing or of printing. McLuhan, for instance, speaks of the world becoming a 'global village' in which 'every human action or event involves everybody in the village in the consequences of every event' (1970, p. 41). John Sparkes sums up more cooly but equally emphatically when he writes of the use of electro-magnetic waves as a technology for communication, epitomized by Marconi's transmission of radio signals across the Atlantic in 1901:

From that moment society was never to be the same again; what is often called the 'Second Industrial Revolution' (I think rightly so) had really started . . . This Revolution in which we are living is sometimes called the 'Scientific Era' but as regards its social aspects, a better name would be the 'Technological Era'. Telecommunication is one side of it and of course there are many more . . . but telecommunication is rather distinct in that not only is it partly responsible for our rising material standards, by its power for organizing, but especially for its psychological effects, its effects upon our minds, our attitudes to one another and to the outside world.

From this point of view then, I have no hesitation in comparing Marconi's experiment in 1901 with that of William Caxton in 1476 when he set up his printing press in the shade of Westminster Abbey. Both led to technologies having the profoundest effects upon men's minds. They are indeed different in kind; the main thing that distinguishes our mass communication today is its universal application to all classes and conditions of people – its unifying, integrating value, relevant to all, not only to a literate aristocracy. (Sparkes, 1973, p. 131)

This, as well as similar passages by a number of writers, makes a clear link between technology of communication and social change – and not just neutral change but *progress*. The overall tone is optimistic.

The general picture of the results of the annihilation of space is an exciting and an attractive one. But there are arguments about it – as indeed one would expect on a subject that so vitally affects not only the academic analysis of society but our whole future well-being. A number of hard-headed social scientists also ask whether technological development must always result in 'progress'. One distinguished writer on communications, at least, is doubtful about this when he speaks in round terms of 'The delusion that, as the global network expands, so the walls of our mental villages are being pushed back: the delusion that increased powers of communication will bring us all closer together into better understanding and a sense of human compassion. There is no foundation whatsoever for such an emotional belief' (Cherry, 1971, p. 8). Some also point out that when space and time are 'conquered' by modern telecommunications this can *also* lead to possibilities which many people would regard as the opposite of good. Conflict and self-interested demands can be transmitted by the media just as easily as peace and harmony! Television and radio can equally well be used, for instance, for government propaganda, for attacks on other nations and groups, and for the consolidation of the views of a small powerful clique. The success of hijacking and kidnapping in publicizing political demands is also facilitated by the modern communications system, as well as the widescale publicity achieved by relatively small pressure groups (including terrorist groups) – hardly a way of leading to greater 'integration'.

Political consequences are a second main area to be considered. They obviously link to some extent with what has been said already about integration and pressure groups, but there are also some specific points worth exploring.

It is often held that modern communication technology makes the practice of democracy and participation by the people more feasible. This belief is built into many of the programmes for aid to developing countries. Telecommunications is seen as playing an essential part in encouraging people to take part in political and economic progress: 'The media teach people participation . . . With the spread of curiosity and imagination among a previously quietistic population come the human skills needed for social growth and economic development' (Lerner, 1964, p. 412). Indeed the extension of modern communication media to developing countries is often seen as an essential step for them to achieve real equality and progress. In the words of various UNESCO statements, improved communication is needed to 'translate human rights into effective reality' and 'expansion of the information media, press, radio, film, television [is] closely linked to economic and social development' (quoted in Cherry, 1971, p. 59).

There are a number of examples too of leaders bypassing the formal machinery to speak direct to the people at large – thus leading (in one sense) to a more 'democratic' appeal, away from the manipulations of party officials, big business or vested interests. In pre-war America, for instance, President Franklin Roosevelt used his famous 'Fireside Chats' to reach his audience direct by radio, bypassing hostile newspapers, while President Kennedy exploited the strength of personal television appeal when 'in five minutes of strong language he forced the most powerful steel companies in the country to rescind a price increase' (Bagdikian, 1971, pp. 300–1); and there are constant contemporary examples.

But of course this direct access to 'the man in the street' through telecommunications cuts both ways. The control of the extensive and speedy media of modern communications can add extra strength to a totalitarian government and additional force to a power-seeking demagogue. It is often said that Hitler's hold on power was facilitated by the radio, and it is also noticeable that whenever a new group comes into power through a *coup d'état* its first step is to seize the radio and television stations and use them to propagate and reinforce its case. More generally, it is sometimes argued that the overall effect of the present system of telecommunications (together with mass-circulation newspapers) in modern industrial society is to lull and manipulate the people into acceptance of the current power structure. Marxist critics of industrial society in particular often see the mass media as playing a key part in upholding the vested interests of the ruling classes.

Access to the means of modern communication has indeed become a significant factor for any group or individual in search of power or influence. Enhanced possibilities for *both* democratic and totalitarian politics are provided by modern telecommunications – but exactly how the system is exploited for political purposes depends on other factors in the society and not just on the *technology* of telecommunications itself.

A third general aspect of the modern communications system is what is usually called its 'mass' nature. Much of it is public, directed to all alike in a society, and often representative of (or conducive to) a 'mass' culture, common to all. When social scientists speak of 'mass communications' or the 'mass media', what they are usually referring to is, to take the definition of one established authority, 'public television and radio, the large-circulation press, the cinema and under some circumstances gramophone records' (McQuail, 1969, pp. 1–2). (It will be noticed that 'mass communications' here do not exactly correspond to 'telecommunications' in general – e.g. they include some *printed* matter and exclude telephones – but there is obviously much common ground.)

This 'mass' quality of modern communications patterns has several implications – some of them touched on earlier. There is the 'open' and public nature of the communication involved in which messages are often (but not always) broadcast to large audiences.[6] The same message can thus be diffused rapidly throughout society, and a whole nation (or indeed continent) can quickly be acquainted with some new event, or information, or pop song.

The mass media as traditionally established are also often impersonal in that communicators are speaking to anonymous audiences: there is not a personal or face to face relationship (as with speech between two people) since two-way interaction is impossible. A number of scholars see this as reinforcing the tendency toward impersonal and bureaucratic systems already introduced by writing and printing. The apparent 'impersonality' of modern urban life is thus attributed, in part at least, to the modern means of communication – yet another instance of the technology of communication perhaps playing a crucial part in the changing forms of human life and society.

This view of modern society is, by and large, held by a number of social scientists (including many mass communications specialists) and certainly a powerful case can be made out for it. But others would argue that, though this view may represent one side of the truth about modern society, it is not the whole truth. They raise the question of how far it is the *means* of modern communication in themselves – their technologies – that bring about mass use and the consequent results, or whether it is only certain media that are of this nature, or certain *uses* of the media. It used to be widely assumed that television, radio, computers, telephones, tapes, and records necessarily depended on public (or mass) circulation. But in fact this is not inevitably so of any of them. It is a fallacy to assume that, e.g. television is most naturally suited to public broadcasts (even though this has been a common use in the UK). Even by the 1970s it was also widely used for teaching (via closed circuit television) in medical schools, etc., and could also be transmitted by cable television, not to speak of the many more personalized uses developing in the late 1980s. The point is that we *use* media for certain purposes, but these purposes are not necessarily inherent in their nature. It was misleading even for the 1960s to suggest (as in McQuail, 1969, p. 6) that 'the basic communication activities' in this country were carried out by 'mass communication', for in fact many different media and different uses were interacting together, some 'mass' and centralized, others more personal.

One final possible consequence of the modern system of telecommunications should be mentioned briefly. This is the effect that it may have on people's *mental* processes, an aspect particularly stressed by writers like

6 There are of course a number of exceptions to this generalization too. The telephone, for instance, unlike the broadcast media is a perfect channel for secret messages, e.g. damning character references which had better not be written down. More recent developments in 'narrowcasting' are also significant.

Marshall McLuhan or Walter Ong. This is not the place to pursue these emotive theories in any detail, but it is worth mentioning McLuhan's thesis that, while print encourages individualism and private experience with appeal to the eye only, television produces a quite different kind of person. 'Electronic man', in his phrase, is emotionally involved in the message he receives, and because *all* his senses are in play he can once again become a whole man. 'In post-literate acoustic space ... we have regained our sensorial WHOLENESS' (McLuhan, 1970, p. 16); we can be 'retribalized' and integrated and give up 'the aloof and dissociated role of the literate Westerner' so long imposed on us by the limiting and dryly academic medium of print (McLuhan, 1967, p. 12).

How far this particular theory seems plausible – and it has many adherents – can be left for the moment (some relevant comments are given in the following chapters). It is sufficient at this point merely to note that it is yet another variation on the theme that has run through most of the previous pages here: that the technology of communication plays an essential part in the formation of our past, present and future way of life. Certainly there are areas of controversy over certain points – how far telecommunications leads to 'integration', for instance, or 'impartiality'. But there seems to be widely held agreement that the new media of communication have in some way played a crucial role in forming our modern society as it now is and as it is likely to develop in the future.

What one ends up with, then, is a highly persuasive theory that the crucial factor in the development of particular forms of society and life has been the technology of communication. The introduction and extension of writing had one set of social, political and economic consequences, printing yet another, and modern telecommunications another again. We can understand both our present industrial society (based on printing and writing?) and the society of the future (based on telecommunications?) towards which we are developing in terms of the dissolution of space, the new political and economic possibilities, the 'mass' emphasis (up to a point anyway) and perhaps the mental and emotional development which can all be attributed to modern telecommunications. The root and basic factor which we keep coming back to is the technology of communication.

A re-appraisal: how valid is the communications-technology theory?

So far, this chapter has mainly presented the argument that the basis of our modern civilization – as well as of the varying forms in the past and likely developments in the future – lies in the various technologies of communication. In this view, technology in general and the technology of *communication* in particular play a crucial part in social development.

As has already appeared, a strong case can certainly be made out for this view. A number of influential writers like McLuhan and his admirers have, furthermore, made the view a popular one. They have represented the development of the media of communication as central to history, and thus have brought to bear one single and powerful viewpoint on the development and nature of society.

However, though this theory is clearly an illuminating one, it also has difficulties and ambiguities. This concluding section points to some of these.

First, just what exactly does the theory imply – or, indeed, is it really a bundle of theories, rather than just one? When it is suggested that the technology of communication is 'basic' in social development, etc., this could mean several things:

1 The technology of communication is the single cause of social development and determines the nature of society in its various phases.
2 It is an important causal factor, but only one among several.
3 It is an *enabling* factor: i.e. it leads to the opening up of various *opportunities* which may or may not be taken up in particular societies or periods.
4 It causes (or influences) some things in society, but not everything.

Several or all of these different possibilities are sometimes suggested by different writers (sometimes even by the same writer) when they stress the importance of communication technology. Yet they are clearly different. The strong view (as it could be called) that communication technology is the single determining cause of social development is clearly very different from the weaker view that it is merely an enabling factor creating certain opportunities, or merely one cause among several. It is worth asking whether perhaps some of the attraction of the general approach is due to this kind of ambiguity: few would easily deny the weakest view, while many might feel doubtful about the strong view if it were stated unambiguously. It is easy to slide from one to another without realizing where one is being led.

One difficulty about the communication technology approach, then, is not that it is necessarily false, but that its actual meaning is sometimes obscure. This sort of difficulty is not, of course, unique to this topic: it applies equally to a number of other broad theories and the difficulty of sorting out definitive single causes and distinguishing them from contributory causes or partial influences is a constant one in social science. It is also a difficulty that can be at least partly overcome (even if not easily) by a greater clarity about just which sense is being accepted by its adherents, whether writers or readers.

It is interesting, therefore, to take the 'strong' or the 'weak' views separately, and see how far they stand up treated on their own. First, the strong thesis that the technology of communication is the single determining cause of social development and of the particular state of society at different periods and places. How solid is the evidence for this?

Clearly there are many indications (detailed in earlier sections) that there is something in this. But does it *always* hold good? And can one prove it?

One large difficulty is that so many of the terms involved are wide and general ones about which it is extremely hard to produce specific evidence: 'rationality', 'individualism', 'bureaucratization', and so on. Even the much simpler term 'literacy', though the basis of much of the argument, turns out to be not without ambiguity: it is in fact extremely tricky to define and to measure. This applies even more so to the larger and vaguer concepts. But unless they are clearly defined in a down to earth and unambiguous way they cannot be proved (or disproved) to have resulted from certain communication technologies. In this sense the strong theory has to be regarded as being as yet unproven and demanding much further research before it could be regarded as empirically established. It is a *suggestive* but not yet solidly based theory.

Further, such evidence as there is available suggests that there are many exceptions to the kind of inevitable sequence seen as arising from communication technology. Admittedly there is still the problem of the vague use of terms. But on the face of it there is some evidence to make one feel doubtful about the claim that media technology is a sufficient condition for certain consequences: i.e. that once the cause is there the consequences *must* follow.

Take the relationship between literacy and a scientific and sceptical approach. Certainly this seems to happen sometimes – but not *always*. One often cited case is China, where, despite difficulties of definition, it seems to be established that scientific method in the western sense was not typical despite long-established literacy. Japan is another example: as one Japanese scholar (Nagashima) concludes his analysis:

A non-rational way of thinking was developed in Japan among the literate section of society although it had also been deeply rooted in the non-literate folk society. This means that literacy itself does not necessarily lead to a scientific way of thinking, as is often assumed (Horton and Finnegan, 1973, p. 111).

The importance of literacy for historical thinking is another point that is often stressed. But this does *not* appear to be a necessary connection: in both traditional India and China there was substantial literacy, yet while in China systematic historical research was established early, there was little or no trace of this in India (Gough, 1968, p. 74). Again, it is true that in western Europe print can be seen as connected with industrialization, mass communications and religious revolution; but that these are not an invariable result of print is shown by India and Japan. It is worth remembering too the many developing countries of the present world in which print *exists*; but, without the intervening social factors of, for instance, widespread education, capital investment or political policies, it does not have the same consequences as apparently it did in western Europe. There is also the case of telecommunications. Some of the consequences suggested as inevitable results of these particular media seem plausible enough at first sight – like greater democratic control, more political integration or increasing impersonality and submergence in the 'mass' – but a number can be interpreted in different ways. On the face of it at least, there seems to be considerable evidence to make one dubious about accepting the strong case as a universally applicable theory.

Much the same applies to the slight modification of the strong case which sees the form of communication technology not so much as sufficient cause but as a *necessary* condition, say, printing as the essential precondition for industrialization. In this view, industrialization is not an invariable result of print but it *is* impossible without it.

This idea of preconditions in communication technology fits rather better with the evidence. But it is still possible to find at least arguable exceptions – and if the strong case is to hold good, there should be no exceptions, or anyway not too many or none that cannot be explained away. A number of the results which keep cropping up in the strong theory look rather less convincing when one examines some of the wider evidence.

A detached analytic approach, for instance, is not easy to define and it seems plausible enough to attribute it to literacy. And yet, on the face of it at least, one can find it among non-literate peoples too. The power to stand back and analyse in a detached and abstract way can be found, for instance, among the basically non-literate Limba peasants of West Africa (see chapter 3 below) and in the unwritten poetry of many non-literate peoples (chapter 4). Again religious revolutionary movements certainly sometimes depend on print and widespread literacy – as did the Reformation – but this is not always so. Witness the millenary movements in earlier Europe or the many religious movements in developing countries today (Africa or Melanesia, for instance) which often reject established religious modes – and which sometimes depend on print and sometimes do not. 'Individualism' is another instance. There are indications that though it often goes with writing or print, it also, in some senses at least, occurs in societies without much or any reliance on these particular technologies of communication. Just to mention two instances among many possible ones: the Tiv people of northern Nigeria are known for their traditional stress on competitiveness and individualism, while the intensely personal and individual tone of unwritten Eskimo poetry has become famous. It is true that definitions here are of the essence – what exactly is 'individualism' anyway? – but perhaps enough has been said to suggest that a blanket acceptance of the strong case without further qualification and research is to go further than the evidence warrants.

Perhaps there are *some* aspects in which the idea of particular communication technologies as preconditions do apply. One might be as an essential prerequisite for industrialization (though even there one might ask whether telecommunications might not, in the future, at least partly replace print). But to concentrate on just certain limited aspects like industrialization is to qualify the previous strong case very considerably.

There is also perhaps something to be said for the strong view *not* as an empirical established generalization but as one model for illuminating reality for us. In the past social scientists (except perhaps economic historians and geographers) have often neglected the significance of both technology and of communication and have tended to take an anti-technological line. It is thus both illuminating and stimulating to have the counter-view stated forcibly. The strong case is perhaps stated over-extremely – but its very extremeness helps to jolt us out of our complacency and draw our attention to a range of facts and possible causal connections previously neglected.

The weak view about the technology of communications – that it leads to certain opportunities which may or may not be taken up – is less exciting and challenging than the strong causal view. It is also much less tidy and more difficult to generalize, since social choices and additional influences also enter in, so that likely results become near-impossible to predict and the range of alternative possibilities is almost infinite. Nevertheless it does accord much better with the detailed empirical evidence.

This view is one that is in any case likely to commend itself to many social scientists. This is because the significance of, say, political and social factors as motivating forces in their own right can be recognized, rather than regarded as primarily conditioned by technological factors.

Certainly the picture of *opportunities* being provided (rather than consequences determined) through various communication technologies seems to fit well with the detailed evidence on social and economic development. The medium in itself cannot give rise to social consequences – it must be used by people and developed through social institutions. The mere technical existence of writing cannot affect social change. What counts is its *use*, who uses it, who controls it, what it is used for, how it fits into the power structure, how widely it is distributed – it is these social and political factors that shape the consequences. Thus the implications of writing are very different when strictly confined to priests and rulers and largely concerned with religion (as in early Egypt) from a society where there is widespread literacy. And this is different yet again from the situation in a contemporary developing country where adult illiteracy may be increasing in absolute numbers and writing is used for a whole range of purposes, but literacy is largely confined to an elite of relatively *young* people who as a result take on the best paid and most powerful jobs with far-reaching political and economic consequences.

Again, it is a social not a technological matter what kind of information is expressed in which medium. This depends largely on the conventions in a particular society (or period) about how knowledge is organized. In our society, for instance, it was long taken for granted that 'proper' and 'high class' literature like, say, Dickens or Shelley should be printed in books and put on school and university syllabuses while other literary forms like miners' songs or army ballads or pop lyrics should not; just as in some periods religious or legal writings in the learned language (often Latin or Arabic) appeared in written form whereas vernacular compositions did not. It is not, to repeat the point, the technology *itself* that brings these results, it is the use and control of that technology in one or another way – in other words, the *social* not the technological aspect.

The same general point can be extended to the other media of communication too. Telecommunications can be used to make a society more democratic or more 'mass' dominated – but could have the opposite result. Again, print provides the opportunity for more bureaucratic organization – but it does not have to be used this way: printed books can form the main learning material in a village school, for instance, without any necessity for it to become bureaucratic. The detachment between artist and audience is often seen as a direct consequence of writing and printing – but some would see this instead as due to Puritanism and class interest rather than the technology of communication, and point to the opportunities that exist now, despite the continued existence of print, to reverse this trend (see Craig, 1973). Many other factors besides the purely technological affect the choice of how particular media will be actually *used* and distributed. One needs to ask, in other words, about such things as political control, class interests, economic pressures, geographical access, educational background, and so on. General attitudes and views too often play a crucial part. Studies on the efficiency of print, radio and television in a political campaign, for instance, have sometimes revealed that the dominant factor was not the *medium* but the recipients' pre-existing attitudes and interests and their choices in the light of the substance of the campaign (Trenaman and McQuail, 1961, pp. 203, 206 and 231). This gives a much more complex picture of the various factors to be considered in communication and its effect on society – but arguably one closer to the facts than the simplified 'strong' version.

The picture is also made less tidy when the ways in which new technologies have or have not become accepted are considered. One often has the impression that once a technology is 'there', then it is inevitably put to use. This is not so. Groups who have a vested interest in the established forms of communication are likely to oppose new technologies. The copyists who saw their livelihood disappearing did not welcome printing, broadcasting companies have not always encouraged competition from cable television, typewriter manufacturers and typists already trained in the traditional QWERTY system are not eager to welcome a more logical keyboard arrangement. Against this stand those eager to promote some particular technical innovation: perhaps for their own commercial advantage, perhaps to overturn the established order, perhaps to use new ways to enhance their existing power. In the real world in which social arrangements are so often a matter of (among other things) political negotiation, economic pressures and sheer accident, there is no inevitable law about which group – the vested interest or the revolutionaries or yet someone else again – will eventually win out, or which is right. Certainly the view that certain technical inventions in communications always go with certain consequences, or the neat equation of broad stages (due to communication) with the pre-industrial/industrial/ post-industrial phases needs to be supplemented by some attention to the social and political factors that complicate the situation.

Similarly, there is little to be said for the impression sometimes given that new technologies inevitably oust the old – as if the spoken, written and printed media were not still of the utmost significance in modern life, despite the emergence of telecommunications and of computing. Perhaps *certain* functions of older media are taken over by new ones – with the spread of radio, for instance, mass adult literacy is not felt so essential for communication in developing countries as it once was, and the increasing use of telephones may encourage the decline of the post. But it is hard to envisage a situation where spoken communication becomes 'outdated', nor does telecommunications, however sophisticated, do away with the written word. Indeed far from giving up writing, people speak of the 'document explosion' over the last generation or so (Cherry, 1971, p. 99) when it has become a problem to keep up with the increasing amount of written information produced and an often costly business, even with computer assistance, to retrieve the necessary information from the huge store available. The Open University is a good example here. For what, despite its justified reputation for using new technology, is its basic medium for staff–student communication? It is surely still the written word.

This is not to throw away the case for emphasizing the technology of communication – it is only to show that it is more complex than envisaged in the simplified strong model. The various technologies of communication *do* provide opportunities, and, conversely, their absence provides constraints. Without writing, extensive and accurate communication over time and space is impossible: and it is essential to bear this in mind in analysing non-literate societies. Similarly it is only with telecommunications that instantaneous communication over distance is possible and that opportunities provided by this fact can be exploited. The very important constraints and opportunities provided by media are forced to our attention by even the weak form of the theory about communication technology. Despite its untidiness and its slightly tame impression compared to the exciting extravagances of the 'strong' case, this weaker but more complex view needs to be considered seriously as providing one model for illuminating reality and leading to further empirical research, for it touches on themes and controversies which are of fundamental importance for understanding human action and culture.

3

Speech, language and non-literacy: the Limba of Sierra Leone

One empirical question about the technology of literacy is whether it *is* a precondition for abstract detached thought. *Are* 'oral' peoples necessarily unreflective, simple or concrete in their thinking? This chapter explores these questions on the basis of evidence drawn from field research among a West African people.

It is still often assumed that non-literate peoples have little or no awareness of the subtleties and depths of linguistic expression.[1] To this is sometimes added the suggestion that they lack the power of analysis (or possess it only in a very small degree) and have little or no capacity for abstract thought.[2] There is also the special image of 'primitive man' as incapable of standing back in a detached fashion, and thus being emotionally involved with the world around him.[3]

It is obvious that this crude picture of non-literate peoples is in many ways an over-simplified one, and one that has been contested for many years. Yet this kind of image has surprising hold on people's imagination – and in Africa too, not just in Europe – and it may be worth yet again disputing it in a particular case. On the other hand, it is also obvious that there is some glimmer of truth behind this crude representation, or, rather, that certain significant questions are being raised by such views. Writing, it is usually assumed, brings about some kind of intellectual revolution (particularly

1 On the persistence of mistaken assumptions about so-called 'primitive languages', see the works cited in Hymes, 1964, p. 82 and the critical discussion in Alexandre, 1967, ch. 3.

2 For the supposed lack of abstract, analytical or 'philosophical' thought among 'primitive peoples', see Bowra, 1962, pp. 31–3; Cassirer, 1953, pp. 118ff.

3 The idea of emotional and intuitive involvement is connected both with the still influential writings of Lévy-Bruhl and, more recently, with the romanticized but ultimately not dissimilar views of many of the *négritude* school and similar writers (see, e.g. Jahn, 1961, ch. 5; Senghor, 1961, pp. 99ff; Abraham, 1962, pp. 193ff; Kaunda, 1966, pp. 29ff; Bastide, 1968). In addition, those concerned with discussing or implementing 'development' are also naturally prone to stress the backwardness, ignorance and 'darkness' of 'traditional' and non-literate cultures (see, for instance, the tone of most UNESCO publications on this subject, e.g. UNESCO, 1966a and 1966b, especially pp. 29, 32–3 and 82).

when it is associated with near-universal literacy). It is sensible enough to ask whether the differentiating characteristics of, say, the Limba on the one hand and modern western peoples on the other should be put down to the distinction between non-literate and literate traditions. The answer to this, it may emerge, is not perhaps quite so obvious as it may seem at first sight.

The present discussion is designed in the first place to assess the truth of this crude picture of non-literate peoples in the light of attitudes to language and speaking among the Limba. In addition, one or two points arise from this particular instance which are relevant to the general question of the possible consequences of non-literacy.

Limba interest in language

First, a word must be said about the general situation of the Limba.[4] This is, in fact, very pertinent to the main topic. The Limba live in the north of Sierra Leone in an irregularly shaped area of roughly 1,900 square miles, which is seldom more than twenty miles across. They are thus in close contact with neighbouring peoples of different languages – Temne and Lokko to the south and west, Koranko to the east, Yalunka to the north and Susu to the northwest. Those on the edge of the Limba areas are often bilingual, or at least able to understand a considerable amount of the neighbouring language or languages, and Limba children there commonly grow up with an ability to both understand and interpret other languages taken for granted. In addition, large numbers of Limba travel throughout the rest of the many-languaged countries of both Sierra Leone and, to a lesser extent, Guinea. Then they return home to visit or to settle down with at least some acquaintance with yet other languages, chief among them being either Krio or the local pidgin English. Within Limba country too there are settlements of 'foreign' peoples, mainly Fula and Mandingo, and travelling traders or cattle herders speaking these languages are constantly to be seen. In addition, though it is certainly true to say that the Limba themselves are by and large non-literate, they have some contact with Arabic literacy, and there are a few elementary Koranic schools within Limba country, run and attended by members of the Fula and Mandingo communities. Finally, in the larger towns like Kabala, Kamakwie or Kamabai, Krio is frequently heard and languages other than Limba widely spoken.

4 At the 1963 Census, the Limba numbered about 183,000. They are mainly rice farmers, and until recently had very few schools in their area. Fieldwork was carried out in the area in 1961 and in 1963/4 (15 months total) under the auspices of the Colonial Social Science Research Council, the Horniman fund and Somerville College, Oxford.

In this situation, the Limba cannot avoid some awareness of the relativity of their own language. It is inescapable that Limba is only one language among many, and that even if it can be asserted to be 'the best' yet there are many alternative and (to the speakers) equally acceptable ways of rendering the same sentiments. The Limba grow up to an acquaintance with many languages and a sense of perspective about their own.

Nevertheless – or rather because of this – they are quite clear about the distinctiveness of their own language. Limba is in fact divided into a number of dialects, some barely mutually intelligible, but this does not prevent the Limba themselves from seeing it as one in relation to the clearly different languages around them.[5] Their language, indeed, is the main mark by which they distinguish themselves from the many other peoples in the area. Thus, in spite of their habit of contrasting their own various dialects, they still assume that one thing that they all share together as distinct from other tribes is the Limba language. 'The Limba language is one. The Limba are one'; 'We are all Limba – we are all of one language/word (*hutha hunthe*) with each other'; 'There are many Limba languages (dialects), but the Limba language is one.'

The native term is *hulimba ha*,[6] 'the Limba language'. The prefix *hu-* is commonly used not only for most terms referring to speech, words or language[7] but as the normal prefix used to transform a root word into an abstract noun.[8] *Hulimba ha* can therefore be interpreted to mean not only the Limba language but Limbahood itself. When I did research among the Limba, my statement that I had come to learn about the Limba people was often passed on as 'she has come to learn *hulimba ha.*' Everything that connects directly with language is often assumed to be distinctively Limba, and I was therefore continuously and spontaneously instructed in new vocabulary, stories, songs and the requisite greetings in the various dialects. 'Speaking Limba' is even sometimes identified with 'being Limba' in the case of individuals of mixed or foreign birth. I was told several times of people of, say, Temne or Fula parents who were 'now Limba' on the

---

5 Limba has normally been considered as one of the 'West Atlantic' group of languages (Westermann and Bryan, 1952, p. 13), but its exact affiliations within this group are unclear and a more recent allocation has been to the newly coined group of 'North-Western class-languages' (Dalby, 1965, p. 1). The orthography used here is basically that employed by Berry in his articles on Limba (1958 and 1960), based on the International African Institute alphabet. In general vowels have roughly the so-called continental values, consonants the English. In addition ɔ and ɛ represent an open *o* and *e* respectively; *gb* a labiovelar plosive; ŋ the velar nasal; and *th* a voiceless interdental plosive distinct from the palatalized *t*. Words and phrases in this chapter are given in the Biriwa dialect.

6 Wara Wara and Sela/Tonko sometimes have *huyumba* or *huyimba*.

7 For example, *hutha ha* and *huluŋ ha* – word; *huthemine ha* – the Temne language.

8 For example, *gbaku wo*, chief, *hugbakine ha*, chiefship; and *thari*, run, flee; *huthara ha* flight.

grounds that not only did they live in Limba country (not in itself a sufficient condition) but that they 'spoke Limba'. Conversely I have heard it said that someone who doesn't understand and speak Limba is not Limba even if both his mother and his father were Limba; and people 'turn into Krios' or 'turn into Temnes' when they take over those languages. Living as they do in a small country inhabited by peoples speaking several mutually unintelligible languages, the Limba recognize that many of their customs – marriage, for example, or some of the 'secret societies' – are shared by others; but that the Limba language is owned only by the Limba, and is their distinctive characteristic.

The Limba, furthermore, are self-conscious about their own language. They like to discuss linguistic matters, whether in comment on their language as a whole or in comparisons between their different dialects. This is perhaps a natural result of their experience of the many different languages around them, their own distinctive forms of speech, and the fact that so many of them speak more than one language or are well acquainted with the principle of interpretation from one language to another.

They sometimes comment on their own language in general. 'The Limba language is old,' said one, 'the old people tell you stories and tell you what is forbidden and so on; you hear that. The Limba language is not new.' Many Limba expressed pleasure that I had come 'to understand Limba' (*ba luya hulimba ha*), and they sometimes contrasted their own language with others, giving imitations of the sounds of various languages; English, for example, was said to sound just like *yɛŋ yɛŋ yɛŋ yɛŋ* or *ŋɛŋ ŋɛŋ ŋɛŋ ŋɛŋ*.

More often the discussion is of the forms of the various dialects, for in other contexts the heterogeneity of Limba is what strikes people (*thalimba tha a bɔi* – 'there are many Limba languages'). This is a constant topic of interested conversation. Comparisons are made between the varying dialectal terms: how, for example, some words are quite different in meaning, others have different connotations (like the regular word in the south which implies an obscenity in the north and vice versa), and the greeting terms distinctive of the different areas. They sometimes cause laughter by imitating or parodying speakers of other dialects. Each group likes to claim that its own dialect is the best or most pure of Limba and people speak of other dialects as 'bad' (*lethe ta*), 'unintelligible' (*yi sa lu*), or 'mixed up' (*faŋitande*) with other languages; they also notice with displeasure when people use a greeting term other than the common local one. They are quite aware of the relativity of their own particular forms – they confess that they not only laugh at the speakers of other dialects who 'can't speak well' but are themselves in turn laughed at by them. In such discussions there are several terms which are used to describe the various characteristics of a language or dialect; it can be 'deep' (*suŋɔi*, i.e. subtle and not easy to understand), 'fine' (*mɛlɛsɛ*, i.e. full of small words, subtle, analytic), 'clean' (*mɛthɛ*), 'broad' (*bukulu*, i.e. with longer words), 'straight' (*thumbɛ*), 'good' (*lɔhɔ*), 'sweet' (*thimɔ*); according to one English-speaking Limba, his own dialect, Biriwa, was the one that 'is sweet and nice and straightforward'. The Limba, then, are very aware of these various ways of speaking their own language, and of the possibility of having dialectical differences within one common language. As one old man answered in some surprise when I asked about the reason for the many Limba dialects, 'But why do you ask? Are not English and Krio the same language but with differences? Well, it is the same with Limba.' The existence of dialects, with their basic similarity and detailed differences, is something, they assume, which everyone can be expected to understand.

Beside such general reflections on the nature of their language and dialects, they also make intentional self-conscious use of language for amusement and joking. They take great delight, for example, in words or phrases they consider particularly funny and bring them in to make people laugh. *Thɛŋthɛŋthɛruma*, for example, is a term used to describe humorously the kind of person not able or willing to carry loads on his head; *kutɛŋtɛŋbɛri*, meaning a hollow beneath a bank or wall, is a Biriwa word thought funny in itself and also used as a test word for strangers. Phrases may be introduced for no other reason but amusement, as with the rhythmic words a boy once used to express his hunger in fun, 'Ho ho ha ha nothing in my mouth' (*ho ho ha ha, ntha ka ka hothi*), the amusing name given to an imaginary country in a story, *Katiŋkiritaŋkarakatarina*, or the punning phrase used by mothers to answer a child's continual whines of *mbɛ?* ('what') with 'what, goat?' (*mbɛ bahu?*), mimicking the conventional cry, *mbɛɛ*, of the goat. A form of reduplication in names – for instance, the pair of fools called Dimping and Dampang or the spirits Ningkinangka and Dingkangdingkangthengku – or the repetition of words or phrases are all also used for the effective ring rather than their sense. Nonsense or semi-nonsense words are enjoyed as, for example, in the chant about a spirit, *kɛŋ kɛŋ kɛŋ kɛŋ kɛŋ kɛriŋ kɛŋ*, or the alliterative words sometimes said to be chanted by the fishes '*thɔ thɔ thɔ* the wet season is ending, we are going to be killed' (*thɔ thɔ thɔ thamɔ thɔi ba thɔye/hiri puthɔi miŋ se ba korio*) in which the little fishes are supposed to be stuttering *thɔ thɔ*, trying vainly to speak like their elders. They also take pleasure in representing bird cries in words, for example, the *kokoro koo koo* of the cock at dawn and the *kutaŋtaŋtaŋtaro* of the francolin. In addition to this, by the various devices of repetition, parallelism, imitation, onomatopoeia, mimicry and exaggeration of tone or length, they have a recognized means of using language for calculated effect as well as in its ordinary use for the communication of fact. Their deliberate use of linguistic forms in these various ways reveals an attitude of self-conscious awareness to language.

The Limba take a certain amount of reflective interest in the analysis of their own speech. Discussion of separate elements and words is made easier by the common Limba word *na* which is used both to introduce reported speech and to put a word or phrase in, as it were, quotation marks. Thus one term, phrase or sentence can be singled out for discussion or elucidation in its own right by prefixing it with *na*. People sometimes came to me spontaneously with the intention of explaining some word or phrase in this way, quoting it for the sole purpose of comment and explication. This habit of considering their own words can also be illustrated by their common use of *hu-* to turn any word into an abstract noun or concept, a device which the Limba employ frequently. The Limba are well aware of the possibility of considering a linguistic formulation in itself detached from its direct social or personal context.

Even what has been said so far should show how far the Limba are from conforming to the picture of the primitive as unreflective and unselfcon-scious, or even – the more extreme view – emotionally involved with the world, unable to stand back or analyse in any detached or abstract way. This picture is quite untrue of the Limba, at least in the sense that they are aware of the distinctive nature of their own language as contrasted with others' and are greatly interested in the language they speak, intentionally using it for play, comment and analysis, not just for the straight communication of fact or expression of feeling.

Limba literature

There are two other aspects in the Limba attitude to language that should be considered here. First, there is the existence of a literature among the Limba. This, it is true, is expressed in an oral rather than a written form. But it can nevertheless be regarded as a literature. The detailed content of this literature – prose narratives as well as poetry of various distinct kinds – matters less in this context than the Limba attitude to it. Contrary to what is often assumed of non-literate peoples, their literature is not valued primarily for functional purposes but for its own sake.[9] Certainly there are conventional social contexts for certain definite literary types – songs, in particular – and the performers on such occasions are fulfilling social as well as literary roles. It is true too that, just as in literate societies, their literature can be used on specific occasions or by specific individuals with a pragmatic intent. But to stress just this side would give a completely unbalanced

9 For a more detailed discussion of the 'functional' approach to oral literature, see Wauthier, 1966, pp. 65ff and Finnegan 1969b.

account of the Limba attitude to their literature. To them, it is something beautiful and wise in its own right, part of *hulimba ha*, handed down to them by 'the old people' and interpreted and re-interpreted through the individual 'heart' (or inspiration) of the composer/performer. They are, it is clear, well aware of the aesthetic function of language as it is expressed in literature.

Further, in their literature they possess a medium through which they can and do comment in a detached way on the social and natural world around them. The Limba story-teller or poet stands back, as it were, from reality and uses his art to bring out the truth that lies below the surface actions of men. And here I am not referring just to the 'morals' that close many African stories, though these do occur from time to time in Limba tales, but to a more generalized and subtle interpretation of how people behave. The different kinds of conflicts inherent in marriage, for instance, may be commented on indirectly through some tale on the surface treating of animals; or the ambivalent role of women, at once powerless and powerful, can be brought out through an individual narrator's portrayal of a girl in one of his stories. Again, people's characters are lightly but vividly commented on in the dramatic way in which dialogues in stories are performed and presented, and humour and observation come out in such passages as, say, the vivid description of a young girl deliberately decking herself out to make a hit with the men, or a local chief walking forward in his voluminous robes and speaking with pompous dignity. Many of these touches fail to come across in a written or translated version, away from the artistry of the actual narrator and from the situation and characters which he is portraying, but it is quite clear to an observer in the actual situation of story-telling that this kind of detached comment on reality is a central element in Limba literature. The composer/performer in story or poem exploits his medium whether humorously or tolerantly, maliciously or tenderly, to stand back from the world around him and express his detached reflections on it.

This aspect of literature among the Limba – and, no doubt, among many other non-literate peoples also – is an obvious one to any observer who takes the trouble to look at it. It too may seem too obvious to state – were it not for the fact that 'functional' interpretations of any literary forms among 'primitive' peoples have been so dominant that the more subtle aspects have been almost completely ignored. It is, then, worth making the point that, among the Limba, literature is used in basically the same kinds of ways as it is in literate societies, and, not least, as a medium for detached and reflective comment on the world. The assumptions that primitive literature arises directly and exclusively from some social occasion and can therefore be explained solely in terms of it; or that it is merely word for word handing down of 'tradition' with no possibility of change in so much as a single word; or that such literature involves mystical participation with the world of nature or consists of childish tales about animals with no depth or subtlety – none of these assumptions are borne out by the actual facts about the Limba. Once these prejudices are removed, the actual way in which Limba literature is used for detached comment becomes unmistakable to the observer.

Limba views of speech

Finally, something must be said about the Limba concept of 'speaking', *gboŋkoli*. A thorough analysis of the usage of this word would take us too far afield, but some account of what could be termed the Limba philosophy of speech and language will throw further light on the main topic of this chapter.

Gboŋkoli, 'speaking', is one of the key concepts of Limba philosophy and society. It would be impossible to give any picture of their social life and relationships without constant reference to this term. A quick look at some of the Limba words built up on this root will help to give some idea of the range of applications of the basic idea.

Hugboŋkila ha means 'speaking' (the abstract verbal noun), as well as 'speech' or 'harangue'; it also refers to the act of arbitration performed by the mediating words of chief or elders as they attempt to reconcile two parties by their 'speaking'; hence it can mean a law case, a formal occasion when the old men hear and speak between the disputants who state their case with due formality: its plural, *thagboŋkila tha*, refers to cases or disputes. *Bagboŋkoli wo* (plural *bagboŋkoliŋ be*), 'speaker', refers to one of the several elders who jointly help the chief to speak successfully between two parties; they speak in turn endeavouring to make the disputants' hearts 'cool' again, and support the chief's speaking by their presence, murmurs of agreement and interjections of 'true' (*thia*). *Gboŋkoliɛ*, 'speak for', is what someone in a position of authority does for those for whom he is responsible; groups tend to have one person to 'speak for' and represent them to others, whether the group is that of uncircumcised boys wishing to be initiated, of workers who make up a hoeing 'company', or of adult men going in a group down-country to tap and sell palm wine; a father or elder also 'speaks for' anyone under his control if he is involved in a law case; the elder's speaking and guarantee for him help the culprit so that he is more easily forgiven or let off lightly 'by grace of' (*thɔkɔ ba*) the one who has spoken on his behalf.

Other forms are found outside the context of formal arbitration. *Magboŋkoli ma*, 'spoken words', can refer to the words of a song, the spoken injunction attributed to someone in authority, 'speech' in the concrete sense (as distinct from the abstract *hugboŋkila*), or forms of speaking, e.g. the different Limba dialects. *Gboŋkilitande*, 'speak together with', is a reciprocal verb which refers both to formal discussion and to mere conversation between two or more people; this is a common term and refers to a quality expected of any leading Limba ('if you are sensible you will talk well with people'); a chief in particular must take pains to 'speak well with others', that is, to greet them well, to listen fully to what they say and to reply to them with respect. *Gboŋkilo*, 'to be spoken to', refers to a formal rebuke to some individual, probably in the context of a long drawn-out and tactfully expressed series of harangues by the leading old men. *Gboŋkilɔkɔ*, 'speak to oneself', is a less common word; it refers to a man's grumbling and complaining to himself when things are difficult or when he has been wrongfully treated; this is disapproved of, for, ideally, if one has been wronged, the right course is not to fight, abuse or complain but to speak out the complaint explicitly in the setting of a formal 'speaking' before the elders – but sometimes individuals who have failed to gain satisfaction feel they have no alternative.

The basic word, *gboŋkoli*, 'speak', is the most common of all. Though it is sometimes used lightly, meaning merely to talk, its root meaning seems to be to speak formally, responsibly and carefully, most typically in the context of a formal law case or transaction. 'Speaking' is the quality of a chief in his role of reconciling people and thus bringing peace to individuals and to the chiefdom as a whole. It is also a desired attribute and activity of anyone with authority over others – a father 'speaks between' his children, a household head between his dependants, an older boy among his juniors, a respected senior wife among her younger co-wives, a *bondo* (women's society) leader among her followers. Formality of speech covers not only speaking to reconcile people but also the whole series of interchanges of formal thanks, requests, offers or announcements which occur in almost every recognized relationship. Formal 'speaking' also includes prayer and invocation by the old men as they 'speak for' (*gboŋkoliɛ*) the other members of the community and 'call on' (*yoŋoŋ*) the dead 'recounting their names' (*kɔndi ŋakeŋ ŋa*); and what makes it correct to apply the term *saraka*, ritual, to a ceremony or material object is the condition that someone in authority has 'spoken' over it, specifying its purpose in achieving a 'cool spirit' and calling on *Kanu* (God) and the dead. *Gboŋkoli* is also used of the formal interchange of speeches at the start of ordeals for witchcraft, of the long rhetorical harangues during memorial ceremonies, and of speaking the words of a story. In all kinds of transactions, whether those to do with farm work, dances, political or judicial proceedings, initiations, ceremonies or negotiations for marriage, formal 'speaking' is an essential part of the proceedings.

There is a further and very relevant point. Not only is 'speaking' a formal activity constantly practised in many different contexts, but the Limba themselves like to describe their own institutions in these terms. A Limba as well as a sociologist will say that the main function of a chief is 'to speak' or that men do not expect women to be able to 'speak' properly only to cry, and people are constantly assessed in terms of their ability to 'speak well'. It is also common to use terms referring to words or speech to describe relationships: two co-wives who are quarrelling are said not to be in 'one word' (*huluŋ hunthe*), a wife is given to one chief by another so that they will be in 'one word' (*hutha hunthe*), orders are described as the 'voice' (*thampa*) of the leader, and 'the word (*hutha*) of the chief should hold the whole country'. Again, the country is said to be 'cool' (in harmony) when people are 'in one word' (*thampa sinthi*); and when 'the words of the chief are heard all through the country', then all is at peace. This kind of phrase is not just extracted from the occasional reference, but can be heard over and over again in daily conversation. For the Limba, 'speaking' in all its forms is assumed to be one of the most significant and profound activities of social life.

Behind this interest in speaking lies the Limba philosophy of *gboŋkoli*. Briefly, this means that only through good speaking is it possible not only to effect certain social actions but to keep people's hearts 'cool' (*thɛbɛ*) – a constant Limba term connoting peace, harmony and well-being whether on an individual or a social level. If a case is decided too quickly, a contract hastily consummated, or a quarrel not soothed with lengthy and sympathetic speeches, people's hearts will remain 'hot' and rancorous, and the quarrel is likely to break out again or the contract be infringed. This question of 'cooling' an individual's heart is crucial. The Limba are aware that a dispute may seem to be patched up or a transaction completed without a truly settled intent by the parties to keep to the decision, and the 'heart' that is not fully acceptant of what has happened is bound to break the peace of the community. Even worse, it may turn to witchcraft, the most heinous and most dangerous sin of all, leading, in the Limba view, both to the deaths of individuals and to the disturbance of the harmony of the whole country.

Even good 'speaking' does not avail against a settled bad disposition – but it is the best resource the Limba have, they feel, to try to ward off such evils. And in cases where wounded feelings or loss of face are involved, they make strikingly effective use of this weapon. They point out that in settling a dispute it is of no use to say quickly, 'he is in the wrong' or 'she acted badly'. Rather you should speak at great length, 'going round for long in parables' (*silɔkɔ haŋ ka thabɔrɔ tha*), pointing to the need for good relations within family or village, to the respect due not only to elders but to children or to women, of the respective duties of, say, husband and wife to each other (not least among them the necessity to speak with honour to the other), and many similar sentiments, platitudinous perhaps and tedious to the observer but extraordinarily effective to the parties involved. Through the various generalizations and analogies (*thabɔrɔ*) uttered by elder after elder, an atmosphere is gradually built up in which it is possible to touch on the faults of the disputants and persuade them to agree. The terminology to describe this process is seldom in terms of 'judging' but of 'speaking well' to each party, 'persuading' them to accept the suggestions, and 'pulling their hearts' so that they will agree unreservedly. Finally they are persuaded to say 'I accept' (*yaŋ yɛrɔkɔi*) and, often, to 'beg' the other party with some token gift to restore peace. The underlying philosophy is that unless the two contenders are reconciled in the sense that their hearts are at peace (*thɛbɛ*) the session has been a failure however 'correct' (from one point of view) the decision may have been.

'Speaking' is, then, central to social action among the Limba, to the making of contracts and cementing of relationships, to their philosophy of society and to their explanation of human psychology. The Limba are not only explicitly aware of the significance of language and of speaking and constantly discuss these topics, but have also developed their own philosophy of speech.

Conclusion: how relevant is literacy or non-literacy for the Limba philosophy and practice of language?

There are, then, three main respects in which I consider the Limba show their awareness of the significance of language. These are their detached acceptance of the relativity of languages and linguistic forms, even their own; their attitude to literature; and their philosophy of 'speaking'. Their reflectiveness strikes an observer immediately in the interest they take in their own language and in their philosophy of speech. Their capacity to stand back and comment detachedly on experience through literature is more subtle and thus less immediately obvious but is nonetheless unmistakable to anyone with any depth of understanding of their life and culture.

What conclusions can we draw from this discussion? First, it is obvious that the crude picture with which we started is very far from the truth in the case of the Limba. Clearly, they are aware of the subtleties and depths of linguistic expression; they possess and exploit abstract terms and forms; and they reflect on and about language and have media for standing back from the immediate scene or the immediate form of words through their terminology, their philosophy of language and their literature. Limba thought and practice is infinitely more subtle and complex than many of the popular generalizations about 'non-literate peoples' would have us assume.

This really is, or should be, too obvious to need saying. The older ideas about 'primitive mentality' are now rejected by modern scholars and to continue laboriously to repudiate out of date notions should be superfluous. But the fact is that this kind of crude image of non-literate peoples is still surprisingly prevalent. There is still plenty of high-flown generalization about African society which, if applied to specific peoples, conveys a totally misleading picture.[10]

10 For example, references cited in notes 2 and 3 above. Most professional ethnographic accounts of particular peoples, by contrast, present a much more realistic and accurate picture.

But perhaps more needs to be said. After all, there clearly are important differences between Limba society (and the Limba attitude to speaking) and, say, corresponding institutions in contemporary British society.

The current trend is to put down many of such differences to the crucial distinction between literate and non-literate cultures. In the case of the Limba, this might lead us to over-hasty generalizations. Their awareness of the relativity of their own language, for instance, seems to have little to do with the question of literacy or non-literacy. The crucial point, rather, seems to be their constant contact with speakers of other languages. Here indeed we might say that their linguistic awareness is in some respects greater than that of the average Englishman who, notoriously, has little direct experience of languages other than his own – and this in spite of an educational system which stresses both literacy and instruction in or about a non-English language. Written sources certainly should be able to help towards some awareness of language. But it seems that it is neither a sufficient nor a necessary condition. It is worth recalling Goethe's remark that a man who knows only one language cannot understand even his own – perhaps this kind of approach is more relevant here than the question of literacy versus non-literacy.

Another aspect concerns the tendency towards abstract thought. Here again literacy can obviously be a factor. The possibility of 'ivory tower' scholasticism and speculative thought very clearly goes with the development of written, private, forms of expression. But in this case too perhaps the significance of bare literacy in itself can be exaggerated. It may not be the only factor involved. One would perhaps say in general that the Limba, in spite of their capacity for abstraction in certain directions, have not developed anything like the complex and systematic symbolic scheme worked out by, say, the Dogon.[11] But the difference here cannot be put down to literacy – for the Dogon are equally non-literate.[12] We could even, I suggest, take the more extreme example of the Greeks. Their capacity for speculative thought is unchallenged and the connection of this with writing is, on the face of it, an obvious one. I do not wish to question this, but merely to point to one factor that is not always emphasized: the fact that writing was not only not universal, it was also not the silent, remote communication that we now tend to regard it. The Greeks read aloud and much of their well-known philosophy was delivered in the form of lectures and discussions. The type of literacy was something very different from that of contemporary Europe and possibly not at all the same thing as that envisaged

11 See, for example, Calame-Griaule, 1965.
12 Though both Limba and Dogon have, of course (like many West African peoples) had some contact with Arabic literacy.

by modern writers who contrast the literacy of modern 'developed' societies with the non-literacy of traditional African cultures. Furthermore, the Romans have never gained the same reputation for speculative abstract thought. Yet they were equally as literate as the Greeks (if not more so). It looks as if the explanation for the development of highly abstract schemes of thought is rather more complex than the mere attainment, or not, of literacy, and that literacy itself is a more complicated and variable factor than one might imagine from many of the facile generalizations which rely on it as the crucial factor.

In other respects, however, the possession, or not, of a written tradition does seem to be significant. One of the characteristics of oral forms of communication, including oral literature, is their lack of fixity. There tends to be more linguistic elasticity, less idea of verbal accuracy. Contrary to what is often implied about non-literate peoples, among the Limba at least there is little of the kind of respect for 'the word' that seems more typical in fact of cultures dominated by written forms.

A further point arises from the Limba lack of association between language and writing. They do not think of words as primarily fixed in written form but are free to concentrate on their significance in social contexts. As we have seen, they are intensely aware of the relevance of speaking for social relationships and social action. They particularly stress what has been called the 'performative'[13] function of speaking – the way in which speech is used to actually perform an action. This comes out in the way in which 'speaking' for the Limba actually *is* the making of a contract. It is the 'speaking' which ultimately makes valid such transactions as marriage, divorce, transfer of rights over land, appointment of a headman, etc. The functions of written documents in literate cultures are performed among the Limba by the very act of speaking – and of this function of speech the Limba are quite explicitly aware.

This social and active aspect of Limba speaking, in contrast to the greater fixity of written forms, also has implications for the whole process of education and socialization among the Limba – the handing on of the culture from one generation to the next. One common picture of this process in 'primitive society' is that the oral tradition is handed downward perfectly with meticulous attention to the minutiae of the verbal forms. This image just does not apply in the case of the Limba (nor, I suspect, of most non-literate peoples), but really forms part of an outdated romantic notion of the nature of 'tradition' among the 'folk'. The Limba, of course, do speak a great deal about preserving the old forms, of the wisdom of the elders and, even more, of the dead, and of the way in which the 'old people' knew best.

---

13 A term introduced by the philosopher J. L. Austin, in *How to do things with words*, 1962.

But when one looks at the practice, innovation and change come in all along the line.[14] This is partly a function of the lack of fixity in Limba linguistic expression that I have already mentioned. It also follows from the point about Limba speech being closely related to its social *context*, rather than to an impersonal written page, and to its performative aspect. Thus 'education' in a sense is a creative process, involving the interaction of specific individuals and specific occasions, rather than the abstract transfer of formalized knowledge. It may be that we, in fact, tend to over-estimate the part played by book learning in the average educational process[15] of our own (literate) society and that this social and individual aspect of learning is always of the greater significance – but in any case it is of obvious importance among the Limba, an importance which it is tempting to associate with their lack of literacy.

Finally, it is noticeable how strongly the Limba connect intelligence and speaking. If you ask a Limba the meaning of *bafunuŋ* (a wise/clever/intelligent man) the explanation is almost always in terms of his capacity to *speak*. Here it is significant to refer back to a point mentioned earlier – that in Limba language the particular noun class which refers to words to do with language is the same as the class containing abstract nouns. The possibility of abstract terms and abstract thought is, for the Limba, directly associated with speech – rather than, as often with us, with writing or perhaps inner thoughts.

The general conclusion I would draw is that, first, the distinction commonly made between literate and non-literate societies may not be as clear-cut as is often assumed; and secondly that some of the specific characteristics of at least one non-literate society may not be as wholly attributable to the fact of their non-literacy as it might seem at first sight. Certainly non-literacy may be very relevant, but the question of the general significance of literacy/non-literacy is not so simple or settled as many dogmatic statements by sociologists, educationalists and development experts would have us suppose. More empirical research and detailed analysis of this topic is needed rather than yet more speculative generalization.

---

14 For how this works in the case of oral literature (stories), see the discussion in Finnegan, 1967, pp. 92ff.

15 As distinct from advanced academic study.

4

Literacy versus non-literacy:
the significance of 'literature' in
non-literate cultures

One way in which the Limba described in the last chapter were able to formulate their insights into the human condition in a reflective and thoughtful framework was through their 'oral literature'. This aspect, introduced only briefly earlier, is taken up for more detailed analysis here in the context of the recurrent question of whether the possession or otherwise of the technology of literacy makes for a basic divide in human cultures.

When people wish to make a basic distinction between different societies or historical periods, one of the commonly invoked criteria is literacy. In particular those who wish to avoid the connotations of 'primitive', 'uncivilized', 'aboriginal' tend to turn to a description in terms of 'non-literate' or 'pre-literate'. Certainly, other characteristics are also employed (particularly that of technology) but that of the absence or presence of literacy is increasingly stressed.

If literacy is to be regarded as a fundamental mark of distinction between two basically different types of society, it is relevant to examine it further. Does non-literacy have consequences for modes of thinking? Do non-literates *ipso facto* think differently from literates? If so, how significant are these differences? In view of the constant use of the differentiating criterion of literacy, this is a question that needs to be faced more directly than it usually is.[1]

One common answer that is often implied is that the presence or absence of literacy is of absolutely crucial significance for the quality of thought in a given culture. Thus in the view of the Director-General of UNESCO, René Maheu, mankind can be divided into two main groups, the difference between them being apparently directly attributable to literacy: 'those who master nature, share out the world's riches among themselves, and set out

---

1 Relatively little solid work has been done to tackle this question directly; see, however, the essays in Goody, 1968 (especially those by Goody and Watt and by Gough); also Finnegan, 1969a (ch. 3 in this volume).

for the stars', and 'those who remain fettered in their inescapable poverty and the darkness of ignorance' (UNESCO, 1966b, p. 29). It is only with the establishment of mass literacy that 'the liberation and advancement of man' is possible, and the ending of 'darkness in the minds of men' (pp. 40, 82). Again, a recent book by Talcott Parsons represents writing as a 'watershed' in social evolution, 'the focus of the fateful development out of primitiveness' (Parsons, 1966, p. 26) and it is almost a commonplace to speak of the 'revolution' brought about by the invention or adoption of writing.

This kind of approach is strengthened by the apparent association between non-literacy and illiteracy. We tend to associate the latter with an individual or group that has failed to master the generally accepted skills of the culture and is thus cut off from the cultural heritage of contemporaries without having anything of his or their own to put in its place. It is easy to assume that a similar kind of picture must apply to *non*-literate cultures where all or most of the community are without written modes of communication. Further, we all only too easily slip into the habit of mind which assumes that those apparently very different from ourselves necessarily have less wisdom, less sensitivity to the beauties or tragedies of life than we have ourselves – and to this extent at least must perforce be said to think differently. This kind of feeling too makes us ready to embrace a view which sets non-literate societies and their inhabitants on the far side of a great chasm separating them from more familiar cultures which rely on the written word.

An important factor which tends to underlie this view is one apparent consequence of non-literacy: lack of literature. *Prima facie* it seems obvious that individuals and societies which are without writing also lack literature with all that that implies. In other words, they have no access to that part of culture which we would normally regard as among the most valuable parts of our intellectual heritage and perhaps the main medium through which we can express and deepen mankind's intellectual and artistic insight. If in 'primitive' societies access to this medium and its riches is truly lacking, then it is hard not to conclude, with Maheu, that there is indeed a basic divide between them and 'civilized' communities and that this is therefore a fact to be taken account of in any consideration of differing modes of thinking.

In this chapter I intend to examine this view about the apparent lack of literature, and its consequences for thought in non-literate cultures. Is it true that the label 'non-literate' necessarily implies 'without literature'? or even if *some*, rudimentary, analogue to literature can be found there, is it perhaps 'literature' of a fundamentally different kind from written literature? Does it follow that societies can be divided into two radically different types so far as their intellectual and aesthetic development goes – the gulf between them being that of literacy and its corollary, literature? What are the implications for some of the more intangible aspects of thinking like self-awareness, detachment or intellectual probing?

There are of course a number of other possible consequences of literacy which could be discussed (see Goody and Watt, 1968). However, the existence of a (written) literature is one of the first to spring to mind and is the only one I intend to discuss here. Unlike the possible connections of literacy with, say, banking, administration or bureaucracy, its implications for literature are of direct relevance for the whole question of 'modes of thought' – in the context, at least, of our common view of literature as both the expression and the moulder of thought.

Literature, written and unwritten

Is it in fact only in literate societies that we find 'literature'? Must literature, in other words, be *written*? Those who have been brought up in a society which, like the contemporary western world, assumes a strong association between literacy and literature will feel inclined to answer in the affirmative. We naturally have a bias in favour of the associations and forms that we know – especially if this is combined with ignorance of those of other peoples.

It is worth, however, considering both the many periods of history and the many recent and contemporary societies which have existed largely or completely without making use of the written word. The period and area in which writing is taken for granted as the main mode of artistic or intellectual communication is relatively small. When one looks beyond our own immediate horizons, it is clear that there are many other possibilities. Some groups are, or have been, completely without writing – like, say, the Australian aborigines, the Eskimos, the Polynesian islanders (so famed for the riches of their verbal art), and some of the American Indian and African peoples. Others again, basically non-literate themselves, have lived at least on the margins of literate cultures and have been to some extent influenced by them: one could instance parts of the West African savannah areas, where Arabic literacy and culture were known (in some areas well known) even though the great mass of the community remained non-literate, or the areas of Asia touched but not pervaded by the influence of China and of India. Other peoples – as in early Ireland, Ethiopia, parts of contemporary North Africa or medieval Europe – have possessed a definite literate and literary class whose compositions were transmitted largely by oral means to the non-literate masses. This shades into the kind of situation of classical Greece, traditional India and China or, indeed, the not so remote past in

Europe where written literature was accepted as the highest form, but for many people access to it could still only be through the spoken or enacted word. Here and elsewhere we may find that the established and respected tradition is that of literacy, but oral literature is still a living art and there is constant interplay between oral and written forms.[2] When we survey these many different possibilities, it helps to bring home how very limited is the world's experience of printed literature and mass literacy – the situations we tend to take for granted as the natural form to which all others must tend.

By now, few who have considered these and similar cases would deny that such cultures possess at least the parallel to what we term literature. Their forms are unwritten,[3] it is true, but in many other respects appear comparable to what we know as literature. Non-literate communities have, for instance, what have been described as lyrics, panegyric poetry, love songs, prose narratives or drama.

The sort of forms that are possible in these oral cultures can best be illustrated by a few examples. Here, for instance, is the opening of a 450-line praise-poem to Shaka, the great nineteenth-century Zulu king and warrior. The figurative and evocative diction makes it obscure to English readers, but something of its tone comes across even in translation.

Dlungwana[4] son of Ndaba!
Ferocious one of the Mbelebele brigade,
Who raged among the large kraals,
So that until dawn the huts were being turned upside-down.
He who is famous as he sits,[5] son of Menzi,
He who beats but is not beaten, unlike water,[6]
Axe that surpasses other axes in sharpness;
Shaka, I fear to say he is Shaka,
Shaka, he is the chief of the Mashobas,
He of the shrill whistle, the lion;
He who armed in the forest, who is like a madman,
The madman who is in full view of the men.
He who trudged wearily the plain going to Mfene;
The voracious one of the Senzangakhona,
Spear that is red even on the handle . . .

                                                    (Cope, 1968, p. 88)

2 E.g. medieval Europe, the nineteenth-century western Sudan or modern Thailand and Yugoslavia. (See Chaytor, 1945, esp. ch. 6; Finnegan, 1970, pp. 49ff; Tambiah in Goody, 1968, p. 116; Lord, 1968a, esp. pp. 23ff.)

3 Or, in some cases, are written at some point but transmitted and 'published' by oral means.

4 A praise-name meaning the rager or ferocious one.

5 Shaka's famous praise-name, sometimes translated 'He who is famous without effort'.

6 Water can be beaten, but to no effect; Shaka cannot be beaten at all.

Again, there is the Yukagir girl's song from northern Siberia,

When our camps separated
I looked after him
He is tall like a mountain ash
His hair covered his shoulders
Like black squirrels' tails.
When he disappeared
I lay down in the tent.
Oh, how long is a spring day?
But the evening came
And through a hole in the tent cover
I saw my love coming
When he came in
And looked at me
My heart melted
Like snow in the sun.
(Trask, 1969, vol. 2, p. 125, quoted from Jochelson, 1928, p. 224)

or the modern Gaelic lament for a hunter in the Western Isles of Scotland:

I am along on the wave-girt island and the birds remain on the shore. Well they may and forever, I have lost the gun-equipped hunter who would leave the brown stag lying, and take the grey seal from the wave mouth. (Ross, 1959, p. 7)

It is tempting to continue endlessly with similar instances of unwritten 'literature'. There are the dirges of the Sea Dyaks of North Borneo, the profoundly meaningful myths of the American Winnebago, Mozambique satirical songs, Somali love poetry, or 'the finest epic poetry of modern times ... from the Kara Kirghiz, tent-dwelling shepherds of the Tien Shan mountains' (Chadwick, 1939, p. 89).[7] But perhaps enough has been said to show that we must approach, as at least analogous to our literature, the unwritten forms of millions of people throughout the world, now and earlier, who do not employ writing.

Is oral art 'literature'?

It could be argued, however, that these analogues to literature in non-literate (and even perhaps semi-literate) societies are analogues only in certain respects and are not essentially 'literature' in our own sense of the term. The

7 For further examples see the various works cited in the present chapter and, in particular, H. M. and N. K. Chadwick, 1932–40; Trask, 1969; Bowra, 1952 and 1962; Finnegan, 1970; Radin, 1957.

differences may be as important as the similarities. It is therefore worth discussing a little further the kinds of expectations we have of literature and whether these apply in non-literate societies. The whole area of 'What is literature?' is of course a controversial and unending one which clearly cannot be covered here even in summary fashion. It is relevant, however, to point to some obvious and common-sense points which would occur to most people considering the subject.

One obvious function that we tend to associate with literature is that of intellectual expression. Indeed for some this seems to be its essence. Literature conveys some truth perceived by the poet[8] and expressed in terms intelligible to his or her audience – not necessarily, it goes without saying, a factually accurate description of something which can be grasped in simple terms, but a form of expression which can be recognized as having its own profound or inner truth. As Aristotle put it, in terms which still influence our attitudes to literature today, it is a representation of reality, it expresses what is in a sense universal.

This may, certainly, not be all we demand of literature – but it is one common expectation of it. If so, it is easy to see how any assumption that non-literate peoples do not have literature in our sense must lead to the view that their thinking is to that extent limited. Connected with this is the old picture of 'primitives' as emotional, close to nature, incapable of standing back and seeing things intellectually. And indeed, if there is no literary medium through which they can express and communicate their insight into the nature of the world and of human beings, this must profoundly affect their whole mode of thought.

In fact an examination of what has been termed the 'oral literature' of non-literate groups shows that this assumption is far from justified. When one reads – or, better, hears – some of the oral literary forms in such contexts one cannot help but admit that expression of insight and understanding by no means necessarily depends on writing. The Homeric epics – to take a well-known example first – would be accepted by all (including Aristotle) as illuminating our knowledge of man and the universe through a literary medium; and yet it is now widely accepted that these poems were composed *orally* and not primarily in writing (e.g. Kirk, 1964). Or take the insight into the problem of poetic composition conveyed, through the image of fishing, in a short Eskimo poem.

I wonder why
My song-to-be that I wish to use,
My song-to-be that I wish to put together,
I wonder why it will not come to me?

8 I am using 'poets' here and later to include creators of prose as well as of verse.

At Sioraq it was, at a fishing hole in the ice,
I could feel that little trout on the line
And then it was gone,
I stood jigging.
But why is it so difficult, I wonder?
              (Rasmussen, 1931, p. 517)

Again an Ewe poet on the West African coast tells of a man who has lost his relatives through death. But in bewailing his fate he also expresses his underlying fortitude and his comment on the human condition.

Last remaining, last to go:
A border mark I stand.
Were I a boundary post
On the farm's edge,
I'd heave myself
Aside and free me.
What can't be cursed must be endured,
Some folk unwisely fret
Under ills they can't prevent.
You who mock my loss of kin,
Know you the will of Fate?
    (Addali-Mortty in Beier, 1967, p. 4)

There is a further problem about regarding oral literature as a form of intellectual expression. This involves the question of artistic 'distance'. One aspect of literary expression is surely the sense of detachment that it somehow involves, so that even when the poet and his public are emotionally engaged, there is also a feeling of standing back, as it were, of universalizing a particular topic or problem, of conveying some kind of detached comment. It could be argued that this kind of detachment and perspective may not so readily be achieved in oral literature when the poet is merely one of his own audience: when, for instance, an African story-teller produces his narrative to a group with whom he has already spent the day and who are predominantly his close neighbours and relatives. There can be no masking of the author from close familiarity, no interposition of the written word between poet and public.

There are however various ways in which, in non-literate contexts, the same function of 'distancing' can be achieved that is performed elsewhere through the written page. In the first place the village story-teller situation is not the only or even the most common type of oral literature. There are many cases, in totally non-literate as well as in semi-literate groups, where we encounter professional poets and raconteurs. Many wander from place to place to perform before unfamiliar audiences, like, for instance, the modern Moorish troubadours (e.g. Norris, 1968, pp. 51ff, 65), the northern Nigerian

Hausa praise-singers (M. G. Smith, 1957, pp. 38–9), the professional minstrels and saga-tellers among the Tatars of the far Asian steppes (H. M. and N. K. Chadwick, 1932–40, vol. 3, pp. 174ff), or the early Irish poets (Knott, 1957, p. 8; Finnegan, 1960, pp. 184ff). Others again stand apart through having some particular position or recognized poetic skill which sets them at one remove from their audiences. There are the official bards of Zulu kings (Cope, 1968, pp. 27ff; Finnegan, 1970, pp. 83–4), the Polynesian *tohunga* priest-poets (Chadwick, 1932–40, vol. 3, pp. 443ff), or the highly trained intellectual elite of Ruanda (Kagame, 1951, pp. 21ff). Even in the absence of such experts, there may be devices which enhance the detached effect of literary forms. It has often been remarked how many African stories clothe their characters in animal form rather than speaking directly about, say, the quirks or the virtues of everyday people, and this clearly has the effect of putting the narrative at one remove from reality by its very setting. As Evans-Pritchard writes of spider tales among the Sudanese Azande, 'the animal forms might be compared to the masks in Greek or in mediaeval drama' (Evans-Pritchard, 1967, pp. 25–6). A somewhat similar point could be made about the element of fantasy that often enters into the stories, or the musical embellishments that sometimes accompany them. Again, the stress on authority – 'we learnt this from the ancestors' – can be taken not so much as a literal attribution of origin but as another means of raising the composition above the ordinary level of communication. It was not only the ancient Greeks, furthermore, who used masks to enact their plays before largely non-literate audiences: the same custom of masking the actors and thus adding an extra dimension of distance between them and their audience also occurs in the dramatic performances of a number of non-literate peoples. In the water-spirit masquerades of the Kalabari fishermen of south-eastern Nigeria, for instance, the masks serve to disguise the individual actors and, with the religious associations of the plays, help to bring about 'psychical distance' (Horton, 1963, esp. pp. 103ff. This article has suggested several of the points discussed here.)

In these cases the audience is still a face to face one, it is true. But it is easy to forget that it is only in a relatively short period of history that dissemination through the written word has been the accepted vehicle for literary communication. In both the classical and the medieval world, oral delivery (even of previously written forms) was the accepted medium – and this does not lead us to assume that the verbal art conveyed through this means was therefore lacking in the artistic detachment of 'literature'. There is then no reason to presuppose that this is a *necessary* consequence of oral delivery in totally non-literate societies either. In all these cases the special nature of literary as distinct from everyday communication is made clear to its hearers by the recognized conventions – whether these are to do with the position, appearance or dress of the poet, the verbal formulae, a special poetic language,[9] or the embellishment in language and music. The very expression of some sentiment in an accepted literary form in itself implies a kind of detachment. Take, for instance, the ironical dance song of the Tikopian islander in the western Pacific, a comment on self-righteous converts. The poet stands back from the immediate situation to comment ironically:

My dwelling is evil,
I dwell in darkness;
My mind is dark
Why don't I abandon it?

It is good that I should die
Die with the mind
Of one who dwells in darkness.

Stupid practices to which I have clung;
Let them be pulled down and caused to slip away
(Firth, 1936, p. 44)

It is clear that for something to be locally accepted as literature (and the *local* appreciation is what is relevant here) there is no need to rely solely on the particular convention of the printed page.

If, then, we think of literature as a condition for the flowering of intellectual and perceptive thought it is hard to see any great divide between those societies which happen to use *writing* for literary expression and those which do not. In the use of literature as communication of insight, there is nothing radically 'other' about non-literate societies – just as there is nothing magic about writing. In this respect writing is just like oral media in that both can be used in a variety of ways – for literature and non-literature, to illuminate and to obscure. Whether we are dealing with literate, semi-literate or totally non-literate societies, there is the opportunity for their literature to both mould and reflect the culture which forms and follows it.

The consequences for the commonly asked question of whether there is a basic difference in modes of thought between western and non-western (or between industrial and non-industrial cultures) are clearly significant. Far from non-literate societies being radically different in that they lack any medium of thought comparable to our literature, they in fact seem in no essentials different from us in this respect. True, their literature may – sometimes – be less specialist, less fixed to the verbal invariability of the

9 E.g. the use of Mandingo as the conventional language for minstrels throughout a wide area of West Africa (including among non-Mandingo speakers) (see Finnegan, 1970, p. 96 and references given there), or the special language of early Irish poets (Finnegan, 1960, p. 187).

written word, more tied to specific occasions. But these are all matters of degree, and do not necessarily affect the functions of literature as expression of thought. Individuals in a non-literate as in literate societies grow up in an atmosphere in which literary forms are there to mould their thoughts, heighten their awareness and provide a form through which they can convey their own insight and philosophy. In some case there is provision for specialist education in the composition and delivery of oral literature – the Maori 'school of learning' (Best, 1923; H. M. and N. K. Chadwick, 1932–40, vol. 3, pp. 459ff) for instance, the Ruanda training in poetry (Kagame, 1951, p. 24) the professional training and public examination of Uzbek epic singers (Chadwick and Zhirmunsky, 1969, pp. 330ff), the Druidic schools of Caesar's Gaul (Caesar, *De bello gallico* 6, 14), or the later Irish bardic schools (Knott, 1957, p. 43; Dillon, 1948, pp. 73, 149; cf. Bowra, 1952, pp. 427ff). But even individuals in societies without such formal institutions are not without an opportunity for literary education in the broader sense. The Akan child in the West African forest areas grows up hearing spoken, sung and intoned poetry, as well as the special verbal poetry for horns and drums and the constantly recurring imagery of proverbs (Nketia, 1958), while a little further east the Yoruba are exposed from birth to 'tonal, metaphor-saturated language which in its ordinary prose form is never far from music in the aural impression it gives and which has produced an extensive variety of spoken art characteristic of the people' (Babalola, 1966, p.v.). In Yugoslavia the future singer imbibes from childhood the complex oral artistry of epic song: 'the fact of narrative song is around him from birth: the technique of it is the possession of his elders and he falls heir to it' (Lord, 1968a, p. 32). And even in quite recent times in the Gaelic-speaking parts of western Ireland there has been the oral intellectual fare of their famous 'fireside literary circles' which has given intellectual enjoyment to those without access to written literature in their own language (Delargy, 1945, p. 192).

It is no longer possible, therefore, to accept the old picture of 'the primitive' (or the non-literate) as unselfconscious and unaware, incapable of contemplating the world with intellectual detachment, a picture conveyed to us through our (perhaps unconscious) association of these attributes with lack of literacy and hence, we imagine, of literature. In some respects one might even argue that individuals in many non-literate societies are liable to grow up with even more acquaintance with literature than those in modern western societies. As Phillpotts put it in her book on Icelandic literature,

Printing so obviously makes knowledge accessible to all that we are inclined to forget that it also makes knowledge very easy to avoid ... A shepherd in an Icelandic homestead, on the other hand, could not avoid spending his evenings in listening to the kind of literature which interested the farmer. The result was a degree of really national culture such as no nation of today has been able to achieve. (Phillpotts, 1931, pp. 162–3, quoted in Goody, 1968, p. 60)

Similarly peasants in an African village or islanders in the remote Pacific – or medieval courtiers for that matter – cannot escape the experience of hearing lyrics, or stories, or sagas throughout their lives. The impact of this literature, we must assume, will influence their outlook on life and their perception of the social, natural and human world around them.

The artistry of oral literature

There is a further point that may still make one want to question the underlying similarity of written and oral literature. This is the awareness of another facet of literature about which I have as yet said little: what might be called its function of expression – aesthetic expression in general and the individual's vision and urge to create in particular. If 'oral literature' cannot also be shown to have some relevance in this sphere – unclear though it is – then we may well feel that, for all its contribution to more intellectual concerns, it must be basically only a limited medium and lacking in what some would regard as the most valued aspect of literature.

There are several popular notions about the nature of non-literate and of 'primitive' cultures which might seem to support this view of their 'literature'. Though few or none of those assumptions would be accepted by most scholars now – at least in their extreme form – they still tend to linger at the back of our minds. In order to assess the aesthetic significance of oral art it is necessary to discuss them directly.

First, there is the idea that *oral* literature, just through being oral, is handed down word for word over the generations. Now there are a few cases where – it seems – this is indeed done (though more likely over the years than over generations),[10] but by and large the most striking characteristic of oral as opposed to written literature is precisely its variability. There is little concept of the verbal accuracy typical of cultures which depend on the written, particularly the printed, word. By its very nature oral literature is changeable: it cannot be checked by reference back to a written standard, and the performer/composer is aware of the need to speak in accordance with the demands of his audience rather than some authenticated but remote prototype. This facet of oral literature comes out, for instance, in a recent description of story-telling in Kenya.

Each person will tell the same story differently, since he has to make it personal and not simply a mechanical repetition of what he has heard or narrated before. He becomes not only a 'repeater' but also a 'creative' originator of each story . . . The plot of the story and the sequence of its main parts remain the same, but the narrator

---

10 For some instances see Trask, 1969, vol. 2, pp. xxix–xxx; N. K. Chadwick, 1939, p. 78.

has to supply meat to this skeleton. This he will do in the choice of words, the speed of reciting, the imagery he uses, the varying of his voice, the gestures he makes with his face and hands, and the manner in which he will sing or merely recite the poetical portions . . . The narrator puts his personality into the story, thus making it uniquely his own creation. (Mbiti, 1966, pp. 26–7)

A similar account can be found in Lord's well-known discussion (1968a) of the process of composition among Yugoslav poets. These singers create long and colourful epics through completely oral composition and dissemination. The formulae and sequences may draw on conventional forms, it is true, but each poem as actually performed on a particular occasion is unique – the product of its particular singer. Passages like the following are filled both with traditional motifs and at the same time with the poet's individual treatment.

The bey prepared himself in his white tower,
And girded on his belt and arms,
And prepared his broad-backed chestnut stallion.
He put on him his arms and trappings,
With a cry to Allah he mounted his beast,
And he drove him across the level plain,
Like a rabbit he crossed the plain,
Like a wolf he ranged along the mountains . . .

Then he summoned the youths:
'Bring me writing table and paper!
I must now send out letters,
To gather the well-dight wedding guests.'
Ever since the world began,
Youth has ever obeyed its elder.
They brought writing table and paper.
See the old man! He began to write letters.
He sent the first to Mustajbey
To the broad Lika and Ribnik,
And thus he spoke to the bey . . .
(Lord, 1968a, pp. 59, 86)

Such passages and the much longer poems in which they occur are not unchanging. As Lord puts it,

Any particular song is different in the mouth of each of its singers. If we consider it in the thought of a single singer during the years in which he sings it, we find that it is different at different stages in his career . . . The larger themes and the song are alike. Their outward form and their specific content are ever changing. (1968a, p. 100)

The same kind of description is given by Radlov of composition among the Kara Kirghiz of the Asian steppes. Here again the minstrel improvises his song according to the inspiration of the moment. He draws on well-tried motifs (or 'formative elements'), it is true, but impresses his own personality on these and never recites a song in exactly the same form.

The procedure of the improvising minstrel is exactly like that of the pianist. As the latter puts together into a harmonious form different runs which are known to him, transitions and motifs according to the inspiration of the moment, and thus makes up the new from the old which is familiar to him, so also does the minstrel of epic poems . . . The minstrel can utilise in his singing all the formative elements . . . in very different ways. He knows how to represent one and the same picture in a few short strokes. He can depict it more fully, or he can go into a very detailed description with epic fullness . . . The amount of the formative elements and the skill in putting them together is the measure of the skill of the minstrel. (Radlov, 1866–1904, vol. 5, pp. xviff, quoted in Chadwick and Zhirmunsky, 1969, pp. 222–3)

In oral literature there is thus not necessarily any requirement that the poet should reproduce word-perfect 'traditional' versions. In non-literate and semi-literate cultures we encounter the same blend, familiar from written literature, between what is conventional (or 'traditional') and the personal inspiration of the individual poet.

It is easy to slip from this into the opposing idea that, if oral literature is not handed down word for word, then it is haphazard, spontaneous, perhaps short and crude, and certainly without deliberate and studied artistry – 'mere improvisation'. If so, this verbal art is presumably very different from what we regard as literature. In fact, many of those who have made close studies of oral literature have commented on its use of style and complex techniques. It is easy to mention the well-known cases of the Homeric hexameter and Homeric epithets, or the forms and formulae of Anglo-Saxon and early English poetry – all, it appears, orally developed. There are also innumerable lesser-known examples: the complicated rhythmic patterns which, together with elaborate tonal techniques, give form to non-metrical Yoruba poetry in West Africa (see Babalola, 1966, esp. pp. 344–91, and references given there), the lengthy praise-poems of the Zulu with their studied use of parallelism and alliteration and their richly figurative style (Cope, 1968, pp. 38ff; Finnegan, 1970, ch. 5), the subtle tonal requirements of Efik poetry (Simmons, 1960) or the careful art of the long oral epics of twentieth-century Yugoslavia (Lord, 1968a). Again, there are the exacting formal conventions of Somali poetry. Here alliteration is the most striking feature – the rule that in each hemistich of the poem at least one word has to begin with a chosen consonant or vowel.

The rules of alliteration are very rigid in the sense that only identical initial consonants are regarded as alliterative . . . and no substitution by similar sounds is admissible. All initial vowels count as alliterative with each other and again this principle is most strictly observed.

The same alliteration is maintained throughout the whole poem. If, for example, the alliterative sound of a poem is the consonant *g*, in every hemistich there is one word beginning with *g*. A poem of one hundred lines (two hundred hemistichs) will therefore contain two hundred words beginning with *g* . . .

While [some] poets find the restrictions of alliteration an unsurmountable obstacle, men with real talent dazzle their audience with their powers of expression, undiminished by the rigidity of the form. (Andrzejewski and Lewis, 1964, pp. 42–3)

On the other side of the world too, in the western isles of the south Pacific, we find in the poems of the Gilbert islanders 'clear-cut gems of diction, polished and repolished with loving care, according to the canons of a technique as exacting as it is beautiful' (Grimble, 1957, p. 200). This technique is a conscious one, employed by poets who, 'sincerely convinced of beauty, enlisted every artifice of balance, form and rhythm to express it worthily. The island poet thrills as subtly as our own to the exquisite values of words, labouring as patiently after the perfect epithet' (p. 200).

It is thus not only in written literature that we find an interest in form and style as one aspect of literary expression. The fact that oral literature is unwritten does not *ipso facto* absolve the poet from adhering to locally accepted canons of aesthetic form (which may be very complex) nor prevent him from delighting in the elaboration of beauty in words and music for its own sake.

There is little to be said, either, for the related idea that non-written literature is somehow 'communally' rather than 'individually' created. This notion is associated with a certain era of the romantic movement and few who know anything of oral literature at first hand would accept it now in its extreme form. There is of course a grain of truth in the idea. While every poet is to some extent influenced by expectations of his public's reaction, the *oral* composer experiences this most directly. Each piece of oral literature is realized in its actual performance and – the relevant point here – before a particular audience. It is directly influenced, and thus moulded, by the audience as well as by the composer. The listeners may even take a direct part in the performance, and altogether make a more obvious contribution than with written literature. But here again this is a matter of degree. The public to which a piece is directed always has some influence and it is never true to think of poets as an island to themselves, unaffected by the society in which they live.

There is a great deal of evidence to show how important the *individual* composer can be in non-literate as in literate societies. In both cases he is to some extent conditioned by conventional patterns but this can of course give scope as well as limits to his genius. In respect of actually communicating his words, the oral performer has even more opportunity for individual expression than one who must commit his imagination to the written page.

He can enhance and point his words by his mode of utterance, embellish them with music, movement and even on occasion dance, bring out the intended humour or pathos or irony of his vision by his expression or tone.

Among many descriptions of the art of the individual oral performer and its contribution to the effectiveness of the actual composition one can quote Ó Murchú's account of hearing an Irish story-teller:

His piercing eyes are on my face, his limbs are trembling, as, immersed in the story, and forgetful of all else, he puts his very soul into the telling. Obviously much affected by his narrative, he uses a great deal of gesticulation, and by the movement of his body, hands, and head, tries to convey hate and anger, fear and humour, like an actor in a play. (Delargy, 1945, p. 190)

In his choice of words and subject too, the individual oral poet has many opportunities. In any community, of course, one can find derivative as well as creative practitioners. But there is no reason to suppose that only the first occur in cultures which happen not to use writing as a vehicle for their thought. Among the Limba peasants of the West African savannah, for instance, I have had the opportunity of comparing a gifted and a merely adequate story-teller working on the same basic plot. The second gave us a competent narrative, enjoyable and perfectly satisfying. But the first – we ended up with a new insight into the ways of human beings: we had joined in his affectionate mockery of a virile young chief's boastful arrogance, his humorous comment on a girl's subtle efforts to attract the youth's attention, and his delight in the beauty of words and music. The imprint of his individual personality, and his personal perception of the world and its artistic potentialities, were too striking to be forgotten.[11]

A similar description has been given of story-tellers among the American Indians.

That far-reaching variants in the manner . . . of telling a tale exist we all know, but a relatively small number of investigators have ever taken the trouble to inquire just wherein the full implication of the variation lay . . . With this object in view, I obtained different versions of the same myth from three individuals. Two of them were brothers and had learned the myth from their father. The differences between these versions were remarkable, but *the significance of the differences lay in the fact that they could be explained in terms of the temperament, literary ability, and interests of the story-teller.* (Radin, 1957, pp. 53–4; my italics)

Or take the Alaskan Eskimo term for poetic concentration, *qarrtsihuni*, literally 'waiting for something to break'. This is not spontaneous communal creation, but a deliberate and personal concentration on poetic composition.

11 For a discussion of differences between individual Limba story-tellers, see Finnegan, 1967, pp. 70ff, 93ff.

The poets must wait in deep stillness and darkness while, as an Eskimo put it, they 'endeavour to think only beautiful thoughts. Then they take shape in the minds of men and rise up like bubbles from the depths of the sea, bubbles that seek the air to burst in the light!' (Freuchen, 1962, p. 281). Again there are the Gilbertese island poets of the southern Pacific of whose poetic compositions Grimble has given so vivid a description.

It is only when the poet feels the divine spark of inspiration once more stirring within him that he deviates from the ordinary course of village life . . . He removes himself to some lonely spot, there to avoid all contact with man or woman . . . This is his 'house of song', wherein he will sit in travail with the poem that is yet unborn. All the next night he squats there, bolt upright, facing east, while the song quickens within him.

The next morning he performs the prescribed ritual for a poet, then goes to the village for five friends whom he brings back with him to his 'house of song'. Together they work on his 'rough draft'.

It is the business of his friends to interrupt, criticize, interject suggestions, applaud, or howl down, according to their taste . . . They will remain without food or drink under the pitiless sun until night falls, searching for the right word, the balance, the music that will convert it into a finished work of art.

When all their wit and wisdom has been poured out upon him, they depart. He remains alone again – probably for several days – to reflect upon their advice, accept, reject, accommodate, improve, as his genius dictates. The responsibility for the completed song will be entirely his. (Grimble, 1957, pp. 204–5; for other examples of deliberate poetic composition, see Finnegan, 1970, pp. 268ff)

It is of course notoriously difficult to appreciate the art of foreign cultures but, even so, it is hard to deny the individual inspiration of such a lyric, created by one of these Gilbertese poets, as

Even in a little thing
(A leaf, a child's hand, a star's flicker)
I shall find a song worth singing
If my eyes are wide, and sleep not.

Even in a laughable thing
(Oh, hark! The children are laughing!)
There is that which fills the heart to over-flowing,
And makes dreams wistful.
Small is the life of a man
(Not too sad, not too happy):
I shall find my songs in a man's small life. Behold them soaring!
Very low on earth are the frigate-birds hatched,
Yet they soar as high as the sun.

(Grimble, 1957, pp. 207–8)

The same applies to the many love poems which have been so widely recorded for non-literate (and thus supposedly 'communally' dominated) peoples like the Maori:

Love does not torment forever
It came on me like the fire
Which rages sometimes at Hukanui.
If this beloved one is near to me,
Do not suppose, O Kiri, that my sleep is sweet.
I lie awake the livelong night,
For love to prey on me in secret.
It shall never be confessed lest it be heard by all.
The only evidence shall be seen on my cheeks.
The plain which extends to Tauwhare:
The path I trod that I might enter
The house of Rawhirawhi,
Don't be angry with me, O madam; I am only a stranger.
For you there is the body of your husband,
For me there remains only the shadow of desire.
                              (Radin, 1957, pp. 118–9)

or the North America Tewa:

My little breath, under the willow by the water side we used to sit
And there the yellow cottonwood bird came and sang.
That I remember and therefore I weep.
Under the growing corn we used to sit,
And there the leaf bird came and sang.
That I remember and therefore I weep.
There on the meadow of yellow flowers we used to walk
Oh, my little breath! Oh, my little heart!
There on the meadow of blue flowers we used to walk.
Alas! how long ago that we two walked in that pleasant way.
Then everything was happy, but, alas! how long ago.

There on the meadow of crimson flowers we used to walk.
Oh, my little breath, now I go there alone in sorrow.
                              (Spinden, 1933, p. 73)

To be sure, there is often little interest among non-literate and semi-literate peoples in the individual personality of the author, particularly of the romantic and intense kind characteristic of a certain period of western literature or western capitalism. Nor is there often an idea of copyright: in societies without the tradition of a printed and fixed version, literary proprietorship is not really relevant.[12] But to deny the effect of individual inspiration and creativity in oral literature for this reason is to ignore the empirical evidence. From the early English ballad singers (Pound, 1921, esp. ch. 1; Entwhistle, 1939, ch. 6; Leach, 1955, esp. pp. 29ff) or recent Yugoslav epic poets (Lord, 1968a) to modern American narrators (Dorson, 1960) or gifted tellers of myths among the Winnebago (Radin, 1956, p. 122), we hear of the skill and inspiration of the individual artist.

What about the 'functions' of this literature? It has often been assumed that oral literature, because it is embedded in 'primitive society' must somehow have essentially different aims from that of literate cultures. Most often these aims are thought of as in some way practical. Perhaps the literature has a magical or religious purpose, or is in some way tied up with fertility, or satisfies some deep psychological need in mythic terms? Among other writers it has been fashionable to represent its function as very specifically 'social': perhaps with a conscious social purpose like education or moralizing, perhaps an unconscious function such as upholding the social structure. This kind of pragmatism is often contrasted with the idea of 'art for art's sake' supposed to characterize 'civilized' cultures. But too often what is given is an over-simplified and over-generalized picture – as if the literary achievements of even one society at one period of history could be reduced neatly to a single aim or a single function.

It is true that there are some special opportunities open to the oral composer. Oral literature can, in principle, be employed in almost any circumstances in which there is an audience, and the practical power of oral poets to eulogize or satirize, and to gain profit thereby, is constantly being mentioned.[13] Similarly certain types of oral literature – some kinds of songs, for instance, and proverbial formulations – can be turned to account in almost any situation. Among the Maori, for instance, sung poems are used for many purposes.

If a woman was accused of indolence, or some other fault, by her husband, she would in many cases retaliate, or ease her mind, by composing and singing a song pertaining to the subject. In the event of a person being insulted or slighted in any way, he was likely to act in a similar way. Songs were composed for the purpose of greeting visitors, or imparting information, of asking for assistance in war, and many other purposes of an unusual nature from our point of view. Singing entered largely into

12 On this see N. K. Chadwick, 1939, p. 78. There are, however, some instances in which songs are 'owned' by individuals, e.g. the Dobuan islanders of the western Pacific (Fortune, 1932, p. 251). (See also chapter 5 below, which qualifies this earlier statement.)

13 E.g. the Hausa praise-poets of northern Nigeria or the 'griots' of Senegambia (see Finnegan, 1970, pp. 96ff), the early Irish poets (see esp. Robinson, 1912) or the Icelandic poets (Einarsson, 1957, ch. 3 on skaldic poetry).

the social and ceremonial life of the people, and in making a speech the Maori breaks readily into song. (Best, 1934, p. 147)

Such uses are not in the same way open to the creator of written forms. On the other hand a writer has *other* opportunities, which he can choose to exploit if he wishes, whether for propaganda, moralizing, satire, or whatever. Beyond certain once-fashionable assumptions, there is no real reason to suppose that there is necessarily and universally a more practical aim in oral than in written literature. Certainly artistic conventions vary from place to place and time to time: it is hard to appreciate those of others, and thus tempting to explain them away in some such simple terms. But in *all* societies literature is likely to have many different aims in different contexts – to delight, propagandize, moralize, shock, cajole, entrance, eulogize, inform – and we can take no such short cut to their analysis as to suggest that these differences coincide exactly with the differences between literate and non-literate. As far as the appreciation of aesthetic and personal expressiveness goes there seems little to choose between the literatures of oral and of literate cultures.

Thus when we consider what are usually assumed to be the basic characteristics of literature (disputed though these are in detail) it is difficult to maintain any clear-cut and radical distinction between those cultures which employ the written word and those which do not. Such differences as there are do not neatly correspond with the presence or absence of literacy, and in both contexts it seems absolutely justifiable to speak of 'literature'. When we reflect how profoundly we expect the possession of literature to colour our own modes of thought we can see that the fact that, after all, it exists in non-literate societies also must greatly affect our estimate of their modes of thought too. We can no longer keep to the old picture of non-literates as without deliberate intellectual probing or aesthetic insight, submerged, as it were, in an unmoving and communal quagmire. In using literature to convey and form their artistic and intellectual awareness they are, at root, not dissimilar from those who live in contexts where writing is prevalent.

Some differences between oral and written literatures

There are also a number of differences between literature in literate and in non-literate contexts which it is interesting to go on to consider. For, however similar in fundamentals, literature in non-literate communities does have the special characteristics of an *oral* literature. Can these special qualities also shed light on our general problem?

One crucial difference as between oral and written literature is the important factor of its dissemination. In literate communities this is primarily through the written word, whereas in non-literate or semi-literate groups it must be orally delivered for its communication as literature. In the oral context, that means, the literature comes across as *performance* as well as a sequence of words. The actual *enactment* of the literary piece is necessarily a vital part of its impact and this fact can be exploited in many ways by the oral poet. His audience, furthermore, sees as well as hears him and the skilful composer/performer takes advantage of this fact. Characterization, for instance, need not be expressed directly in *words* when it can be as clearly and as subtly portrayed through the performer's face and gestures; conversations too can be lavishly introduced, a sure technique for the performer to convey personification and drama – points that have been made for recited literature as different otherwise as medieval narratives or contemporary African tales (Chaytor, 1945, pp. 3, 12, 55; Finnegan, 1967, pp. 52, 83ff). Similarly, the styles of these pieces may be related to their form of delivery. Repetition may be particularly marked and also the use of various well-known formulaic phrases and runs,[14] or the highlighting of particular dramatic episodes or detailed descriptions in a way not altogether in keeping with the unity of the whole when *read*. In medieval literature, 'the whole technique of *chanson de geste, roman d'aventure*, and lyric poem presupposed ... a hearing, not a reading public' (Chaytor, 1945, p. 13) – and the same point can be made of orally delivered literature generally.

This is something which it is essential for us to bear in mind when we attempt to *read* publications of literature originally designed for oral delivery. When one misses the interplay of ear and eye, of audience and performer, which is an essential part of oral literature, it is hard for it not to seem pale and uninteresting. 'The vivacity is lost: the tone of voice, the singsong of the chants, and the gestures and mimicry which give emphasis to what is being said and are sometimes a good part of its meaning' (Evans-Pritchard on Zande stories, 1967, p. 19). We similarly miss something by following the modern habit of reading classical Greek and Roman literature silently, through the eye only; it too was expected to be read aloud and it was a common practice in antiquity to publish a work by recitation before an audience. Medieval literature too was commonly chanted to a musical instrument and is 'filled with expressions which indicate the author's intention that his work shall be read aloud, shall be heard' (Crosby, 1936, p. 98; cf. pp. 88–9).

---

14 There is a large and increasing literature on this topic, ranging from treatments of Homeric epic to Gaelic songs in the Western Isles of Scotland. The main earlier references include: Lord, 1968a; Kirk, 1964; Magoun, 1953; Waldron, 1957; Ross, 1959; Jones, 1961; Benson, 1966; Rosenberg, 1970; Duggan, 1973; recent work is summarized in Foley's comprehensive bibliography, 1986. On larger units see also Propp, 1958 on 'functions', and Benedict, 1935, on 'incidents'. See also ch. 5 below.

This stress on literary impact through the *spoken* rather than the written word, sometimes further enhanced by the visual element, should not in fact seem so strange to contemporary European culture. With the spread of radio and television we are beginning to capture something of the same effect. To some this is a matter of regret. It is interpreted as a threat to the more scholastic form of education and outlook which had been so much admired earlier. Maheu speaks with alarm of the danger arising from the new media of mass communication:

Unless we take care, we shall have a form of communication . . . based purely on images, visual and sound, which will develop, parallel but independent, alongside instruction based on writing. This dualism endangers the spiritual unity of civilization because of the deep psychological differences that separate the two processes of mental training, one of which – that based on the image – appeals mainly to feeling, emotion and reflex response, while the other – based on writing – is, on the contrary, essentially an exercise in critical thought. (UNESCO, 1966b, p. 32).

Others will think that these 'deep psychological differences' are exaggerated and that this kind of assessment arises more from one particular cultural background in a particular period than from a dispassionate assessment of the available facts; and the suggestion that the use of non-written media necessarily leads to 'conditioning as opposed to education' (UNESCO, 1966b, p. 33) may seem an extreme one. But the relevant point to stress here is that, even if one does accept such a view, this in fact tends to undermine the assumption that any great divide between cultures (and their thought) coincides with that between modern western peoples on the one hand and those of the rest of the world on the other. For if more reliance on non-written media involves – as some have suggested[15] – a 'revolution' in communication and hence perhaps in thinking, then it is the highly industrialized nations that are moving fastest towards this – and moving, it would seem, in the direction of something taken for granted in societies which already make use of auditory means in the transmission of literature. Again, we find that the simple view of two basically different types of society, characterized by radically different communication media, just does not accord with the facts. There are differences *and* similarities between non-literate and television-influenced societies just as there is clearly neither a sharp break nor complete continuity between recent periods in European countries characterized, respectively, by the presence and absence of electrical media of communication.

15 See in particular the widely acclaimed writing of M. McLuhan, especially *Understanding media*, 1967.

A further factor in the actualization and transmission of oral literature is the audience. In a non-literate context an audience is in practice essential[16] – there is no written form in which it can be expressed otherwise than in front of those to whom it is directed. This contrasts with a written literature: even when his ultimate public is clearly in the writer's mind, his essential task is to get his composition on *paper* rather than directly to his audience. It is different too from the mass media of television and radio. Here an audience is, certainly, implied; but it is not face to face and has no direct and immediate impact on the poet. In the more direct oral context of non-literate cultures, however, the audience's reaction is an integral and continuing part of the whole artistic situation. It contributes not only to the mode of delivery but to the actual words used, by its overt reactions and additions, even by its passivity or at times evident boredom. Radlov has given a vivid description of this role of the audience in his account of the Kara Kirghiz poets of nineteenth-century Asia.

Since the minstrel wants to obtain the sympathy of the crowd, by which he is to gain not only fame, but also other advantages, he tries to colour his song according to the listeners who are surrounding him . . . By a most subtle art, and allusions to the most distinguished persons in the circle of listeners, he knows how to enlist the sympathy of his audience . . . The sympathy of the hearers always spurs the minstrel to new efforts of strength, and it is by this sympathy that he knows how to adapt the song exactly to the temper of his circle of listeners . . .

The minstrel, however, understands very well when he is to desist from his song. If the slightest signs of weariness show themselves, he tries once more to arouse attention by a struggle after the loftiest effects, and then, after calling forth a storm of applause, suddenly to break off his poem. It is marvellous how the minstrel knows his public. I have myself witnessed how one of the sultans, during a song, sprang up suddenly and tore his silk overcoat from his shoulders, and flung it, cheering as he did so, as a present to the minstrel. (quoted in Chadwick and Zhirmunsky, 1969, pp. 225–6; cf. pp. 221ff)

The audience is thus more involved, more imbued with literary creativity than is possible when communication is through the more remote medium of writing. This may have certain consequences for the nature of literary activity in such societies. It is likely, in many cases at least, to be somewhat less specialist and remote than it has – sometimes – been in societies where the interposition of writing can create an extra barrier between the creator and his audience. But there are obvious exceptions to this, in the many non- and semi-literate societies where it is possible to speak of an intellectual class: the Polynesian *tohunga* (H. M. and N. K. Chadwick, 1932–40, vol. 3,

16 Songs and poems are sometimes chanted by individuals while alone, so oral literature is conceivable without an audience. But in practice the normal situation involves an audience.

pp. 443ff), for instance the Mandingo 'jellemen' of West Africa, or the poetic order of early Ireland or modern Ruanda. But even in these cases the very fact of delivery before an audience must have kept the compositions of such poets from becoming too remote from their audiences. Again (the same point put in a different way) in non-literate societies individuals may be less likely in some respects to escape direct experience of the literary achievement of their local culture.

It is clear, however, that this whole question is a complex one and demands much further research. Obviously the significance of the audience as a direct factor in oral literature must be taken into consideration. But for the nature and impact of the literature it may be that the *kind* of audience or public to which it is directed and the functions expected of it by composer and public are equally important – and these seem to have varied as much *within* as between non-literate and literate communities.

A further obvious difference is in the degree of verbal flexibility. Variability seems generally to be the norm in oral cultures in contrast to the fixity of the written word with which we are more closely acquainted. Surprisingly to one brought up in a literate culture, those without writing often have little concept of verbal accuracy.[17] There is no possibility of a written document to act as the yardstick of accuracy and the whole conjoint process of composition/extemporization in oral literature tends to get away from the idea of a fixed and correct archetype. By contrast, it is in literate cultures that we tend to find the magic of the written word and the concept of a text as the immutable and once-for-all authentic version. There have been plenty of examples in western history of the reverence for the written word for its own sake, whether in a transmitted manuscript tradition or on the printed page. This is a sphere in which the difference between literate and non-literate culture can be profound, and perhaps one of the first prerequisites for an appreciation of the subtleties and individual inspiration of oral literature is to understand this difference.

It is so important, indeed, that it is tempting to regard it as a key to all other differences. But we cannot, alas, push this point too far. Even in literate cultures there are many differences of degree in the respect accorded to a fixed text. There seems to be somewhat less of this attitude in parts of western Europe now, say, than in the last century; there are variations according to the type of text involved (sacred books like the Bible, Koran or – an oral example – the Rig-Veda, attract more reverence for word-perfectness than more popular writings); and even within a single community different groups will take, say, the immutability of a particular form of prayer or of a well-known textbook more, or less, seriously. It is possible indeed that we

17 For some exceptions and a qualification of this comment see ch. 5 of this volume.

should regard *printing* rather than writing in itself as the most important factor here. This at any rate is the view of one authority on medieval literature.

The invention of printing and the development of that art mark a turning point in the history of civilisation ... The breadth of the gulf which separates the age of the manuscript from the age of print is not always, nor fully, realised by those who begin to read and criticise medieval literature ... We bring unconsciously to its perusal those prejudices and prepossessions which years of association with printed matter have made habitual. (Chaytor, 1945, p. 1)

The degree of verbal fixity is, then, one very important sphere of difference between the literature of oral and literate cultures and as such must affect the outlook of the corresponding communities. But, like the other differences discussed, it does not produce a clear-cut and fundamental division between them, and, if there is a divide, perhaps it is between societies with and without printing rather than with and without writing.

There is not space to treat other possible differences that spring to mind,[18] but one further point should be mentioned. This is the suggestion that non-literate societies as such necessarily have less comparative perspective – i.e. less awareness of other cultures, less realization that their own ways are not unique. This is probably true to some extent and as such must affect the general outlook in such societies. But again it is easy to exaggerate. The isolation of non-literate communities has for various reasons often been over-estimated in the past. Ethnocentricism, further-more, is by no means limited to 'primitive' societies. More important in the present context is the possibility that it may not necessarily be non-literacy itself which leads to such isolation as there is – various technological factors seem more relevant here – and its presence need not therefore of itself imply a limited outlook. Written literature, particularly the printed word, does indeed provide certain opportunities for wider communication. But so too can an *oral* literature. We can instance the travelling 'jellemen' of the great western savannah region of Africa who created a vast cultural area throughout many different kingdoms and linguistic groups by their arts of word and music (Finnegan, 1970, p. 96), the wandering *azmaris* of Ethiopia who helped to bring about the striking uniformity of Ethiopian poetry among the many groups of the area (H. M. and N. K. Chadwick, 1932–40, vol. 3, p. 525), the unifying effects of their reverence for Homer among the disparate Greeks, or the early poets of Ireland who 'in the absence of towns or any centralized political system ... were the only national institution' (Greene in

18 In particular the question of historical perspective often said to be lacking to those without written literature. On this see the discussion in Goody, 1968, especially the comments by Goody and Watt, pp. 44ff, and Gough (with whose sceptical approach on this question I am very much in agreement), pp. 74–6.

Dillon, 1954, p. 85) – all performing the same kind of functions as the medieval jongleurs and minstrels of western Europe or their counterparts in the Arab world. Here again it turns out that the differences are not clear-cut and that the detailed forms and impact vary with the general nature and outlook of the society as much as or more than the question of whether or not that literature appears in writing.

This brings us to a final difference that should be mentioned here – though strictly it has not necessarily to do with the presence or absence of literacy. This is the difference in outlook and general development that exists between any two cultures unknown to each other. It is very hard to believe that people very different from us can really have anything approaching the depth of understanding or grace of expression that we know in our own society and its literature. This barrier cuts us off to some extent from all other cultures. But it often seems particularly insurmountable for those brought up in a largely literate culture contemplating the arts of non-literate groups – particularly (if irrationally) when the groups are very different from us in *material* development. How few Englishmen, for example, would have been prepared to recognize in the ragged Russian peasant, Yakushkov, one of the greatest composers and singers of the famous local epics? (N. K. Chadwick, 1939, p. 79). Again, scholars have acquainted us with the rich and elaborate poetry of early and medieval Ireland; but from the point of view of their conquerors these Irish *literati* could be dismissed as 'rebels, vagabonds, rimers, Irish harpers, bards and other malefactors' (quoted in O'Rahilly, 1922, p. 86). It is not only the literate who are ethnocentric. It is salutary to remember the comment of a native of the Gilbert Islands – the Pacific group so imbued with their rich heritage of song – when he heard about aeroplanes and wireless: 'It is true the white man can fly; he can speak across the ocean; in works of the body he is indeed greater than we, but' – his voice rang with pride – 'he has no songs like ours, no poets to equal the island singers' (Grimble, 1957, p. 199). The fact that an unfamiliar literature is not immediately pervious to a foreign observer need not therefore mean that it lacks its own depth and richness for those who practise it or that there is some fundamental mental difference between the two.

Modes of thought

What emerges is that there are indeed many differences between the literatures of literate and non-literate cultures, and that some of these may be relevant for their modes of thinking. But there are a number of difficulties about taking the sum total of these differences as marking a fundamental division between the two. It is perhaps worth summing these up at this point.

First, the implication that non-literate societies do not have 'literature' turns out to be without foundation. This literature, furthermore, can achieve the same range of things we expect from written literature, with all that this means for the mode of thinking in such contexts. It is true that, as with most foreign literatures, it is not always easy for us to appreciate that of cultures very different from our own. It is also true that much research remains to be done on the different psychological and social effects of reliance on oral as opposed to visual media, as well as on the differences both between direct and indirect (or mass) oral media, and the psychological processes involved in visual communication through written *words* on the one hand and non-verbal visual images on the other. But these problems merely show that the subject is a complex one – much more complicated than the clear-cut chasm between 'oral' and 'visual' (or non-literate and literate) cultures which some people assume. Questions for further thought do not invalidate the main point being made in this chapter: the presence of literature as a vehicle for intellectual and aesthetic expression in non-literate as in literate societies.

The final point to make is that, though there are indeed interesting differences between the literary media in non-literate and in literate groups, these seem to be no more fundamental than differences *within* each of these. To take just one relatively short period of western European history and the many vicissitudes that have affected literature there: we have experienced the change-over from script to print, then the expansion of the range of print with increasing literacy, the move from a reliance on the Greek and Roman 'classics' as the eternal standard to more local and contemporaneous writing, the recent paperback 'revolution', and the expanding influence of radio and television. Thus to take as our yardstick the present circumstances of literature in western Europe – or rather perhaps those of a generation or so ago – and assume that this is the standard by which we estimate all other literatures is to show a profound lack of historical and comparative perspective. There is no reason to suppose that our peculiar circumstances are the 'natural' ones towards which all literature is somehow striving to develop or by which it must everywhere be measured. In particular there is no reason to hold that it is only through the written – far less printed – page that man achieves literary and artistic development and that we can ignore as wholly other the literary expression of thought and artistry in other forms. As Levin put it in his preface to Lord's analysis of Homeric and Yugoslav sung epics, 'We live at a time when literacy itself has become so diluted that it can scarcely be invoked as an esthetic criterion. The Word as spoken or sung, together with a visual image of the speaker or singer, has meanwhile been regaining its hold through electrical engineering. A culture based upon the printed book, which has prevailed from the Renaissance until lately, has bequeathed to us – along with its immeasurable riches – snobberies which ought to be cast aside' (Lord, 1968a, p. xiii).

This chapter has perforce skated over many highly controversial questions and has not ended up with any clear definition of either 'literature' or 'thinking' – or of the exact relation between these. The subject tackled is a huge one and all I have tried to do is to make a few obvious (if sometimes ignored) points about it. What I hope I have established is that it *is* a huge and complicated subject – far too complex to be reduced to trite classifications or the categorization implied when we facilely define certain groups as 'non-literate' and unthinkingly go on to assume consequences from this for the nature of their thought. Much work clearly remains to be done on these questions, including careful comparisons among different non-literate cultures themselves. But despite the scattered nature of the illustrations given here it does seem at least clear that one cannot assume that individuals in non-literate (or largely non-literate) cultures are *ipso facto* less creative, thoughtful, self-aware or individually sensitive than people in literate cultures, and therefore fundamentally different in their modes of thought. Non-literacy itself is unclear and relative enough as a characterization; but the further assumption that non-literate cultures and individuals necessarily lack the insight and inspiration – the modes of thought – that we associate with literature seems on the basis of present evidence an unjustified conclusion.

5

Oral composition and oral literature: some evidence from the Pacific

One of the arguments for a basic divide between oral and literate cultures rests on the assumption that, even given the existence of oral literature in non-literate societies, the oral technology behind this 'literature' makes it fundamentally different in its compositional (and hence transmission) patterns from written literature. This view is particularly, though not exclusively, associated with the influential Parry–Lord 'oral school' and has received apparent support from studies of oral composition not only in Yugoslavia in the 1930s but also elsewhere in the world. The universality of this particular form is queried here in the light of the evidence from traditionally oral cultures of the South Pacific where the processes of creating and disseminating oral literary forms have both parallels and contrasts to those of written literature in a way which undermines the generalized Great Divide theories of an opposition between orality and literacy.

The oral literature of the Pacific is an extremely rich and developed one, with its traditions of panegyric and cosmological poetry, dance-songs, religious poems, war and abusive poetry, love lyrics, topical songs, hymns, story-telling and oratory. All through the Pacific Islands – from Hawaii in the north through Kiribati or Nauru near the Equator, to Fiji, New Hebrides, Tonga, Samoa or, in the further south, the Maori of New Zealand – verbal art is treasured and developed not only in the traditional forms of Polynesian, Melanesian and Micronesian culture, but also in the context of the modern political and economic order or the ceremonial of the Christian churches of the Pacific. Even now, it is an art form whose development strikes the student of the modern nations of the Pacific, while in the past its elaboration and high prestige surprised European visitors to the region, reaching perhaps its highest peak of specialized concentration in the traditional hierarchical Polynesian societies such as Hawaii, Maori or Tahiti, of which Katherine Luomala remarked that their literary specialization 'ranks the area with Ancient Greece, India, and Scandinavia in the earliest era of the bards' (Luomala, 1950, p. 879).

This remarkable literary development in the Pacific has been relatively little noticed by the recent students of comparative literature.[1] Certainly the Pacific evidence has not appeared much in recent discussions about the nature of 'oral culture' or of the type of composition or style likely to be characteristic of oral literary forms. Yet in fact the Pacific material can throw interesting light on a number of the controversies involved and in some respects seems to provide a counter-example to the apparent trends established by current research into oral literature, which has mainly drawn upon evidence from Eurasian, African and to some extent American traditions.

It is the contention of this chapter that, in certain respects, oral literature in the Pacific stands out as different. This claim touches on a number of aspects, but applies in particular to the way in which literature (especially poetry) is often composed, where the evidence from the Pacific in part runs counter to commonly accepted assumptions about the characteristics of oral composition and performance.

Theories and assumptions about oral composition

In recent years there has – rightly in my opinion – been a reaction against the older romantic ideas of oral composition as a communal, even 'tribal', activity which, by the time most oral forms came to be collected, rested more on memorization and transmission by passive 'traditors' than on any active creativity by present-day individuals or groups. This reaction has been in part due to one fairly obvious characteristic of oral literature that was pointed out, notably, by early researchers on East European and Asian forms, such as Radlov on Kirghiz heroic poetry or Murko on Yugoslav, and reinforced by the close study made possible by the taperecorder: that is, the *variability* of oral literature. Unlike the written word there is no fixed and 'correct' text, for oral literature is a performed not a printed art form and its expression depends on the effectiveness of the performers and their sensitivity to the audience's wishes as much as on a *text*. As the Chadwicks summed it up, 'on the whole we must regard the free variety which allows more or less scope

---

1 Among earlier scholars, the Chadwicks and more particularly Nora Chadwick did pay due attention to Polynesian oral literature (see H. M. and N. K. Chadwick, 1932–40, vol. 3 pt. 2). However, the relative ignorance of Pacific forms among students of comparative literature comes out in authoritative reference works (Cassell's *Encyclopedia of World Literature*, 1973 edition; *The Penguin Companion to Literature*, 1971; and Seymour-Smith's, *Guide to World Literature*, 1986) which say nothing about Pacific literature apart from a few brief notes on Polynesia (and coverage of New Zealand literature in English) in contrast to extensive coverage given to Asian and even African literature – not to speak of Europe and America.

for improvisation as the normal form of oral tradition, and strict memorisation as exceptional' (H. M. and N. K. Chadwick, 1932–40, vol. 3, p. 868).

This emphasis on the variability and lack of fixity of oral as contrasted to written literature has of course been further focused by the research on Yugoslav heroic poetry by Milman Parry and Albert Lord, with their explication of 'composition-in-performance – improvization during the actual performance through the use of formulae and formulaic expressions (Parry and Lord, 1954; Lord, 1965, 1968a and 1975). Their work has been profoundly influential in all areas of oral literature research. It can be said to be the currently ruling theory about the nature of oral composition – taken as the basic point of reference in studies as far apart in historical and geographical coverage as Tamil heroic poetry (Kailasapathy, 1968), English and Scottish ballads (Jones, 1961; Buchan, 1972), early Hebrew poetry and biblical studies generally (Culley, 1967), Greek folk poetry (Beaton, 1980), West Sumatran sung narrative poetry (Phillips, 1981), the Nibenlungenlied (Bäuml and Spielman, 1975), the Song of Roland (Nichols, 1961; Duggan, 1973) or Hittite epic (McNeill, 1963).

As such there is presumably no need to summarize the main theories and findings of the Parry–Lord analysis of oral texts or their composition.[2] There are certain points, however, to which I wish to draw explicit attention as basic presuppositions in the current orthodoxy about the nature of oral literature and oral composition. A number of them are also accepted by scholars who would not necessarily go along with all the detailed theories of the 'oral formulaic school' – or may not even be explicit aware of them – but who are nevertheless indirectly influenced by the current consensus on the nature of composition in 'oral cultures'.

These presuppositions, I suggest, basically come down to four main assertions:

1 *The text of oral literature is variable and dependent on the occasion of performance, unlike the fixed text of a written book.* Thus Bäuml and Spielman can assert with apparently no fear of contradiction that 'it is well known that . . . each performance of a poem [i.e. an oral poem] will vary from each other performance' (1975, pp. 63–4). Following Lord's 'any particular song is different in the mouth of each of its singers . . . [and] each performance is more than a performance; it is a re-creation' (Lord, 1968a, pp. 100–101).[3]

2 *The form of composition characteristic of oral literature is composition-in-performance, i.e. not prior composition divorced from the act of performance*: 'For the

---

2 The standard texts are of course the writings of Parry and Lord themselves, which can be supplemented by the general surveys and discussions such as Whallon, 1969; Watts, 1969; J. D. Smith, 1977; Finnegan, 1977, ch. 3; also Haymes, 1973; and Foley, 1985.

3 Quotations here are illustrative of a wide range of similar statements or assumptions.

oral poet the moment of composition is the performance,' writes Lord, 'for singing, performing, composing are facets of the same act' (Lord, 1968a, p. 13).

3 *Composition and transmission of oral literature is through the process mentioned above and not (as we once thought) through word for word memorization.* Claims that an oral poem, for example, is re-delivered in memorized form 'exactly (word for word) as I heard it' have been shown in many cases to be unfounded through comparing recorded versions. In Lord's assessment 'oral narrative is not, *cannot* be, memorized' (Lord, 1965, p. 592); or, in the more modest form in which Jack Goody indicates the general evidence about oral culture, 'reproduction is rarely if ever verbatim' (Goody, 1977, p. 118).

4 *In oral literature, there is no concept of a 'correct' or 'authentic' version.* There is no fixed text and all versions are equally authentic as actually performed. This is another fundamental difference between oral literary forms and *written* texts – indeed in some of Lord's works *the* crucial difference: it is when the oral poet takes over 'the concept of a fixed text and ... memorization' that he ceases to be a true oral poet (see Lord, 1968b, pp. 4–5).

These four assumptions have all, of course, been queried before now, at least if taken to be universal and unvarying characteristics of *all* oral literature (or even all oral poetry),[4] and there are a number of instances in different parts of the world where their application has been questioned. Nor would all the writers referred to necessarily hold to every aspect mentioned. Albert Lord himself, it should be said, while at times expressing himself in somewhat universalizing terms (e.g. Lord, 1965), does not claim universal applicability to *all* genres of oral poetry for his findings on Yugoslav oral *epic* (see Lord, 1968a, pp. 4, 141, etc., together with comments in informal discussion). In this respect Lord's disciples have sometimes taken his 'oral theory' further than he would himself. Overall, however, these four characteristics have been widely accepted as *the* typical form of oral literature (not just oral epic) to be found widely and predictably in 'oral cultures', and one which it is reasonable, furthermore, to predicate of oral culture in historical periods of which we can no longer obtain the full contextual evidence.[5] Indeed, this general set of ideas has been widely influential even

4 See e.g. Stolz and Shannon, 1976 (essays by Kiparsky, Aspel, Finnegan); J. D. Smith, 1977; Finnegan, 1977, esp. ch. 3. Lord himself, be it noted, does not make such universalist claims as some of his disciples.

5 See, e.g. Nichols, 1961, p. 9; Notopoulos, 1964, pp. 19ff, 50ff, etc; Kirk, 1965, pp. 22, 29ff; Curshmann, 1967; Burke, 1978, pp. 141ff (the last by no means, however, a full or uncritical acceptance of the oral-formulaic theory).

among those who would not necessarily align themselves uncritically with the oral-formulaic school, and has a kind of self-evident quality about it which has led many (including myself[6]) to take it as more or less providing the given parameters within which work on oral literature should be set.

It is thus remarkable that in the case of the rich and developed oral literature of the Pacific the model indicated above is apparently not the most appropriate one. Or rather, there *are* instances where it does more or less apply but there is also a definite sphere where the exact opposite seems to be the more typical form. In fact if one were forced to explain in a brief sentence the 'characteristic' mode of performance and composition in Pacific oral literature one would have to say, after a bit of hedging about there being a number of different recognized modes according to genre and situation, that – on the current evidence – the most highly regarded and specialist form of poetic composition commonly involved precisely the *opposite* characteristics from what one might expect starting from the prevailing orthodoxy. Much Pacific poetry is composed *prior* to performance, depends for its performance on a fixed and memorized version, and does involve the concept of a verbally 'correct' text. In other words, the oral literature of the Pacific area provides a fascinating counter-example to the currently accepted model not in just one or two scattered and perhaps specially explicable instances, but in a model widely accepted and revered throughout a wide culture area in which oral literature plays an extremely important part.

I want to exemplify this claim in further detail shortly. Let me, however, begin by qualifying it a little and explaining that not *all* oral literature in Oceania is of this prior-composition-and-memorization form. In fact there are a number of differing modes in which oral literature in the Pacific is produced. This of course in itself throws some doubt on the universalist assumptions implicit in the oral-formulaic school and its disciples who give the impression that only *one* form – that epitomized by the Yugoslav model as explicated by Parry and Lord – characterizes the composition of oral literature: 'a special technique of composition outside our own field of experience' (Lord, 1968a, p. 17), one which is characteristic of 'all oral poetries' (Parry and Lord, 1954, p. 4) and perhaps, according to some extensions of the theory, of oral prose and oral tradition generally (e.g. Nichols, 1961, p. 9).

Before turning to a consideration of some of the variants in modes of literary composition and performance in Pacific cultures, I should explain that I will in general be concentrating on composition of the *words*, even

6 I was particularly influenced by the insights of *The Singer of Tales* in my earlier work on Limba story-telling and oral literature in Africa (1967 and 1970). Though I still consider the book one of the great classics in the field I now think I earlier accepted some of its apparent corollaries (as noted above) rather too uncritically.

though in the case of poetry the music – and in some cases the dance gestures – are important components of the full artistic performance. This concentration is partly because I do not have the space or expertise to cover everything, but it also has some justification in what seems to be a common attitude to oral literature in the Pacific: that the verbal element is in some sense prior. When people speak of 'composing a new song', most often what is meant is composing new *words* to an already existing tune. As Jacob Love sums it up, 'In Polynesia and probably in Melanesia the essence of a song is in the words; gestures and intonations are perceived to be secondary' (Love, 1977; cf. also Kaeppler, 1976, p. 210; Karoua, 1977).

Composition, performance and rehearsal in the Pacific

Among the various forms of oral composition and performance in the Pacific the evidence suggests that some do fit with the model of composition-in-performance put forward by the oral-formulaic scholars. The performers of certain literary forms draw on the kind of 'ready-made diction' and traditional themes that Lord found with Yugoslav poets, and it is through relying on this conventionally accepted 'stock-in-trade' of phraseology, style, themes and plots that performers can produce a suitable and in a sense 'new' piece of literature suited to the occasion and audience for which they perform.

This is obviously one aspect of many story-telling situations. It is widely noted that individual story-tellers impress their own personalities on the content and presentation of a story – even a 'traditional' story – and that this is partly a matter of how they deliver it (in a sense 'compose' it) during the actual performance. As Luomala puts it in her discussion of the stories about the trickster-hero Maui which are so widely known throughout the Pacific, the 'author-raconteur' (i.e. story-teller) is 'the individual who is both the creative agent and the perpetuator of the oral literature. An author-raconteur's creative reinterpretation and synthesis of the mythological stock-in-trade peculiar to a certain island at a particular time achieves the "uniqueness of the real", to use Hegel's phrase to describe the rich individuality which distinguishes each variant of a myth or a cycle from another even though from the same island . . . Each biographer interprets Maui in the light of the culture not only of his era and island, but of his particular social and intellectual set' (Luomala, 1949, p. 23).[7] The same kind

---

7 For a more detailed account of how a particular performer (the Maori narrator who was the source of John White's well-known translation of the Maui story) created his own unique version of the story by drawing on and manipulating traditional themes and skills see Luomala, 1949, p. 52.

of process is depicted in Wheeler's description of Mono-Alu stories from the Bougainville Straits (Wheeler, 1926). Here the stories are not unchangeable wholes, handed down in fixed form through oral tradition, but rather a series or combination of 'motives' – themes and plots. One story-teller will put these together in one way, another in a different way, so that there is not one final and 'correct' version of any tale – only the way the story is put together by an individual narrator on a particular occasion. Among the Tangu of northern New Guinea similarly story-tellers may change and innovate and then run the gauntlet of popular reactions: 'Miming, gesturing, struggling for words, ready to initiate as well as forgetful, a story-teller may leave out some passages and incidents, and he may add new ones' (Burridge, 1969, p. 417).

Though the extent of improvization – and hence of composition-in-performance – is not always clear in all these cases, it does seem that one way in which the teller's individuality is brought into play is through his selection of words, phrases and dramatic expression, as well as his reactions to the audience during the actual process of delivering the story. The general picture that emerges certainly throws doubt on earlier assumptions about long communal transmission through the ages, with no part left to the individual but memorization, and fits reasonably well with the currently accepted view: that individual narrators are in fact responsible for the final composition of the story (at least in large part) when they are actually performing it for their audience.

The same general point applies to oratory, one of the great literary forms of the Pacific. Here certainly the stylistic forms, appropriate themes and accompanying actions may be clearly laid down by convention (or 'tradition') but the detailed wording, form of phrase and insertion of particular content frequently depend on the circumstances of the actual performance. In the often competitive setting of Samoan oratory, for example, a speaker trying to ward off an interruption-attempt with proverbial expressions and mythological and allegorical references, or responding to his opponent's speech in oratorical contests (*fa'atau*), cannot rely on memorization of old speeches but must be responsive to the sensitivities of his audience and the obscure metaphorical allusions of his opponent which he must understand and cap to come out the victor (Holmes, 1969, pp. 346, 350).

Similarly, in formal Maori oratory there are certain points within the set structure where the speaker can indeed exercise the skills of composition-in-performance, which include building on a set of formulae and 'frames' appropriate to the occasion (at other points the wording is set and invariable once the basic and known texts have been selected). He has the

option of choosing among a wide range of set phrases, or deciding to coin his own. The set phrases include formulae for the recitation of genealogy, proverbs, and a more flexible set of oratorical clichés . . . These clichés can be varied by minor word changes and the selection of new images to fit almost any situation. The appropriateness of the speech is made specific by the introduction of proverbs and genealogy, which demonstrate that the speaker is well-acquainted with historical kinship links between the groups present . . . The other option of innovation is most likely to be taken up by a speaker who has thoroughly mastered the standard forms. He has the expertise to manipulate familiar routines so that they emphasise his breaks into creativity. (Salmond, 1975b, pp. 53, 54)

Apart from differences in setting and format (prose rather than poetry) this process sounds remarkably like the 'oral composition' delineated by Lord and Parry.

This is also sometimes found in accounts of the composition of poetry. Far from being all handed down from the remote past, some poems can be improvised on the actual occasion on which they are performed. Ifaluk word songs are sometimes composed, for instance, as they are needed (Burrows, 1963, p. 102), and the same is true of Maori songs for paddling canoes. An early account by Hochsetter in 1867 makes this clear

In large war canoes manned sometimes by 60 or 70 men there are generally two *kaitukis* acting as leaders, one placed near the bow and the other the stern. They either sing by turns, one responding to other, or they sing together, extemporising at the same time, various jokes and witticisms, by introducing into the traditional songs new verses having references to the momentary situation. It is remarkable to see how the pullers are in this manner guided in keeping time. (Mitcalfe, 1974, p. 183, quoting from Hochsetter, 1867, pp. 297–8)

This extempore quality is still noticeable in many modern Maori work songs (Mitcalfe, 1974, p. 183).

Similar comments are made by a number of early observers of Maori singing in general. John B. Williams, American Consul at the Bay of Islands in 1842–4, writes with, as Mitcalfe puts it, 'slight exaggeration':

Songs [are] quite original, made up as they go along upon any being, subject or matter. A circle will be formed for the purpose of singing, which is extempore. They sing of persons and things around them and of the beautiful works of creation . . . If at work for anyone, they sing of the person who employs them. Thus they sing of every stranger who comes in the place, without premeditation, causing laughter and merriment among them. (Mitcalfe, 1974, p. 184, quoting Kenny, 1956, pp. 79–80)

Another occasion very much recalls the composition-in-performance so stressed by Lord.

Ensign Best describes how a song was improvised for him as he paddled up the Waipa in March, 1842: 'I stripped to my trousers, hid my clothes under my big coat, seized a paddle and worked away with such effect that a *Tuki waka* was instantly composed'. (Mitcalfe, 1974, p. 184, quoting Taylor, 1966, p. 345)

A parallel process occurs in taunting and competition songs where capping the opponents' words is part of the aim. Thus in East Aoba in the New Hebrides, weddings are the occasion for teasing and sexual jokes between the two groups of in-laws. When one side has sung a song full of sexual innuendo the other replies suitably on the spur of the moment, also in song (Mera, 1977). Similarly in the singing contests so popular in many parts of the Pacific, it seems that improvising is sometimes part of the singers' response to their opponents' efforts. In Easter Island rival clans or families used to challenge each other to an *ei* competition – offensive but funny couplets, whose singers used to hire themselves out to display their powers of wit and improvisation (Campbell, 1971, p. 4: English summary); while the traditional singing contests of master bards and intellectuals in Polynesia provided the occasion to show quickness of composition as well as mastery of traditional wisdom (see, e.g. H. M. and N. K. Chadwick, 1932–40, p. 415; Luomala, 1955, p. 48; Beckwith, 1919, p. 28).

These instances of improvisation seem to fit much better with the theory of composition-in-performance than with the 'communal creation' idea according to which present-day literature derives from composition dating back many years or generations before the present, transmitted through word for word memorization by the performer.

There are also the interesting cases where a new poem is deliberately built upon an older one. This is a common practice among the Maori, where songs of lament are adapted to the particular circumstances of the dead person though constructed according to certain basic and existing patterns. Similarly old *haka* (Maori war songs) are modified for new purposes and new personnel whether this be a VC investiture ceremony or a conflict on the sports field. In general 'it was the custom of the Maori to adapt an old song to a new circumstance' (Mitcalfe, 1961, p. 11), just as old Hawaiian praise-songs were revised and rededicated to living persons (Pukui, 1949, p. 255) while in the Marquesas praise-songs were 'flexibly composed . . . quickly adaptable to any customer who could pay to have his name publicly celebrated' (Luomala, 1955, p. 51).

It is not always clear how the adaptation of these older songs took place. Sometimes, it seems, long and deliberate re-working took place *before* a special occasion, with the new song being composed as a special undertaking separate from the performance. Elsdon Best describes a Maori lament for the death of a neighbour's small child in which the final song was largely adapted from older forms through prior re-working by a group (Mitcalfe, 1974, p. 7, following Best, 1925, p. 116). On other occasions it may be that this adaptation took place partly at least during the actual occasion of performance – but on this point as on so many others to do with composition, further research could be most illuminating.

From the evidence, then, it is certain that in some instances the process of composition is a deliberate act by individuals and *not* based primarily on far-off communal creation; and that in some cases at least the kind of composition-in-performance described by Lord and others is rather closer to what happens in practice than is memorization. This 'composition-in-performance' seems to apply in particular to *prose*, which tends to be more subject to variation according to context and teller than poetry. For though certain themes and plots in prose literature are old – those of the well-known stories about the hero and trickster Maui for example – the way they are actually told is 'much more plastic' than poetry. Their original authors may not be known (in contrast to the known authorship of much poetry) but in compensation the 'author-raconteurs', to use Luomala's phrase, can make their own unique and personal performance when they present the story for a given audience and context.

This, then, is one style of composition in the Pacific. But it is not the only one. For there is also a second form – and a very highly regarded one too: deliberate and planned composition *before and separate from* the performance.

This second form of composition in the Pacific applies mainly to composition of poetry associated with the dance. In this the poet works out his composition some time before the planned time of performance (often several months or more). He or she then teaches it to the future performers, and a series of concerted rehearsals takes place before the final public performance.

The case of the Fijian *mekes* (dance-songs consisting of around three to twenty pages when transcribed as texts) provides one instance of a process that in one form or another seems to be common throughout the Pacific. In Fiji a *meke* is composed in anticipation of a particular ceremony or special occasion. A group or a local chief decide they want a *meke* for a particular occasion, and commission it some time beforehand from a known local composer. A group goes to the poet (who can be a man or a woman) and asks him to compose a *meke* for them, taking care to gain permission from the local 'priestly' clan if the poet himself is not a member of it. Certain rituals then have to be performed, varying in different areas of Fiji, to enable the composer to gain the desired inspiration. In one case, the requesting group brings the composer flowers. He sleeps under the flowers and from them he draws his spiritual inspiration. In a sleep or a trance he sees a vision in which the words, the music and the dance gestures of the *meke* are given to him. He wakes, and calls his apprentices to him. They listen as he expounds the *meke* to them line by line together with the music and the gestures. It is the apprentices' responsibility to memorize the *meke* given to them by the poet, for once he has delivered the content of his vision to his followers he himself forgets the details of the poem. This is then followed by a series of rehearsals, after which the *meke* is finally presented in public. At this performance the composer's initial responsibility is recognized and rewarded, but after a series of ceremonial exchanges he or she gives up the ownership of the *meke* to the local chief or the village who then controls it (Seniloli, 1976; Kubuabola et al., 1978).

A parallel process obtains in the Gilbert Islands (now Kiribati), where again there is prior composition by the poet well before the time of performance. The details vary in different accounts, but all agree that it is not a matter of composition-in-performance, as the 'oral-formulaic' theorists would expect, but a separate act of composition totally divorced from the performance itself and dependent on groups of people memorizing the words composed by the poet. In one account (by Grimble, 1957) the poet goes by himself to some lonely spot to compose the poem and there performs a series of rituals. At dawn he intones to the rising sun:

O Sun, thou art reborn out of darkness;
Thou comest out of deep places, thou comest out
    of the terrible shadows;
Thou wast dead, thou art alive again.
O Sun behold me, help me:
The word of power died in my heart,
Let it be reborn again as thou,
Let it fill me with light as thou,
Let it soar above the shadows,
Let it live.
So shall I be eloquent.

This incantation (age-old inheritance from his magic-loving ancestors) he repeats three times, then rinses his mouth with salt water, thereby making his tongue 'pure for song'. (Grimble, 1957, pp. 204–5)

Following this he enlists the help of a group of friends. He brings them back with him to his 'house of song' to help him work on his poem.

He begins to recite the 'rough draft' of his poem, which he has ruminated overnight. It is the business of his friends to interrupt, criticize, interject suggestions, applaud, or howl down, according to their taste. Very often they do howl him down, too, for they are themselves poets. On the other hand, if the poem, in their opinion, shows beauty they are indefatigable in abetting its perfection. They will remain without food or drink under the pitiless sun until night falls, searching for the right word, the balance and music to convert it into a finished work of art.

When all their wit and wisdom has been poured out upon him, they depart. He remains alone again – probably for several days – to reflect upon their advice, accept, reject, accommodate, improve, as his genius dictates. The responsibility for the completed song will be entirely his. (Grimble, 1957, p. 205)

This is then followed by a long series of practices by the chosen choir and dancers – a chorus up to two hundred strong – who memorize the song phrase by phrase and develop the dancing gestures under the guidance of a dancing expert. The process may be long drawn-out:

There are interminable repetitions, recapitulations, revisions, until the flesh is weary and the chant sickeningly familiar. But from a ragged performance of ill-timed voices and uncertain attitudes, the song-dance becomes a magnificent harmony of bodies, eyes and arms swinging and undulating in perfect attunement through a thousand poises, to the organ tone of ten score voices chanting in perfect rhythm. Then dawns the poet's day of glory. (Grimble, 1957, p. 206)

The other main published account of Gilbertese composition, by P. B. Laxton, differs in certain details,[8] but resembles the first in the essentials: prior composition by the poet, a religious-magical setting, and memorization by others for later public performance.

The composers of these songs . . . are often recognized poets and to a certain extent the skills and magic rituals observed are handed down in families. The magic is that of the *kario*, which may be translated as to 'bring down'. The performer of the *kario* magic will go to the ocean side of the atoll at a propitious time accompanied by an assistant. He will enter the sea before dawn and swim beyond the ocean reef, a feat in itself involving no little danger. There, just beyond the line of breakers he will lie and swing up and down in the rollers as they pile themselves to crash on the reef and chant his *tabunea* or invocation . . .

The words and the music then come to him and he sings them out line by line so that his companion will hear and repeat them until the song is done. The companion, standing in the reef-shallows will never, owing to his part in the magic, forget or vary the song thus obtained. (Laxton, 1953, pp. 343–4)

Descriptions of actual composition have seldom been given with even the detail of the two accounts quoted here, but the general pattern of a poet deliberately composing beforehand for important occasions seems a common one in the Pacific. Some of the classics of Maori poetry were composed by great poets (and poetesses) for great ceremonies, and both their names and the occasions are sometimes remembered for years (Mitcalfe, 1974, pp. 7–8). In the Marquesas, a song for a festival was commissioned by the head of a family approaching a specialist (*tuhuna*) in composition and teaching. 'The composer retired into seclusion to evolve from his mind the verses and melody . . . After his compositions were ready, the next step was the assembling and teaching of the chorus that was to

---

8 In view of the discrepancies further research on this topic would be interesting – though perhaps difficult in view of its esoteric and secret nature. Other evidence also supports the conclusion that Gilbertese composition is clearly separated from the performance and that song composition is commonly regarded as a specialist and esoteric activity (Hughes, 1957; Xavier, 1976; Karoua, 1977).

perform them ... The composer himself taught his chants to the chorus, all members of which, like the teacher, were subject to certain restrictions during the period of training' (Handy and Winne, 1925, p. 11). The Trobriand song *Kaduguwai* was first composed in an inspired trance and this was then followed some years later by a specially produced occasion for its performance, organized by the local chief, the composer's husband (Baldwin, 1950). Here too the same basic pattern can be detected: the separation between the act of composition and the act of performance. In these and similar cases the procedure might be compared rather to the considered and deliberate literate tradition, than to the oral composition-in-performance discussed by Lord and others of the 'oral-formulaic school'.

In these and other accounts of composition in the Pacific there are a number of points of great interest for the comparative study of composition and of oral culture more generally.

First, it is interesting how many references there are to group participation in the act of composing. In the Cook Islands, for example, 'Christmas hymns' (*imene tuatua*) are jointly composed by a working group of church members who try out various different lines and evaluate them according to how well (among other things) they fit with the intended scriptural message (Tongia, 1977). Similarly for certain Hawaiian poems, members of a group had to provide a line each (Beckwith, 1919, p. 28), just as the Maori lament mentioned earlier was composed by a group 'selecting and rejecting images – until they had the song they wanted' (Mitcalfe, 1974, p. 7), and in modern Samoa songs are sometimes composed by a group of three or four people working together (Love, 1977). For Kiribati too Grimble mentions the part played by a group of the poet's friends in working over his 'rough draft', even though he himself retains final responsibility (Grimble, 1957, p. 205), while in Buin in the Solomons the composer sometimes goes alone to the forest to be undisturbed but may also 'sit at the fire in the evening ... together with his pals' (Thurnwald, 1936, p. 6).

Obviously composition by or with a group is only one form of the composing process in Pacific literature for, as commented on below, there is great variety in composition modes even within one culture, and individual composition is also often important. Nevertheless group composition is common enough to be worth remark. It also has interesting implications for the more general theories about oral composition mentioned earlier. It is in fact far from the kind of 'communal' composition or 'folk creation' that used to be believed in by many folklorists, for it is usually a small selected group who carefully and consciously work together to try out various wordings. Nor does this group composition fit with the oral-formulaic model of composition-in-performance by an individual poet – not only because a group, rather than a single individual, is responsible but also because of the deliberate act of composition divorced from the situation of performance.

There is a second and perhaps even more striking characteristic of many of these descriptions of composition in the Pacific. This is their association with spiritual inspiration – with the idea of a trance, dream or vision through which the poet is inspired. The words and music are often thought of as not really his own but from some outside spiritual source. Once the poet – whether individual or group – has thus received the words from divine inspiration, they cannot be changed, but must be preserved and repeated faithfully by the performers.

This theme comes out again and again in accounts of poetic composition in Pacific cultures. The Fijian poet Velema in the 1930s who composed the narrative poems about 'The Flight of the Chiefs' translated and published in Quain's well-known collection, grew up as a seer with special powers to 'speak with ancestors who perhaps joined personally in the battles of ancient Flight-of-the-Chief' (Quain, 1942, p. 8). Even when he used recent events for his songs these are represented as given to him by the dead. Thus one song composed to commemorate a death was not, in the local view, made up by the composer himself 'but, as the song itself relates, the soul of the deceased chanted it to the composer' (Quain, 1942, p. 9). Velema 'communes with true ancestors . . . In trance or in sleep the songs come to him, taught him by his supernatural mentors. He takes no personal credit for his composition . . . All contribute to the glory of his ancestors' (Quain, 1942, p. 14).

Although the details have changed, the same general picture of the process of composition is given by Fijians today: the poet receives his compositions in trance or vision, through the spirit dwelling within him; and once the lines and actions have been given him in this form, they must not be changed by composer or performers but remain exactly as they come from the spirit.

Similar references to the spiritual and esoteric nature of composition are found in many Pacific cultures. It is not perhaps surprising that the new songs taught by the spirits (of various kinds) revered in the local religious movements known as 'cargo cults' are held to be transmitted to believers in a state of trance or dream (see, e.g. Freeman, 1959, pp. 189ff; Chinnery and Haddon, 1917, pp. 449, 452–4), but this situation is not just confined to specifically religious movements. In Hawaii some chanters were said to have been taught by the gods of the hula in dreams (Pukui, 1949, p. 257), among the Kiwai of Papua New Guinea many of the serial songs are associated with Adiri (the spirit land of the dead) and with rituals to do with the dead spirits

(Landtman, 1927, p. 428), while for the Tangu 'myths and dreams are interdependent' (Burridge, 1960, p. 253). The Trobriand songs described by Baldwin were seen as inspired in a series of trances. In one case the composer was in deep mourning for her son when 'the spirit came and spoke to her, felled her in a trance, and took her soul to the sunset isles. There she met . . . all . . . Uweilasi's [her husband's] departed relatives. They composed together the tunes and words of the *Kaduguwai*. They gave her a commission to sell Uweilasi to make a grand celebration to end all the mourning.' The composer, Igali, 'named herself and spoke in the third person. She insisted that it was a spirit song' (Baldwin, 1950, p. 264). A rather similar view is held by the Ifaluk of the Carolines. Their song-poems are regarded as having been composed by one of the gods, for 'a god can take possession of either a man or a woman and so dictate a song which issues from between tranced lips' (Burrows, 1963, p. 7).[9]

This view of composition seems on the face of it to be closely tied up with 'old' religious forms and therefore likely to die out with the establishment of Christianity. But this does not necessarily follow. Trance-like composition or the notion of divine inspiration is far from incompatible with Christian forms. Indeed one specifically religious song about Noah in Uvea came to its composer 'in a dream' (Burrows, 1945, p. 13) and of course the cargo cult movements are often influenced by Christian beliefs and forms; in the Maori Hau Hau movement, the leader received the hymns directly 'from Gabriel' (Winks, 1953, p. 206). Furthermore a number of the poets who compose Fijian *mekes* today following the inspiration and ceremonies described earlier are themselves Christians, some of them leading church members.

The model of divine and trance-like inspiration for poetic composition clearly goes deep in the Pacific. In some ways it may – like all models – not fit the facts exactly; it seems clear, for example, that while in some cases immediate and rapid inspiration does take place, in others the poet perhaps works rather harder at his compositions and makes more alterations than it might seem if we took this local model too literally. The Gilbertese process as described by Grimble is one case in point. So perhaps is the *series* of trances – over about a month – in which the Trobriand poetess composed her song: it did not, perhaps, come complete the first time; and maybe was also worked up later for performance. The picture is also complicated by descriptions like the following from Hawaii, where the idea of divine inspiration is *combined* with that of preparatory hard work beforehand.

A single poet working alone might produce the panegyric, but for the longer and more important songs of occasion a group got together, the theme was proposed and either

9 For some further references to trance, dreams, inspiration from spirits, etc., see Layard, 1944, pp 121–2 (Malekula, New Hebrides); Gunn, 1914, pp. 238–9 (Futuna, New Hebrides); Fischer, 1970, p. 207 (Truk).

submitted to a single composer or required line by line from each member of the group. In this way each line as it was composed was offered for criticism lest any ominous allusion creep in to mar the whole thing by bringing disaster upon the person celebrated, and as it was perfected it was committed to memory by the entire group, thus insuring it against loss. Protective criticism, therefore and exact transmission were secured by group composition. (Beckwith, 1919, p. 28)

Exactness of reproduction was in fact regarded as a proof of divine inspiration.

It seems then that a number of problems remain to be investigated about the exact process involved in the actual composition, even when the overall local model is clear.[10] More research on the detailed practice is certainly needed, together with fuller analyses of parallel texts than has so far been carried out. Nevertheless it is now clear at least that there is a subject here that would repay further investigation in a comparative context.

The general picture that emerges of the importance of prior composition and the frequent model of poetry as divine inspiration is thus a striking one. This particular model of poetry is not of course unparalleled (a number of other instances were mentioned at the Urbino conference on orality in 1980 as elsewhere), but the way that it is specifically linked with the process of oral composition and memorization in some Pacific poetry gives it a particular interest for wider discussions on the nature of 'orality'.

The relevance of the Pacific evidence

It is time now to relate these findings to the presuppositions about the nature of oral composition and performance listed earlier. It can be seen that the second mode of composition in the Pacific as explained here is far from fitting with that particular model.

First the fact of prior composition in many cases is indisputable; the pattern is composition *followed* by a series of rehearsals – sometimes over many months – *followed* by performance. Unlike what would be expected on the currently accepted view there is a clearly observable and locally recognized split between composition and performance. Second, there *is* memorization by the listeners and the performers for the words to be recorded, as it were, in the first place and then later performed by the group. How much variability there is in practice between the poet's first inspired version and the actual performance later does indeed demand further controlled research but it is clear not only that the local view is quite definite

10 For a similar point in the context of musical composition see the interesting discussion in Merriam, 1964, ch. 9, esp. pp. 170–1.

about the verbal identity of each, but also that a degree of verbal memorization is certainly involved (it has to be to make the later joint performance possible) and that, contrary to what we might predict, there is definitely a local concept of the 'correct' and 'authentic' version of the kind we normally expect only of written literature.

This apparently unusual form of composition and performance can perhaps be linked to a number of other aspects of Pacific culture and to the situation in which these poems or dance-songs are produced.

First, because of the joint and public nature of the final performance, there is obviously some need for an agreed form of words rather than freedom to compose during the performance. Sometimes the poet is also the composer (or the inspired medium) of the music and dance gestures as well as of the words, and in this case the whole performance is his responsibility (though he may have assistance for the rehearsing). In other cases he is primarily responsible for composing new words to tunes that are already in circulation – apparently a common practice in the Pacific – and he may or may not be the one to work out the details of the dance. But, whatever the exact division of labour, it seems that the music, the dance gestures and the words (the latter always the responsibility of the composer) must be reproduced more or less exactly for a rehearsed performance to be possible with the dancers either themselves singing the song or accompanied by a singing group. This is recognized as a necessary element particularly in the Pacific context where so many dance forms depend on performance of a definitive version by a concerted and well-drilled troupe rather than individuals, but it could be that there are parallels in predominantly oral culture elsewhere. Joint performance of, for example, celebratory or panegyric poetry by a group – as perhaps, say, in the case of Pindar's compositions[11] or of Zuni unison songs (Tedlock, 1985) – often involve not only prior composition but to some extent the acceptance of a definitive version.

This is also related to the second point: the emphasis on exact memorization and on the concept of a correct version. In part this is simply the practical point mentioned – the need for a group to sing accurately together. But there are also other aspects. One is the strong emphasis on the divine or spiritual inspiration which lies behind the poet's composition (or reception) of the poem, and which must not be betrayed by those who receive it from him. Another is the emphasis in many aspects of Pacific culture on the concept of memorization and correctness.

---

11 A point suggested to me by Dr E. Cingano, who is currently working on oral composition in relation to Pindar's poetry.

There are constant references to this in the context of the transmission and performance of poetry. In Tonga 'a poet may recite . . . his own, or another's compositions or teach them to bands of singers and dancers', writes Collocott in his great collection of Tongan poetry (1928, p. 64). He also speaks of a Tongan poet chanting a one-hundred-and-one-line poem as a gift when making a formal visit of condolence to a friend, himself a poet. His friend responded by thanking him for his gift: 'Thanks for the . . .' and recited the whole poem back again even though he had only heard it once a few minutes before (Collocott, 1928, p. 81). Luomala comments, 'The incident illustrates the value laid on poetry and the remarkable memories of the bards, not only in Tonga but throughout Polynesia. Over and over again, poems are given and received as gifts and feats of memory are described' (Luomala, 1955, p. 43). Again, in the Cook Islands the composition of Christmas hymns (*imeme tuatua*) depends on the process of memorization as well as composition. These hymns are composed by a group, in stages, and after each session 'the women were given the task of memorizing the hymns . . . They were the keepers of the hymns until the next practice session'; on occasion, when a tape recorder was available, this would be used instead for the memorizing function (Tongia, 1976–7). Similarly both the Maori and the Hawaiians lay great stress on the *correct* rendering of songs: in Maori areas 'memory lapses are still regarded as a sign of death or disaster and some young people say they would sooner not try to learn songs than run the risk of not performing them correctly' (McLean, 1964, pp. 34–5). Sir Apirana Ngata gives a vivid account of this when discussing his own education as a Maori:

I learnt one outstanding feature in the education of a Maori, that he must know a thing in one lesson: in two lessons, if his teacher is indulgent. To learn a song in one lesson, words, air and all its graces seemed an impossible feat. But it was demonstrated in many cases within one's knowledge. There were illiterate elders among my relatives in the sense that they read with great difficulty and could barely sign their names to paper. But they could memorize genealogies, land boundaries and strange songs with ease. They took no written notes, showed in fact from the commencement of any narration or recitation that they were committing to and holding the matter by an effort of memory. . .

There were the song leaders, who attained to that position by a process of selection in practice. A fundamental feature of recitation or singing in Maori is that there must be no hitch of any kind. So a leader must not only know his matter, but must also remember it in all its phases. A fault was an *aitua*, a presage of ill-fate, even of death. (Ngata, 1959 (1972) pp. x–xix)

On first reading one or two of these references to memorization in the Pacific it is easy to be sceptical, specially for one acquainted with the findings of Lord and his followers. Indeed, my own first reaction was to recall the many cases where local claims of exact memorization had been disproved by the more precise test of comparing different recorded versions. This may still happen with particular instances in the Pacific (and I hope that further detailed field investigation of these will indeed take place), but it is quite striking how firmly references are made to the idea and practice of exact memorization. This does indeed seem to be a feature of at least a number of Pacific cultures (perhaps most notably in Polynesia) and to find expression, among other things, in the particular mode by which poetry is often composed and performed.

A further related point is the admiration and recognition accorded to the composer himself. It might seem that, with the stress on inspiration from divine forces outside the poet combined with an emphasis on joint performance and exact memorization, we are back with the theory of communal composition with little part for creativity by the individual. But not at all. The Pacific model of composition–rehearsal–performance is combined with a respect for an individual's poetic originality and even, in some cases, of some idea of copyright held by the author over his own compositions. Even if a poet later relinquishes control of his composition to the patron for whom he composed it, his own responsibility (under divine inspiration) is apparently clear. It is true that the composition takes place within the constraints of certain conventions of style, content and attribution (as surely happens to some degree with the composition of *any* literary genre, written or unwritten); but even so the poet's own and original contribution is recognized and rewarded. Indeed originality is sometimes highly prized and sought after if Fortune's description of Dobuan composition is any guide: 'There is as much emphasis on originality of content and of words used for expression as in our own [i.e. European] literary tradition' (1932, p. 251; see also Grimble, 1957, p. 200 on Gilbertese composition). All in all, we seldom seem to encounter evidence of cases which could be considered as 'communal authorship' but rather of known poets composing individually (or sometimes in small groups), prior to performance, and in due course receiving the recognized reward for their achievements. Both the prized originality of the individual artist(s) and the value attached to the completed poem – a piece of intangible property as it were – once again help to explain the apparent stress on the preservation of the correct version of compositions in the Pacific and the frequent memory of their authors' names.[12]

It is not the case, then, of mere mechanical repetition of known forms which an outside analyst could perhaps try to argue was not really oral poetry

12 On this see Alpers, 1970, p. 37, and instances cited in Merriam, 1964, pp. 171–2. There is not space here to discuss the complex question of 'copyright' but some relevant references are Kubuabola et al, 1978; Layard, 1944, p. 315; Fortune, 1932, pp. 251, 261.

in its proper sense,[13] but original oral compositions by known and named poets composing within an oral framework – though they happen to do this in a way very different from the one we would expect from the current assumptions about oral composition inspired mainly by the work of Lord and Parry.

Some conclusions

How are we to explain this somewhat unexpected finding? Albert Lord's reaction is interesting here. After hearing some of the instances mentioned above, he queried in an earlier discussion whether 'the kind of composition in which the singer makes up his song beforehand and memorizes it . . . is, indeed, oral composition . . . I think there is a possibility that the kind of composition in which the singer makes up the song orally, and doesn't commit it to writing, but commits it to memory, may not be oral composition, but rather written composition without writing' (Lord in Stolz and Shannon, 1976, pp. 175–6).

His remarks are worth pondering. One possible suggestion that might arise from this is that the particular form of oral composition in the Pacific might in fact be due to the influence of writing – that Pacific Islanders have already through their contact with European cultures somehow acquired a 'literate mentality' (as Lord would put it, Stolz and Shannon, 1976, p. 175) and so naturally compose in a 'literate manner' even though in practice the poets and their disciples may not happen to use actual writing.

In so far as this suggestion is not just playing with words, it is worth following up a bit further. Certainly many areas of the Pacific have had quite long enough contact with European culture – at any rate over the last 200 years – to be well acquainted with writing and written literature, and this has included profound influence by Christianity. It is natural to wonder how far this influence has introduced an unusual emphasis on 'correctness' or prior composition which is not really the 'natural' form of oral composition in the Pacific; just as one wonders whether the stress on correctness, memorization and prior composition among Somali poets (which is somewhat unusual though certainly not unparalleled in African oral literature) is to be connected with the co-existence of written Arabic literary forms in Somali literature (Andrzejewski and Lewis, 1964; Finnegan, 1970, p. 106).

But though this may be an interesting line of thought to pursue, I am not convinced ultimately of its validity. After all we have to take the facts as we find

13 A line that Lord seems prepared to take of texts that have been memorized word for word (1968a, p. 280) – a rather extreme way of legislating out of court forms which do not fit his own theory (see J. D. Smith, 1977, p. 143).

them, rather than speculating about some 'natural' or 'primeval' form in the far past. And the facts suggest that whereas in Yugoslavia the composers of oral poetry normally followed the 'composition-in-performance' procedure, in the Pacific oral poets commonly (though not invariably) used the contrasting composition–memorization–rehearsal–performance procedure that I have delineated – yet Yugoslavia is an area which actually has a much *longer* contact with literacy than the Pacific, with written forms directly contributing to the oral poetic tradition. Furthermore the evidence suggests that this type of prior composition and emphasis on memorization goes back some time in the Pacific and is *not* just a recent phenomenon; and it seems to take place as readily – perhaps more readily – in the early periods and in the more remote islands as in modern urban contexts or missionary centres. Pending the emergence of new evidence on this, it is at present somewhat difficult therefore to be satisfied with explaining away this particular oral procedure in the Pacific, in contrast to Yugoslavia, as essentially due to the influence of writing or the outside imposition of a 'literate mentality'.

Another reaction to Lord's comment might of course be that he is merely ruling out possible counter-examples to his own theory by redefining the term 'oral' so narrowly that it can *only* be applied to examples which fit the Yugoslav model on which his own analysis is built – i.e. those manifesting the characteristic of composition-in-performance. However, more constructive than this rather cynical assessment would be to consider further the area in which the Pacific procedure *might* be regarded as a form of 'written composition without writing'. This raises the point that, quite apart from the oral-formulaic theory, we do indeed usually associate certain patterns such as lack of verbal variability, prior composition away from the involvement of the actual performance or situation of oral delivery, and the idea of a fixed and authentic text, with *written* and *not* with oral communications. As Goody puts it, in a non-dogmatic and reasoned discussion of the evidence with which most researchers would agree, 'most of the standard oral forms of non-literate societies fall towards the variable rather than the repetitive ends of the continuum . . . each reciter [of oral myths, in contrast to written forms] is an author . . . [In oral unlike written sequences] reproduction is rarely if ever verbatim' (Goody, 1977, pp. 119–20, 29, 118; cf. also Goody and Watt, 1968).

In the case of the Pacific, however, these associations do not seem to hold as we would expect. Perhaps instead of trying to query or explain away the *oral* context involved we should instead query the necessity of the assumed associations. Is it *only* with writing – and written literature – that these characteristics can appear? It seems not. Certainly, they are commonly (and understandably) associated with the written word. But perhaps we are wrong to assume that a *common* association is a *necessary* one.

Those of us who have grown up within the traditions developed over the last centuries of western culture are perhaps too steeped in the idea that fixity of form together with the facility for the multiplication of identical copies *must* be associated with writing (and more especially printing). Are we perhaps in danger of assuming too readily that that is therefore the *only* way things can be: that fixity can *only* go with a visual medium? After all, a fixed auditory form or the multiplication of identical *auditory* copies is not in principle impossible. Indeed, through the developing technology of auditory reproduction, above all of tape/cassette recorders, we are already beginning to see precisely this happen in our own culture. Even in fully literate societies therefore it is no longer just through *written* forms that fixity and multiple identical copies are achieved: a development whose significance we are perhaps only beginning to appreciate. In cultures where oral forms have for long played a central role, it would not therefore be totally surprising to discover cases where some of the characteristics which in our own culture are linked with writing appear in association with auditory forms. This, I hold, is exactly what we find in the Pacific – a culture area which has developed a tradition of achieving what elsewhere would be a fixed text through auditory forms. And along the same lines, there is the concept of a fixed 'correct' version, held orally rather than through writing. The contemporary use of tape recorders in the Pacific fits easily with this tradition – something which achieves the same end, once again in an auditory not a visual medium, but this time mechanically rather than (so to speak) by hand.[14] So we may need to widen our own ethnocentric assumptions about the 'natural' form for achieving and recognizing fixity in verbal versions to realize that in some cultures this can sometimes be in an auditory (oral) and not just in a visual (written) medium.

Not all 'oral' cultures have laid emphasis on fixed and exact versions through auditory forms. Indeed, it seems to be somewhat more common for this association *not* to hold and for orally composed and transmitted versions to be subject to a great deal of verbal variability. To this extent, the common paradigm contains much truth. But this should not blind us to the cases where this association *does* hold or, still worse, tempt us to deny its existence when it *is* found. Oral literature in the Pacific, I suggest, is one area where in *certain* forms (not all) there is the demonstrated occurrence of verbally fixed forms, retained by *oral* not written means, together with both the concept of a 'correct' version and the institutionalized means for achieving this over a limited time span.

---

14 The reliance on tape recorders to record and reproduce (auditory) versions, probably as a satisfactory means in itself rather than just a second-rate substitute for writing, is also of course documented outside the Pacific too (e.g. Tedlock, 1985; Sherzer, 1985).

This may be a somewhat unfamiliar idea to those of us brought up in a highly literate culture with its emphasis on the importance of the written word. But, on reflection, it should not really be a cause for much surprise. After all it is now well established that writing can be used for different purposes and with different philosophies in different societies: there is not just *one* context for writing or one established stage (evolutionary or otherwise) to which it corresponds (see, for example, the discussions in Hoenigswald in Stolz and Shannon, 1976, p. 277; Meggitt, 1968; Clanchy, 1979, esp. Part II; Goody, Cole and Scribner, 1977, p. 299). The same variety, it seems, applies to oral communication: it too can take a number of different forms and appear with different characteristics in different cultures. There is perhaps after all no one abiding set of characteristics that *always* appears in 'oral culture' (any more than in 'literate culture'), but there are instead a number of different options and differing possibilities, as exemplified by the varying arrangements that have proved possible for the composition and performance of oral literature. Once the question has been opened up it can be seen that, though there are a number of differences between oral and written communication, these differences are not necessarily absolute and universal ones: in many cases they are found, in some they are not, in others they are a matter of degree rather than kind.

The main conclusion then must be that one particular form of oral composition which is widely found in the Pacific does in fact possess characteristics which in our experience of western civilization have more commonly (till recently at least) been associated with written than with oral composition.[15] This, if true, is a conclusion of some significance, and one which forces us to revise some of the assumptions not only of the oral-formulaic school but also about the nature of 'oral' as opposed to 'literate' culture in general.

This leads on to the final point. Why should we in any case feel some need to explain – let alone explain away – the Pacific (and similar) examples? The answer presumably lies in the assumption that we can somehow find *one* theory, *one* model of the nature of oral composition (or of oral culture more generally) – if not Parry and Lord's then another. Thus if we meet what seems to be a counter-example to the established theory we have to explain

15 This particular syndrome comes out especially clearly in the Pacific, which is why this area has been singled out for particular discussion here. But it is of course not unparalleled. Elements of this appear in a number of other instances of oral literature where prior composition or a measure of memorization are involved, sometimes with the sanction of divine inspiration: for example the Rig Veda; the nineteenth-century Finnish epic and lyric poetry which formed the basis of *Kalevala* (Kiparsky, 1976, pp. 94ff); and certain forms of Somali and Rwala Bedouin oral poetry (Andrzejewski and Lewis, 1964, p. 45; Meeker, 1979, p. 113), to mention only a few (for some other examples, see Finnegan in Stolz and Shannon, 1976, pp. 146ff).

it. But it has in fact become obvious, not just in this chapter but in many accounts of oral literature, that there are a number of *different* ways in which oral composition can be organized. This is certainly so in the Pacific, and I hope my insistence on what is (admittedly) one very important and admired form of Pacific literature has not obscured the existence in *other* cases of the composition-in-performance mode in the Pacific. Indeed this variety goes even further, for even within a single Pacific culture, a number of different methods of composition may be recognized. In the Cook Islands, for example, the Christmas hymns (*imene tuatua*) are jointly composed and worked on by a local group; the *ute* songs are individually composed by a single poet whose words are memorized for him by a group of women; young men individually try out new words to the tunes they have first heard in songs by Elvis Presley, Jim Reeves or others on the radio; while the religious poems known as *karakia* are primarily handed down from tradition, with great emphasis on exact memorization and correct rendition (Tongia, 1976–7, 1977). Stories on the other hand are apparently told in a freer context, much more in accordance with the composition-in-performance model. Similar situations with differing modes of composition for different genres even within a single culture are recorded in, for example, Hawaiian and Maori literature (e.g. Beckwith, 1919, p. 28; Pukui, 1949, p. 255ff; Mitcalfe, 1974, pp. 7ff, 183ff) and may well apply in many other cases too: writing also sometimes plays some part, interacting with more oral modes.

Thus, contrary to what we would expect from the general theories about oral literature – whether the communal composition or the oral-formulaic theories – the variations cannot easily be subsumed under one uniform theory, nor is there just one unvariable process by which oral composition takes place.

This is indeed the other assumption of the current orthodoxy which is challenged by the example of the Pacific – an assumption which is perhaps even more basic than the four stated earlier. That is, that it is possible to find *the* universal characteristics of all oral literature or at least of 'all oral poetries', as Parry puts it (Parry and Lord, 1954, p. 4), and from this draw up a theory of universal application. But even if this venture was feasible in principle and not, as expressed in the oral-formulaic model, already subject to modification from counter-examples elsewhere, the Pacific evidence would render it extremely doubtful. For here, it seems, oral composition not only does not always follow the uniform procedures of the composition-in-performance model, but often, in a widespread and highly prestigious procedure, appears in forms involving memorization, prior composition, and the concept of a correct version – all processes which must lead us to query many of the characteristics of written as against oral communication which we usually take for granted as the norm.

6

Oral and written interactions:
the South Pacific experience

Orality and literacy, far from being mutually contradictory poles, can interact and support each other. This is illustrated from literature in the South Pacific, where the writing down and codification of their 'myths' or 'legends' was not a neutral or merely 'technological' procedure of capturing some exotic and impervious 'Old Tradition' but a social process influenced by familiar political, ideological and religious pressures.

Many of the collectors and analysts of literature in the Pacific have deliberately set out to find 'old' forms. We can see here the influence of the romantic back-to-nature model common to many writers about the South Pacific, depicting the 'Noble Savage' in his free and 'natural' state, uncontaminated by the influence of modern civilization. This model has led many analysts to look for the form supposedly characteristic of that 'primitive and unspoiled original state', and to reject as later distortions anything which seemed to smack of the impact of western traders, officials or missionaries. This attitude, understandable perhaps in view of the nineteenth-century romantic and evolutionist fashions which still influence so many writers today, has resulted in a misleading picture of the actual facts. For literature and communication in the South Pacific have inevitably been affected by the historical processes of the last centuries. To pretend that songs, chants, stories or proverbs recorded in the nineteenth or twentieth century in the Pacific arose in a situation untouched by Christianity or by foreign contacts is merely to shut one's eyes to the facts.

This does not make the literature created and collected during the last century or so any the less interesting. On the contrary it is fascinating to study how once-foreign ideas and stories (from the Christian tradition especially) have been taken over by Pacific islanders and moulded according to local styles and insights into truly Pacific literary genres. It is impressive too to study how poets and narrators have not been content just to take over word for word verbalization from the past but have also worked with new ideas and developed new forms built on the old. It seems unfortunate that the romantic search for 'the primitive' has so often blinded investigators to the fascination of contemporary and developing forms of Pacific literature and to the richly creative ways in which new ideas have been moulded into Pacific culture.

Overlap

In this process, writing has played an important part. Indeed, there is a striking *overlap* between oral and written literature. It is true that when one speaks of 'oral literature' the obvious model is of literature that is composed, transmitted and performed orally, and this indeed is true of some cases. But there are also instances where literature is oral only in *some* of these senses. For example, a piece may be composed in writing, but then transmitted and performed orally; or it may be composed and performed orally but writing may be used in its transmission. These – and other – combinations can be observed extensively in the Pacific both today and in the past and show how careful one needs to be in using concepts like 'oral literature' or 'oral culture' as if they are simple ones. In practice they are sometimes accurate but in a complex sense that does not necessarily exclude all interaction with written modes. This will come out more clearly through some examples.

Maori literature provides a number of instances of forms originally composed in an oral context but then depending partly on writing for their circulation and transmission. In New Zealand, people like to learn Maori songs but sometimes find them difficult to memorize easily. McLean explains how they find that 'the best way of getting around lack of memorizing ability is to begin with a text. Some learners are already taking song texts with them to meetings' (McLean, 1964, p. 35). Maori orators often 'carry a small notebook around with them to *hui* [ceremonial meetings], filled with random jottings [on] . . . genealogies . . . and . . . fine turns of phrase for future use' (Salmond, 1975a, pp. 120–1). Similarly many Maori families have manuscript *waiata* (song) books. In fact, as Biggs explains, 'In New Zealand it was, and is, usual for Maori families to keep manuscript books in which are recorded genealogies, the texts of songs known to members of the family, and local tradition . . . Great numbers still exist' (Biggs, 1964, p. 25). Maori newspapers for their part printed hundreds of texts sent in by correspondents in the nineteenth and early twentieth centuries (Biggs in Ngata and Hurinui, 1961, p. vi) and there are many collections too of poems and other texts; altogether it has been calculated that the number of songs published 'runs into thousands' (Biggs in Ngata and Hurinui, 1961, p. vi). Literary forms of this kind continue to circulate in clubs, special performances and schools, and by now this normally implies some reliance on *written* texts as the vehicle through which these compositions are learned. Writing is not the only mode of course. Face to face performance is still important; as well, Maori poetry is performed in both radio broadcasts and gramophone records, and at the same time is preserved in recorded form through the New Zealand Broadcasting Corporation and in similar recordings and transcriptions organized through universities (e.g. by the University of Auckland), a number of them circulated yet again through the pages of the Maori magazine *Te Ao Hou*.

A similar process of interaction between oral and written forms is widely found in the Pacific, often supplemented by transmission through the radio. Hymns, songs and sometimes stories are recorded in written texts, which in turn preserve them and also serve as the basis of further oral performance. Thus in the Carolines, Burrows found that a number of Ifaluk people had notebooks containing song texts which they were sometimes prepared to pass on to him. They did this not by showing him the notebooks themselves – they were secretive about these – but 'by oral dictation' (Burrows, 1963, p. 409). Similarly in his great collection of Tongan poetry, Collocott mentions that a number of poems have appeared in written as well as oral form (Collocott, 1928, e.g. pp. 84, 93–4) and the same applies to a number of the sources for Gifford's classic edition of Tongan 'myths and tales'. As he writes:

The printing press has undoubtedly done more to preserve the extant Tongan myths and legends than has oral transmission. Fortunately both the Wesleyan Methodist and the Roman Catholic churches in Tonga adopted the broad policy of publishing in their Tongan language magazines many stories from raconteurs now long dead. A number of tales presented in the following pages are drawn from these sources. (Gifford, 1924, p. 5)

Written sources also play a part in literary forms which in other respects may be oral in their composition or performance. Many forms of literature involve reference to biblical themes. To take just a very few instances: modern Samoan oratory is shot through with biblical references; the popular Fijian *same* are specially composed poems on biblical themes; Christian hymns in local languages are common throughout the area, including those associated with separatist religious cults; the detailed study of songs in Uvea and Futuna by Burrows revealed that most songs in these islands are Christian ones (Burrows, 1945, p. 13); one of the popular poetic genres in the Cooks is that of *imene tuatua* ('Christmas songs') specially composed on biblical themes (Tongia, 1977), and Christian themes are common in their dance-songs; at the celebrations in Tuvalu in 1976, during discussions of the independence constitution, by far the largest proportion of dances involved songs on topics drawn from the Bible – Moses and the tablets, the Israelites leaving Egypt, Daniel and the lions, or the wise men following the star (Murray, 1977). The same kind of interaction comes out in the way books of proverbs and myths are sought after by orators as a basis for their speech-making in modern Samoa (Holmes, 1969, p. 351). Similarly contemporary Maori orators like to refer to their small notebooks for speech-making at ceremonial gatherings (Salmond, 1975a, pp. 120–1) and old people sometimes carry round copies of Ngata's collection of Maori poems *Nga Moteatea* (Salmond, 1975a, p. 122). The Bible serves as a frequent resource for the same purpose. Assumptions about some acquaintance with written sources or the techniques of writing may also enter in. Thus in the song of congratulation composed for the then President of Nauru, Hammer De Roburt, when he was made an OBE, one of the highlights was a play on the letters OBE – Boe (a district in Nauru), with the witty suggestion that he got the OBE because of coming from a district named by the same three letters (Agir, 1977).

All in all, it seems clear that even where a particular form has been composed and delivered orally, writing may still play some part. This interaction between oral and written forms is in no way 'unnatural' or surprising for such overlaps can in fact be found in many areas of the world, but it is worth emphasizing since it is so often overlooked in the accounts of Pacific oral literature.

The written origins

Another way in which written and oral forms interact is where some piece is originally composed partially or wholly through writing (perhaps partly from oral antecedents) and thence passes into the 'oral tradition', i.e. is transmitted and performed orally. The story-tellers in Rennell and Bellona, for instance, used to write out their stories before telling them to the collectors. Their stories are nevertheless published under the title of 'the oral traditions' of these islands (see Elbert and Monberg, 1965, p. 32).

Perhaps the best documented example of written composition leading to oral circulation is that of the 'Kaunitoni myth' in Fiji. This myth tells the story of the first origins of the Fijians and where they came from. Their ancestors, it is told in the myth, set out in their canoe, the *Kaunitoni*, from a land far to the west and sailed towards the rising sun, led by the chief Lutunasobasoba. They were driven by a storm onto the coast of Viti Levu and landed there at Vuda. Lutunasobasoba's brother Degei searched out a place for them to live in the high northeast mountains and after a successful settlement there the people were finally scattered throughout Fiji after Lutunasobasoba's death.

This myth is widely known and told throughout the whole of the Fiji group and has been mentioned by a large number of scholars in the present century. It seems to be a clear case of 'oral literature', indeed 'oral tradition' from the far past.

The surprise is to discover that this is not so. A carefully documented historical analysis (France, 1966) has shown that it originated in the late nineteenth century and that its composition rested as much on the written word as on oral forms. For it turns out that this famous 'traditional' Fijian myth was in fact unknown in Fiji earlier in the nineteenth century. The evidence for this seems clear, for the many nineteenth-century authorities with close familiarity with Fijian customs are all unanimous that there were no tales about the origins of the Fijians, much though they wished to discover them. Then, in 1892, a brief reference to a story was published by Basil Thomson, 'an amateur anthropologist and enthusiastic observer of Fijian culture', as France describes him. In this story the ancestors of the Fijians had been washed up on the west coast of Viti Levu, though the story apparently made no mention of the name of the group's leader or of their canoe. Thomson was eager to find further elaboration. By then, as France explains it,

quite a lot of people knew what Thomson was looking for. The mission schools had introduced Fijians to the knowledge of distinct racial groups occupying different areas of the world, and several of the mission teachers had evolved definite views on the origins of the Fijian race. A graduate of the Navuloa mission school, who studied there from 1892–1894, has described the history lessons in which he was told of the African origins of his ancestors. (France, 1966, p. 111)

In 1892 the editor of the Fijian language paper *Na Mata* held a competition to discover and preserve a definitive history of the Fijians. The version that was selected and published was almost certainly written by Thomson's clerk (France, 1966, pp. 112–13). It follows the main lines of the history that was currently being taught as fact by European missionaries in some of the mission schools building on the current (but now rejected) speculations about ultimately African origins; in this account names of Fijian villages were equated with those in Tanganyika, and Fijian customs compared to those of the ancient city of Thebes. It is surely no accident then that the entry chosen by the editor and published in seventeen episodes from September 1892

told of the departure of the ancestors from their native city of Thebes; their journey up the Nile and settlement on the shores of Lake Tanganyika; the eventual quarrel with neighbouring tribes which resulted in the great migration from Africa to Fiji, led by the chief Lutunasobasoba, on his canoe, the *Kaunitoni*, and the establishment of the settlement at Nakauvadra. Later instalments described in detail the spread of the

Kaunitoni voyagers and their descendants to all parts of Fiji. It was this story which, shorn of its Egyptian and Africa incidents, was translated and published by Thomson in 1895 and which, as described above, subsequently established itself among the traditions of the Fijian people.

The establishment of an oral tradition authenticating the teachings of mission schools was not solely motivated by the natural courtesy of graduates towards their mentors; new forces of enquiry were at work in Fiji, and it was the pragmatic habit of Fijians to satisfy all investigators who represented authority. Legend acquired a new significance . . . the clerks of the Native Lands Commission sought for evidence of how the tribes came to be occupying the lands they claimed . . .

So the *Kaunitoni* legend was born, of missionary parentage, and nurtured by the enquiries of the Native Lands Commission. Its general acceptance at the present time is one of the products of Fiji's transition from a geographical expression to a nation; it has the same socially cohesive qualities as the national coat of arms and the flag. But it is no more closely related to Fijian culture than they; it does not, apparently, antedate them. (France, 1966, pp. 112–13)

Clearly one can no longer claim the *Kaunitoni* story as arising from oral composition, far less as going back to 'prehistory' as used to be believed. Nevertheless it is now a widely known tale, told throughout Fiji and giving a sense of unity to a people otherwise widely scattered over scores of islands and speaking different dialects. As such, it is no imposture, but has a genuine reality for many thousands of Fijians. The fact that its original composition was partially through the medium of writing, and stimulated by the interest of foreign scholars, is no reason for rejecting its current reality and popular oral circulation among Fijians.

This is not, in fact, an unusual situation; for the influence of writing and the interest of foreigners have encouraged the systematic collecting and formulation of stories, often partly moulded by their own interests and preconceptions (for an excellent account of this in relation to myths about Maori origins see Sorrenson, 1979). In practice, writing has played a major part in the preservation and formulation of so-called 'oral tradition' in the Pacific. Take, for example, the Maori 'myths' about creation, the primary gods, the peopling of the world, and the occupation of particular tracts of land by its owners. Many of the original traditions about these topics recorded in the classic collections by Grey, White and others, did not, as might be assumed, just find their way spontaneously and in their 'traditional', 'natural' form into these collections. Rather they were sought after by the collectors, their recording and transcription were carefully organized, and they were in many cases written down specifically for the collectors by literate Maoris.

Consider, for instance, one of the early and most authoritative collections of Maori traditional material – Grey's *Nga Mahinga a Nga Tupuna* (1854) (and his translation of this as *Polynesian Mythology* (1855)). In a detailed analysis of the sources Simmons (1966) describes one of Grey's main informants for the Arawa region: Te Rangikaheke, also known as William Marsh or Wiremu Maihi, the chief of the Ngati Rangiwewehi tribe of the Rotorua district and the son of a famous chief. He was also literate, wrote down the traditions himself, and in fact contributed some 500 pages of manuscript to Grey's collection (Simmons, 1966, pp. 179–80). For the Ngati Toa, Grey's main source was the young chief Matene Te Whiwhi. He was a Christian who against the wishes of the elder chiefs travelled from Wellington to the Bay of Islands in 1839 to obtain a missionary for his people and in 1843 went on a dangerous voyage around the South Island to take Christianity to yet other groups. He too contributed in writing to Grey's collection, and his manuscripts, which are still extant, 'comprise some 78 pages of tradition, genealogy and poems' (Simmons, 1966, p. 181). Simmons also lists many other manuscripts written by local Maori informants. It was these which Grey used and interwove into a single account in his famous collection. It is obvious that writing as well as 'oral tradition' played a part in the formulation of the narratives published in Grey's classic collection.

A similar comment has been made by Luomala with reference to the version of the famous Maui story in Grey's volume. As she explains in her classic treatment (1949) of the Maui stories, there never has been one 'correct' version of these tales about Maui, but rather as many versions as there are (and were) tellers. So it is not surprising that the version that appeared in the collection is in the event just one among many possible ones, one composed by a particular individual (probably in writing), using his own insights and his own way of presenting the traditional episodes. Luomala comments on the unique characteristics of the way in which the composer-teller of the story created his own personal composition:

> Its unity, coherence, and depth of feeling point to the work of a literary genius reinterpreting the mythology of his people . . . Its author-raconteur saw the possibility of using an error in the father's rites over Maui as a point of departure in building up suspense to a climax. The narrator has integrated various stages of Maui's career from birth to death into a composition which resembles a novelette in its closely woven plot. The Arawa cycle is a masterpiece of primitive literature. (Luomala, 1949, pp. 38, 63)

The same general point applies to many, perhaps most, of the 'myths' and 'legends' recorded in the nineteenth century and published as classic collections of Pacific traditions. It is often forgotten that by fairly early on in the nineteenth century – and certainly by mid-century – there were many literate Pacific islanders, particularly in New Zealand and Hawaii but also increasingly in other countries like Tonga, Fiji, Samoa and many others, the majority of them deeply influenced by Christianity and mission teaching.[1] It

1 For some detailed accounts of literacy, see Parr, 1963 (Maori); Clammer, 1976 (Fiji).

was men like these who were responsible for organizing the collection of 'traditional tales' or acting as scribes to write them down in answer to requests from administrators, missionaries, and other enthusiastic collectors from abroad.

Writing has therefore been involved from the very start of systematic collecting. In fact, there is nothing very surprising about this situation nor does it mean that the 'traditions' thus recorded are in some way not 'genuine'. It is true they do not represent any pure 'natural' and 'primeval' state; but then perhaps there never was such a state, for individuals presumably always made their interpretations and presented their own versions of the accepted plots and motifs. In any case, we have to remember that in any recorded and printed version a *number* of factors are likely to have entered in: the personal views and ambitions of the narrator and/or composer, the context in which the collecting took place, the personality and known desires of the collector, and, in many cases, some use of writing.

Feedback

There is another aspect of writing that it is worth noting: the potential 'feedback' into oral forms from written sources. Since there were a number of literate people around in the Pacific in both the nineteenth century and more recently, as well as books of various kinds (not only the Bible but accounts of the classic voyages and of local traditions), many people had the opportunity to know, directly or indirectly, the contents of these works. One can never assume without question, therefore, that the accounts in 'oral narratives' came purely from 'oral tradition'.

In a number of cases there is quite definite evidence of direct or indirect influence from written works. Perhaps the most obvious is the use of ideas from the Bible in Polynesian creation narratives. Henige sums this up:

The co-optative impulse seemed to have been greatest for the Polynesian creation myths. The introduction of the Bible, with its own creation myths – supported, as one might expect, by genealogical scaffolding – presented certain problems for the Polynesians. Their acceptance of Christianity required either the acceptance of its genealogical/aetiological concomitants and the consequent rejection of their own myths, or an attempt to assimilate the two discordant bodies of material. Several attempts at assimilation were in fact made. Some were more obvious than others. These included the introduction of Garden of Eden concepts into Polynesian creation myths, the banishment of evil spirits from a paradise, purgatory, the Flood, and the interpolation of prominent Biblical figures into Polynesian genealogies. (Henige, 1974, p. 98)

Some examples of these are of interest. Take, for instance, the 'very generally received Tahitian tradition' reported by Ellis in 1829, that the first human pair were created by the god Taaroa: he made man from red earth, but then sent him to sleep and 'while he slept he took out one of his *ivi*, or bones, and made with it a woman, whom he gave to the man as his wife, and they became the progenitors of mankind' (Ellis, 1829, vol. 2, p. 38). Is this a Polynesian 'traditional' story? Ellis was himself doubtful but adds that Tahitians 'have repeatedly told me it was a tradition among them before any foreigner arrived' (p. 38). But many will consider that Ellis's informants were mistaken, and that there was indeed biblical influence here. As Barrère comments in her interesting discussion of 'Revisions and adulterations of Polynesian creation myths',

Between the time of Tahiti's discovery by Wallis in 1767 and the arrival of the first missionaries from London in 1797, the Tahitians had had a good deal of contact with Europeans and several individuals had had opportunities to become acquainted with Christian mythology (Henry, 1928, pp. 10–31). However much the Europeans did or did not tell of their Biblical stories, the story of the creation of first man and first woman would probably have been the most common, and, of course, completely consistent in each telling. Twenty to thirty years before the first missionaries arrived in Tahiti, and forty years before Ellis and his associates were recording native traditions, a number of Tahitians had no doubt heard the Biblical account of man's creation. In Polynesian terms this represents two or three generations, and it is not surprising to find the natives insisting to Ellis that the story of the creation of first man out of red earth, and the first woman from his bone, were sincerely thought by them to be a pre-European tradition. (Barrère, 1967, p. 106)

Again in the 'traditions' written down by the Hawaiian scholars Kepelino and Kamakau in the mid-nineteenth century there are obvious influences from biblical stories on their versions of Hawaiian creation narratives. Like any other narrator, these two writers moulded the stories according to their own insights and it is not surprising that they demonstrated the influences they had both received from their mission education. What in fact they were doing was, as Barrère describes it, to manipulate Hawaiian traditions to bring out parallels to Christian beliefs: 'in the process the Hawaiian gods Kane, Ku and Lono (Tane, Tu and Rongo) became a "threefold god", and Kanaloa (Tangaroa) became a Satan' (Barrère, 1967, p. 109). They described the creation of the universe and of man in a way obviously patterned on Genesis, and later elaborated these in conversations with the great Hawaiian collector Abraham Fornander (1919, 6, pp. 266–76) to include the fall of man and the Flood. These stories were later taken seriously (by Fornander) as evidence of the early history of the Polynesians. But in view of the most recent analyses of these and similar texts it seems obvious that a major part was in fact played by feedback from written literature.

This affects genealogies too. Kelly gives an intriguing example of this in his article on Maori genealogies in the context of the effect of missionary influence. The name of Kaitangata was associated with cannibalism (which the missionaries particularly condemned) and yet appeared in the accepted genealogies.

The question was debated at several meetings and a suitable substitute sought for. Finally someone had a brilliant idea! In Maori genealogies the son of Kaitangata was Hema, which also happened to be the missionary translation of Shem. What better substitute could be found than Noa? And so it came to pass; the name Noa replaced Kaitangata in the genealogies of the mission tribes. Now, a hundred years later, and the circumstances of the change largely forgotten, we find natives repeating their *whakapapa*, Noa, Hema, Tawhaki, Wahieroa and so on. (Kelly, 1940, p. 241)

Another example of the way writing can affect 'local traditions' comes from Tahiti, this time also accompanied by influences from other areas in the Pacific. Henige explains what happened.

Before the introduction of Christianity in Tahiti, Ta'aroa appeared as a supreme Creator (Barrère 1967 p. 104–5). After Christianity was introduced into Tahiti, however, the Ta'aroa myth was embellished by various Biblical accretions, for example, his creation of a pair of primeval ancestors (Barrère 1967 p. 105, Monberg 1956, p. 270). Initially Ta'aroa was the family creator god of the Pomare family, which by the last quarter of the eighteenth century, was beginning to become predominant in the Society Islands (Newbury 1967). With the ascendancy of the Pomares in Tahiti Ta'aroa became the recognised creator god on the entire archipelago (Monberg 1956, 277–8). In the half-century after Cook's visit to Tahiti in 1773 the concept of Ta'aroa as creator god spread throughout much of Polynesia . . . Inter-island communication became much greater with the regular visits of Europeans after Cook's voyages. Tahitians are known to have visited many other islands on European ships . . . The obvious implication of all this is that this relatively brief period of fifty years was sufficient to permit the widespread absorption of a Tahitian myth into the traditional cosmologies of several other Polynesian islands. This propensity to absorb data from other oral traditions was accentuated by feedback from written European sources. (Henige, 1974, pp. 98–9)

This is an instructive case for it helps to show how older ideas about the 'pure' and isolated state of the 'traditional Pacific societies' are often just not true. Certainly from the eighteenth century onwards there were many contacts between different islands which, combined with the influence of writing, sometimes had direct and extensive influence on so-called 'oral tradition'.

The older idea that published Pacific narratives all arise from 'pure oral tradition' (in the sense of tradition involving no contact with or influence by writing) needs to be questioned in the Pacific – as indeed it has been elsewhere. At the least, one cannot assume without question that where one encounters a narrative, whether of creation or of more 'recent' events, such as the visits of Captain Cook or other early explorers,[2] these are necessarily all due to purely 'oral' tradition with no influence at all from written accounts.[3]

Against this general background it is perhaps no longer surprising to find overlap between written and unwritten literary forms. For there is, after all, no reason why forms should *not* overlap, when those using them see no necessary contradiction between them. Thus to the Maori there was no incongruity about using songs (basically an 'oral' mode) in written communications: in the nineteenth century, we are told, Maoris 'almost invariably in writing a letter or a note, began it, after the introduction, with a few words from a song' (Mitcalfe, 1974, p. 6, quoting from Colenso, 1880, pp. 57–60).

Again there is surely nothing inappropriate in the use of schools as one important context for the transmission of oral literary forms in the Pacific today – stories, riddles, lullabies, dance-songs and others. Schools indeed play an important part in the circulation and even the revival or oral literary forms. This is so notably among the Maori.

Today Maori high schools, especially the church boarding schools and the Maori clubs at the various teachers colleges and universities, have been in the forefront of the Maori cultural revival, introducing new literary or musical forms and amalgams, ranging from George Webby's 'Story of Wiremu' at Wellington Teacher's College in 1959 to the various Maori operettas devised and performed by Turakina Maori Girls' College and by St Peter's School at Auckland and Ardmore Teachers' College Maori Club during the early sixties. (Mitcalfe, 1974, p. 195)

Cultural clubs and radio play their part too, as does the church, using writing as well as oral media. In fact, even if it was desirable for either practical or analytic purposes, there is by now no way in which purely 'oral' literature could be fully separated off from written literature or from that in which writing has some influence.

The future of oral tradition

Does this mean that the use of writing is now driving out oral literary forms? Is oral literature bound to 'die out' and disappear? This question is often asked, and creates a sense of urgency in many collectors. I will end this chapter with a brief comment on it.

2 E.g. those told in Niue or the Cooks (Loeb, 1926, p. 30; Gill, 1894, p. 259).

3 One must be especially cautious in excluding written texts as a possible source where the collectors comment – often as apparent evidence for the accuracy of oral transmission – on the closeness between the 'oral' account and that in some printed volume (as with the examples of Cook's visits cited in the last footnote).

In one way, perhaps the extensive use of writing does mean some decline in the relative position of oral literature. For there are now other kinds of literature as well as that expressed orally. But in another sense, oral literature shows no sign of disappearing. Songs (and the dances that often go with them) continue to be composed and performed, oratory is a constant feature of the Pacific scene, and stories are still exchanged based on recent events as well as old traditions. In some areas schools and churches, far from 'driving out' these forms, have stimulated and fostered them. The radio too – together with gramophones and tape recorders – has an important part to play in the modern Pacific. Over the radio, truly oral forms of art can come into their own, as stories, poems, songs, and speeches are broadcast over areas much wider than the 'traditional' narrator or minstrel could reach with his individual voice. All in all, it is hard to see a quick death for oral literature in the Pacific, or any inevitability about its 'decline'.

It is true that some forms are less popular than others and may be on their way to oblivion, and others have already disappeared in the sense of being no longer performed. Collectors are understandably eager in their efforts to trace such instances, so that some record may be made of them before they are totally lost to human knowledge. But this does not mean that these now less popular forms are of any greater *intrinsic* interest than those that have remained popular or that are now being developed; the latter are equally examples of Pacific oral literature with the former, and, in themselves, equally worth recording. It is also not unprecedented for some forms to lose their relative popularity, others to gain it, and yet others to be developed on new lines – this after all is what 'the history of literature' is about. Though there may have been many changes in the Pacific over the last two centuries in literature as in many other aspects of life, this is nothing unique in the comparative history of literary taste.

The change in the circulation of particular genres need not therefore lead one to the extreme conclusion that oral literature as a whole is on the way to extinction in the Pacific. On the contrary, it is likely that in a whole variety of contexts (not least the radio) it will continue to flourish for the foreseeable future. It may no longer be circulating in some pure 'natural' and 'uncontaminated' state – if such ever existed – but in the perhaps even more interesting and variegated situation of the modern Pacific, interacting with writing, broadcasting, Christianity, education, entertainment, planned and unplanned change, contemporary politics and a whole host of other activities in the contemporary world.

Conclusion

It is commonly assumed that the technology of writing provides the opportunity for a neutral record of oral forms, or, alternatively, that it is somehow intrinsically opposed to or even 'kills' *oral* literary expression. The evidence from the South Pacific suggests that both of these assumptions are questionable.

The writing down of narratives and 'traditions' in the nineteenth and early twentieth centuries (from when many of the great collections of Pacific literature date) was a formative and creative act rather than merely neutral collecting. It not only turned an oral into a written form, with consequent stress on the significance of verbal text, linear formulation and length as distinct from performance, but also emphasized certain aspects of content or form in the selection of texts according to the current preconceptions of the publisher, collector and/or transcriber. And the effect of these particular preconceptions has in turn often led to misleading conclusions about the 'age-old' and 'traditional' characteristics of Pacific literature or the nature of traditional mythology or religious beliefs. At the same time, the increasing availability of these written versions fed into the *oral* literary tradition. In the South Pacific, it seems, these were not (as sometimes supposed) two separate and opposed modes but, both now and in the past, form part of one dynamic in which both written and oral forms interact.

7

The relation between composition and performance: three alternative modes

This chapter discusses another context in which orality and literacy can interact rather than be kept apart. Although contemporary British culture would formally be considered 'literate', in practice oral modes of composition and performance are still important in many cultural forms. This is illustrated in this chapter from a study of local urban music. Once again it appears that there are no single forms of either oral or literate transmission dictated by the technology, but a number of different uses and combinations of oral and written modes through which, sometimes in cooperation with modern electronic technology, people can achieve their cultural ends.

Oral transmission has often been neglected in musicological research. It is, however, a topic of great interest, the more so when it is considered in the context of the interplay of the oral and literate in musical transmission. The most fruitful strategy for pursuing this topic would seem to be not to get tied up with grand theoretical terms or uncritical generalized concepts like 'literacy', 'oral tradition' or 'orality', but rather through elucidating some of the *specific* ways in which oral and literate elements are used in differing forms of music. This more specific approach may form a better basis than *a priori* model-building for the formulation of general insights into oral and literate processes in music.

I will therefore explore the place of the oral and literate in a musical context from two main points of view. First, I consider the relevance of research on oral literature to this question. Second, I draw on some field research on music-making in a contemporary English town, using this to exemplify the *different* ways oral and literate elements may be combined even within what – from the outside – looks like a single tradition.

The oral in literature and in music

First, then, some comments on work on oral literature (or verbal art, the term preferred by some scholars). Here too we encounter oral and literate elements used in differing ways in the processes of composition, transmission and performance, and *varying* relations between these which are arguably analogous to those in music.

Over many years studying aspects of oral literature, I have been increasingly struck by the strength of the European preoccupation with *written* forms and the way this colours thoughts and definition – the 'literacy paradigm' of scholars, as it is well put in Treitler (1986). Over the last centuries of European history written modes have been taken as *the* paradigm for education, scholarship and artistic activity, a dominant cultural view widely accepted even beyond the narrow circle of academics. What was written was to be valued and analysed; and what was not written was not worth scholarly study. This unquestioned assumption determined how literature has been defined and interpreted. Thus the essential thing about a literary work was for long taken to be its *text*, a permanent written formulation distinct from, and seen as somehow possessing a timeless validity quite other than, the ephemeral process of writing, reading, enacting or experiencing that work.

The consequences of this taken-for-granted view for the study of oral forms were far-reaching. In the first place it made it seem that non-written artistic forms 'couldn't' be 'literature' or have 'literary qualities', demonstrated both by the claimed etymological contradiction in the term 'oral literature' and, more seriously, by the apparently self-evident conclusion that if it was not written it was not suitable for scholarly analysis – and *therefore* not 'literature'. Even when oral forms like tales or song lyrics did become objects of interest (albeit often as 'folklore' or 'popular culture' rather than as 'literature' proper), the same implicit assumption affected the terms in which they were defined and analysed. Whether taken down from dictation or transcribed from recording, they were presented as *texts*. Thus it came to be accepted that oral forms could perhaps be studied, but only in the sense of capturing the texts which were presumed to constitute their essence and treating them in a similar way to written literature: as fixed forms which could at times be corrupted (for example by imperfect memory) but essentially existed in correct and permanent texts.

A great deal of interesting and important work was carried out following this text-based paradigm of oral literature – but there was the problem of all the things *left out*. The object of study was removed from the act of performance with its richness of specific occasion or succession of variations, and all the performance elements were ignored. But in oral performance such elements play an essential part. The style of delivery (tempo, mood, dynamics or tone, to mention just some aspects), the drama and characterization conveyed by the performer, the audience's involvement through interjections, responses, verbal interplay or choral participation in response to the main performer's lead – all these are not extra, optional embellishments, as they might seem if we follow a written paradigm, but a central constituent of the literary act.

The performance elements are thus essential to the art form but totally missed if we concentrate on the text alone. It is for this reason that many analysts now insist that texts give a seriously incomplete account of most oral performances as they are actually experienced by performers and listeners. Some American anthropologists and folklorists go even further in their 'performance-centred' approach, which sees any telling as a communicative event in time rather than a spatially defined text (e.g. Bauman, Tedlock, Ben-Amos, cf. Finnegan, 1981). Whatever the detailed terminology and approach, however, it is now accepted among serious students of verbal oral performance that the *text* alone is an insufficient guide to the art form, and that to understand it fully one must go further and also study the processes of performance and audience reception as they actually take place in space and time. This point becomes obvious once one has become involved in the observation and experience of oral performances, but it is worth emphasis because the continuing focus in western thought on written forms makes any move away from the idea of timeless, permanent texts as constituting art forms something that still seems to need explicit justification.

The relevance for music will now be clear. In the study of music we find the very same western assumptions about the dominance of writing. Musical art too tends to be equated with its *written* form, so that if something is not written it is assessed as not 'really' music, or at any rate not worth serious scholarly study. In traditional western musicology 'music' is usually defined as the musical work, itself in turn defined as its written formulation – the score – rather than for instance, the process of playing or singing or the act of performance. This emphasis on text is reinforced by the western educational system – at least in England – where formal music training even in unassuming local schools as well as in conservatoire settings is usually taken to consist in learning to *read* music: to cope with notation, learn musical theory, and pass written (not just practical) music examinations. Even the conventional English vocabulary supports this view of music as essentially constituted by written text. Ask any member of a local choir or orchestra if they have 'their music', and they will understand you to mean not musical skill or memory or experience but a copy of the requisite printed (or occasionally hand-written) notated text.

As with oral literature, this definition of music as text leaves out essential elements of the art form as actually practised by performing musicians and experienced by audiences. Further, it misleads us as to what people actually do and value in music, particularly in the context of performance. In practice, probably most people with any personal experience of musical activity know very well that other processes than those enshrined in the written text are in fact involved. But because of the strong literacy paradigm in musicological study these other aspects tend not to be verbalized, with the result that they are too often treated as just not there, in an analogous way to the suppression of performance attributes in a text-based approach to oral literature.

Traditional musicology in the west seems in the main to be blind to such points, continuing its long emphasis on music as written score and on works of art as somehow timeless, existing beyond social conventions and removed from the humanly organized act of performance or processes of composition, rehearsal or transmission. There are now a few voices even among musicologists of western music (many more, of course, among ethnomusicologists) who query this traditional concentration on text. But it seems that in music the same change of emphasis as for the study of oral literature still needs fighting for (only perhaps even more fiercely, given the strength of the traditional musicological establishment in the west): that music as an art form is more than notated text, and that concentrating on written aspects to the almost complete exclusion of the very real oral elements gives a misleading account of music.

This is the main point, it seems to me, that emerges from comparing current moves in scholarly work on oral literature with issues in the study of the oral and literate in music, and one of the very greatest importance in the study of art forms as they are actually practised, whether in the west or the east. But before leaving this section, I would mention one further lesson that it may be useful to draw from the analogous work on oral literature. This is the increasing awareness that, in contrast to some earlier simplicist assumptions, there is no *one* way in which oral elements in verbal art are necessarily expressed and formulated. Rather, according to the socially accepted conventions of a given society or a particular genre, there are a whole series of different ways in which, say, oral composition, oral performance or oral transmission may be related and arranged. 'Orality' or 'oral tradition' can be realized in manifold different forms which cannot be predicted *a priori* but must be discovered through detailed investigation and in full appreciation of the variety and complexity inherent in oral, as in written, modes of expression and communication.

The oral and the literate in music-making in a modern English town

I now want to try to illustrate these points through the specific example of musical activities in a contemporary English town. This is drawn from field research which I have been undertaking on amateur music-making in the early 1980s in Milton Keynes (a growing town in Buckinghamshire, then of around 100,000–120,000 population), a study based on participant observation, local documentary sources and some limited survey work. The study encompassed all forms of local music-making; that is, not only the classical art tradition (represented by local choirs, orchestras and instrumentalists) but also jazz, brass bands, musical drama as enacted by local Gilbert and Sullivan and 'amateur operatic' groups, country and western music, folk clubs and their music, and pop and rock groups.[1]

I began from the assumptions of the classical music tradition in which I myself had grown up – one kind of ethnocentrism perhaps even *within* western culture. But I soon began to realize that these assumptions were not necessarily accepted by all musicians. In practice, I discovered, there were a number of different 'musical worlds' – to adapt Howard Becker's seminal concept of 'art world' – even within the single town of Milton Keynes. Each had different, but usually unspoken, assumptions about, for example, musical training and learning, the conventions of performance, the nature of composition, or the mode of transmission. These were often different from what the dominant ideology of western classical music would lead one to expect, differences which commonly led to misunderstanding between members of these worlds when they tried to judge that of others by their own taken-for-granted but deeply powerful conventions.

I will take certain of these 'musical worlds' within Milton Keynes as case studies to illustrate some of the different ways in which, even in a single culture, oral and written elements may be related in music. To do this I will focus specially on the relations between composition and performance in the three 'worlds' of classical music, jazz and rock, and the implications these three differing modes have for transmission. Before embarking on the detailed exposition, I should stress that, though the patterns I isolate may well be found more widely, the present research depends essentially on musical activity as it was realized and performed in practice in Milton Keynes in the early 1980s. I am not claiming that my account can be taken as necessarily applicable to these forms at other times or places.

1 I am grateful to the Social Science Faculty Research Committee of the Open University for their support for this project, and to the assistance of Liz Close in the interviewing. A fuller account of the project as a whole will be found in Finnegan, forthcoming.

Composition and performance among local classical musicians

There were many classically trained musicians in Milton Keynes playing or singing in local choirs, orchestras and small instrumental groups, and this represented one strong musical tradition in the area. Within this world the standard view was that musical works were composed before, and totally separate from, performance and that composers were specially gifted individuals above and beyond present everyday practice, notably those in the great canon of classical composers (Bach, Mozart or Beethoven, for instance). In this view these works were essentially composed and transmitted in *written* form and constituted by the printed texts which could be read and disseminated by present-day performers. Performers, furthermore, were merely executants of musical works composed by others, reading each composition from its written, notated text and under an obligation to render it correctly. In this view the performers, despite needing certain performance skills, were essentially passive traditors of music formed and written out by others rather than themselves taking an active part in its creation. The behaviour of audiences at classical concerts fitted the same paradigm. Its role was silent acceptance of the great music of the past: sitting still, in an almost temple-like hush where moving a single limb or hand during performance of the work was frowned on. The audience was provided with printed or typed programmes in which the names and composers of the works to be performed were always included, sometimes supplemented by written 'programme notes' summarizing the main features of each work which could be followed by the listeners during the performance.

This paradigm of music as consisting in works written by the great authors of the past, transmitted in writing and accepted by the current generation through its enactment by basically non-innovatory performers supported by written programmes was reflected in the actual practice in Milton Keynes. It was the framework within which most formal music teaching took place, both in the schools and by private music instructors, with a stress on the necessity of being able to read written music and reproduce it correctly. The concerts put on locally by both visiting and local performers followed the same model, one accepted, furthermore, by the local classical music societies and the choral and instrumental amateur groups. As will emerge later, the situation was more complex than this mode allows, but it was nevertheless a powerful one both as a set of ideas moulding people's perceptions of the nature of music and music-making, and as an account, up to a point accurate, of how people actually behaved within the classical music tradition.

Composition-in-performance: the jazz mode

The particular relation of composition to performance of the classical music world was not, as I had at first assumed, the only developed form within Milton Keynes music-making. For the very different jazz mode was taken for granted by a number of Milton Keynes musicians and presented a very different combination. I do not intend to enter into the long-worn arguments about exactly how 'jazz' should be defined nor to discuss the different possible varieties of jazz, merely to describe the musical practice of those musicians in Milton Keynes who classed their music as jazz – members of such local groups as *Momentum*, *Mahogany Hall Jazzmen*, *Original Grand Union Syncopators*, *Fenny Stompers* or *T-Bone Boogie Band*. Such performers were emphatically *not* primarily playing written compositions by named composers who had created the music in written texts (though there were occasional examples of this mode). Rather, the typical jazz form was for the performers themselves to play a part in the composing of the music in the act of performance. In contrast to classical music, there was no correct text fitted and finalized beforehand, and composition was not a primarily literate process but rather – in the sense at least of being basically developed without reliance on a written text – an oral one.

This of course is not a new point about jazz performance, but it was strikingly well illustrated by jazz bands in Milton Keynes. One interesting indication was the reaction of local jazz performers when asked if their groups played their own original material. This question was immediately clear to classical and rock players, but jazz performers puzzled about the concept of 'original': no, some said, they did not make up their own compositions but at the same time and in another way their performances were '100 per cent original because we improve and change standards'; this was explained further by noting that tunes were used as vehicles for improvising 'so everything the group does is original'. Another band explained that they played little of their own original material while at the same time their actual performance was 'very fluid – the numbers are practically made up on the spot', while others reckoned that many of their numbers were 'improvised out of nowhere – we could go on all night'. This experience of personal creativity in actual performance was also very evident to the observer in the way Milton Keynes jazz performers looked at each other in recognition and pleasure as they played, particularly after the alternating solo spots by one of the leading wind players – a sense of freshness and innovation. The performers were creating on the spot across a much wider spectrum than was open to classical players, and in ways which went further than just performance skills in the narrow sense, but also extended to the ordering and content of the music: elements which in classical music would be laid down in the written text.

These conventions about the specific relation between composition and performance in jazz were also in keeping with other patterns in the organization of local jazz playing. Learning jazz was usually not through the formal graded instruction from written texts typical of classical music teaching, but rather a self-introduction to the skills of jazz playing either as an individual (usually by using a sound recording as a basis) or, as their instrumental skills developed, playing together with others in a group: learning-by-doing. Local jazz bands went in for fewer joint practices than most classical or rock groups – understandably so, given that they were not trying to perfect their performance of a fixed already-composed work (for which regular rehearsal would be needed) but rather drawing on their musical skills in the act of performance to produce, on each occasion, a new and unique performance. For the same reason it was easier for jazz than for rock players to be members of several different groups or to accommodate visiting players who wished to 'guest' with them. This too lay behind the success of jazz groups as 'resident' bands in local pubs, appearing regularly every fortnight or so over a period of months: their performances, unlike those of rock or country and western bands, were different enough each time to prevent listeners from getting bored. The participation of the audience was significant too, for far from remaining quiet and consulting written programmes, jazz audiences played an active part in each performance, showing their pleasure in the performers' creativity, encouraging them, sometimes joining in as guests or even, with some local bands, singing or dancing to the music. Many local jazz bands had built up keen groups of local fans who followed them from gig to gig, and helped to make each performance a special event by their enthusiasm and participation.

The bands' statements about 'improvisation from nothing' or 'made up on the spot' should not be taken literally. Their performances were certainly *not* made up 'from nothing', but arose from a whole series of shared musical skills and themes. There is a useful analogy here in oral literature research, in the 'oral-formulaic' mode so well explained by Albert Lord (1968a) and others (discussed and summarized in, e.g., Foley, 1985; Opland, 1986; Finnegan, 1977, ch. 3). Their central point was that lengthy oral narrative verse did not consist of fixed texts which could be transmitted or performed in a single correct form, but were in practice extremely variable, depending on the poet's individual skill and interests, the audience's reactions, and the actual occasion of performance. Poets did not memorize their texts beforehand, but neither did they have to hesitate for words and lines as they performed, for they were drawing on a familiar store of 'formulaic' phrases, themes, incidents and plots, all of which could be combined and recombined according to the requirements of a particular occasion. The composition-in-performance that resulted, in which performing and composing were not separate but facets of one single activity, proceeded on a different set of assumptions from the concept of the fixed, correct text of written literature, for *each* performance was equally authentic in its own right.

In jazz performances, the activity was arguably even more complex, resting on the interaction of several players at once, but the same basic process would seem to apply, by now well established in scholarly writing on oral composition: composition-in-performance drawing on a set of shared tunes, musical devices, harmonies, rhythms and musical structures. Jazz musical performances were not 'correct' or 'incorrect' renditions of fixed texts but were individual performances on specific occasions, each valid in its own right. In keeping with this, local jazz players relied little on written music. Occasionally they made limited use of memory aids in the form of written-out lyric sheets, tunes, or chord charts or followed cassette recordings, but basically what was transmitted was neither a written nor an oral memorized text but a set of musical skills and themes: a shared musical storehouse.

The jazz mode therefore contrasted sharply with classical music in the relation between composition and performance and, by consequence, in the respective roles played by oral and literate aspects in both the transmission and the definition of the music.

This basic composition-in-performance mode has parallels in artistic performances throughout the world (verbal as well as musical) and has been taken by some as *the* 'oral' mode of composition and transmission. It is therefore worth emphasizing its existence in the urban setting of a contemporary English town. It was, furthermore, considered nothing at all unusual by either the musicians or audiences that applauded it, many of whom were highly literate in other spheres, including (in some cases) in classical music. The use of writing for other purposes did not, then, undermine the enthusiasm of jazz performers and listeners for the role of oral elements in the composition, performance and transmission of jazz as it was realized locally.

But it must also be noted that this 'oral-formulaic' form was not the only alternative to the classical mode in Milton Keynes music nor, as is sometimes implied, the only form in which 'oral composition' in some sense of that term can take place. This, then, brings me to the third main mode.

Prior composition through practice: the rock mode

In Milton Keynes in the early 1980s there were at any one time around one hundred bands playing music which could broadly be termed 'rock'. Here again precise definitions are difficult, not least because popular bands seldom used the term 'rock' on its own, preferring instead to label themselves under more elaborate heads such as progressive rock, acid pop, heavy metal, soft rock, punk, futurist, new wave, blues rockers, high energy progressive folk rock, and many other. There were differences between these forms but in general they shared certain conventional expectations about the relation between composition and performance. This turned out to be different from both jazz and classical music.

My own expectation, perhaps over-influenced by Lord's analysis of verbal performances, had been that the rock mode would be like that of jazz, emphasizing improvisation in performance or, where that did not happen, memorization of the broadcast or recorded versions of well-known bands. My expectations turned out to be unjustified. There were some cases, it is true, where local bands did memorize music composed by others, almost always learning it from performances on cassette, disc or tape rather than from written texts. But much more important for almost all the local rock bands was a third process, which I am here dubbing the rock mode, in which rock bands engaged in prior composition through joint practice, followed by a separate performance of the work that had by then reached a relatively fixed form through this joint development.

It was a surprise to me to find how many bands played their own compositions. Between thirty and forty local rock bands were questioned about this in 1982/3 and of these nearly four-fifths said they played mostly or (in over one-third of the cases) solely their own original material. Of the remaining fifth some used just one or two songs of their own, for others their normal repertoire had up to 25 per cent of their own material or 'three or four songs a night', while only two of the bands currently performed *no* material of their own.

Admittedly the extent of original composition claimed by local players may have been exaggerated – a significant point in itself, if so, indicating the value locally placed on 'originality'. But it was clear not just from the interviews but also from observations and comments from yet other players that the standard expectation was indeed for their bands to play mainly material composed and worked out by themselves.

How did this widespread form of composition take place? This turned out to be different from both the jazz and the classical modes. In the first place *written* music typically played little or no part at all in rock composition and transmission. Nor was it, like jazz, a process of improvising on the basis of shared material and skills in the actual moment of performance. Rather, each band worked out its own numbers through a series of practices over weeks or months which they then played in more or less fixed form for public performance or recording session.

What actually happened was that one or two of the players came up with some initial idea for a piece: a bit of a tune, a set of rhythms or chords, or a verbal fragment for a song. This was then taken up by the band as a whole and worked out jointly. There were several different ways this could take place, summarized in some of the bands' own comments: 'We develop the tune from the bass line: we go over it together and improve it'; 'at practices we always have ideas, we work on them together'; 'Anita usually gets the original idea, everyone adds ideas and modifies the song – [it's] collectively composed and learnt'; 'one person comes up with a riff or song, we work on it from there'. One pattern ran through all the personal variants, however. This was that the band itself had to work out the piece through actually trying it out and developing it in practice, and it was only when they reckoned that it had been fully completed and learnt that they were prepared to commit themselves to a public performance. In this sense, then, it was their *own* jointly composed number which they had by then memorized and reproduced in predictable form, a contrast to the more fluid nature of jazz performance. Musicians who played in both jazz and rock modes were very aware of this difference. As one player put it, rock performances can be less interesting for the players because there 'it's all happened, the work's already been done', whereas in jazz it is still happening anew during each performance.

This third mode also fitted with the social organization of rock bands. As with jazz, the process of learning was not typically through the formal instruction of classical music, but was self-teaching on the job alongside other players. In rock this was even more emphasized, for many rock players had first formed a band in their teens at a point where they had as yet practically no instrumental skill (sometimes none at all) and had learnt through jointly experimenting with chords, tunes and ensemble creation with their fellow players. Consequent on both this and the emphasis on developing their own material, most rock bands had frequent and regular practice sessions together, typically at least once a week, often more. Having built up this investment in their own jointly created material, which might amount to just a few numbers for a fairly recently formed group or up to twenty or thirty, even fifty songs for an established band, there was a crisis if any member of the (typically four-man) group left. Named bands were often short-lasting and their players moved on to re-form under different names and thus create a new sequence of original material.

What was involved was not, therefore, a set of shared musical resources forming the basis for composition-in-performance in the jazz style, but was nevertheless, like jazz, a primarily oral set of precedures without the written texts of classical music. In the rock mode, writing typically did not enter in at all. Indeed the only band that said they used written music was one of the two that reckoned to play none of their own material and while a few made temporary use of hand-written song lyrics or chord charts, they expected to dispense with these fairly soon in the practising process, and certainly in performance. What was transmitted was nevertheless a memorized piece: in one sense more of a fixed text than in jazz (albeit an unwritten one), but at the same time a performance-centred work (rather than a series of 'correct' notes and sequences). It involved both musical performance skills – *central*, not peripheral, to the actual number – and the visual and kinetic effects which also formed part of the performance. This was emphasized too by the role of the audience at rock gigs, for though their specific participation varied with the particular brand of music being played, some direct and immediate audience reaction was an essential part of the work-as-actually-performed. This was not through the study of written programmes (never part of a gig) but in the form of movement, response to visual and auditory effects, vocalized acclaim and sometimes dancing. Unlike the classical model, the piece as actually performed by the band which had created it was what defined both the music and its execution.

Here, then, was another essentially non-literate form of musical composition, performance and transmission, different both from jazz and from the reproductions of classical works composed by others. It should be emphasized, though the typical reaction of classical musicians (and no doubt of traditional musicologists) to this form of musical activity was to regard it as the outcome of uneducated and probably uncouth teenagers who did not know any better and could not be classified as making 'real' music, nevertheless this *was* a distinct form of music-making in its own right, with its own standards and canons of excellence. Not all players were necessarily so very young either (some of the keenest were in their late twenties, thirties or even forties) and several had begun in the classical tradition and could in fact read notated music – but chose not to use this (for them) inappropriate skill in the independent rock art form with its essential reliance on oral rather than literate interaction. This oral mode, it should be stressed finally, is not being differentiated here just as a theoretical possibility drawn from comparative study (although it has some interesting analogies with certain modes of oral literature composition such as the prior composition–rehearsal–performance typical of the South Pacific, see Finnegan, 1985). Rather, it was something being actively practised by around one hundred rock bands in Milton Keynes in the early 1980s.

The three main modes I have distinguished are not the only possible ways in which composition and performance can be related, nor were they the only forms to be found in Milton Keynes. But they did comprise three leading modes to be found in Milton Keynes in which oral and literate elements entered *differently* into the musical process. Their co-existence demonstrates clearly that no *one* process of musical composition, performance and transmission can be taken as the 'natural' or 'authentic' form even in one culture (even, that is, in what is usually taken to be the highly literate culture of contemporary urban Britain) and, furthermore, that the more 'orally' dependent forms are not just pale reflections of the proper written process – 'failed' classical music as it were – but developed and independent art forms in their own right in which literacy happens to play relatively little part.

Some wider implications

Distinguishing these three modes can also be helpful in a comparative context. They help us to identify some of the factors which can enter into the processes of musical performance, all factors which – in a range of ways – may or may not make use of oral or literate media respectively. For consider the three modes presented here, taking them now as a possible basis for analytic discussion rather than just descriptions of Milton Keynes players. To understand the relation between composition and performance in each case (and, indeed, the nature of the musical 'work' itself as actually realized and conceived by those involved) it proved essential to take account of factors that in narrow musicological terms would seem 'extraneous': mode of training and learning, nature and organization of practising, formation of musical groups, transmission and performance conventions and – very important – expectations of audience behaviour. For all these aspects, we can ask about the expected role of 'orality' or of 'literacy', with different detailed answers for each of the three main modes discussed here (as, doubtless, for yet others that could be distinguished).

This consequent widening of the sphere of investigation which was for me one consequence of treating these modes seriously as alternative but equally authentic patterns of musical execution, also paradoxically raises further questions about the analysis of the specific examples themselves, in particular the first one – the classical form with which I started. For once we take into consideration those other elements which turned out to be important in jazz and rock, it starts to appear that the conventional account of the relation between composition and performance in classical music as essentially a *literate* process is misleading. It leaves almost totally out of account such factors as performance conventions, learning, the process of rehearsing and audience conventions – all factors of real importance in actual music-making and ones where oral processes may in practice be of much greater importance than is indicated by the widely accepted high culture model. A classical notated score, for example, provides only incomplete guidance for performance. How this is translated into actual performance depends *not* just on the written text but also – as is well known in practice – on a whole series of other inputs such as contemporary performance conventions, learning techniques or additional written indications supplementing written scores. One could also point to such very real processes in classical music activity as, for instance, agreements about tempo, dynamics, balance, timbre, or dramatic impact worked out in practice in a choir or instrumental group through a series of rehearsals; the interaction between contemporary composers and the known musical limitations or resources of a local performing group for whom a composition is initially intended; or the varying forms of learning – in the case of amateur choral singing, at least, much more 'oral' than is often recognized.

The role of audience too is of greater significance than at first appears. Their apparently 'passive' reception is in fact a positive convention of classical music performance which has had to be learnt by the audience (a point which comes over clearly when inexperienced attenders, including young children, break the accepted norms and suffer consequential disapproval or rebuke). This is the culturally approved form of audience contribution without which a live classical performance cannot be successfully enacted. Nor is classical performance just the 'pure' *musical* exposition of a written text, for both physical movement by performers (and constraint on movement by audience) and visual effects through special costumes, layout and lighting arrangements also form part of a classical performance as characteristically experienced by musicians and audience alike. It appears that a concentration just on written media is to leave out much which in practice gives even classical music its reality as one distinctive musical tradition in western culture.

I would conclude from these reflections on the different musical modes discussed here that some of the assumptions often made about western music can mislead us about its actual nature. In the first place, not all western music falls within the classical tradition, despite the impression given by scholars who, following the traditional western emphasis on *written* forms, tend to highlight the classical high art form and ignore the rest. It turns out that even in one not very large English town, at least three different modes co-exist, the second two of these by no means self-evidently of lesser importance in terms of numbers of adherents or intensity of appreciation. Second, our long western ethnocentric paradigm of literacy may also mislead us even about the nature of classical music itself, playing down the unwritten elements that in practice play an essential part in its realization.

These points are important, I suggest, not just for the analysis of western music for its own sake but because international comparison can otherwise proceed on misleading assumptions. It is only too easy, for example, to contrast the 'multiplicity' of Japanese music (as it is put in the *New Grove Dictionary* article) with the apparent single and increasingly 'rational' tradition of the European classical art music tradition. In practice multiplicity also characterizes British music even in just one single contemporary town, a multiplicity that tends to be played down, even concealed, by much musicological theorizing. Furthermore, it is only too easy to take the *theory* of western musicologists (a theory presupposing the dominance of literacy) and suppose that by contrasting it with the *practice* of music elsewhere one has reached a valid comparison. On the contrary, the most interesting comparative perspectives may come from comparing practice with practice (or perhaps theory with theory) and refusing to accept – at least without further discussion – the models of the high art specialists at their face value as the only and complete accounts of actual musical processes. If we try this wider approach, it may be that, though we may discover more and more riches in the manifold and variegated ways through which humankind has used both written and unwritten modes to formulate and assist musical expression, some of the once self-evident *contrasts* between east and west or even between orality and literacy may turn out to arise in part from a misassessment of the nature of western musical processes and an underestimation of the role of non-written elements in actual musical realization.

This brings me back, then, to the points I raised at the beginning in the context of oral literature: that a concentration on the text is not enough for a full understanding, but that – whether for verbal or, it now seems, musical art – many other elements need to be analysed as well, among them performance and composition processes, audience behaviour and the cultural background of learning, appreciation and realization in actual performance. Widening the questions to such matters once again challenges the simplified view that one can talk about 'orality' or 'literacy' in general terms, far less (as Steven Feld has so convincingly shown (1984)) contrast whole cultures or groups as 'oral' or 'literate' respectively. Rather, there is the complex challenge to consider the *specific* ways in which the differing aspects of musical processes may be formulated or expressed or furthered by various oral or visual or written media, whether in terms of the three modes I have suggested here or in the (doubtless) many other patterns in which these elements can be related.

Above all I would end with the plea, drawn both from my earlier background in oral literature study and from my present venturing into the musical arena, that such questions be explored by looking at musical *practices* and not just at musicological *theory*, specially theory biased toward western ethnocentric assumptions about the centrality of writing. Professor Tokumaru Yosihiko has reminded us (1986) that we should not be content just to accept the common contrast between the 'originality' of western music and the 'tradition' of that of Japan, for if we examine this in terms of the *actual* amount of variation, the supposed differences may turn out to lie more in evaluative theorizing than in contrasts in actual music-making. His comments point to a fundamental theme not just for my own paper but for the effective examination of the oral and literate in music more generally: the need to look not just at isolated texts or abstract musicological theory but at the actual processes and practices of the realization of music.

8

Transmission in oral and written traditions: some general comments

Following up earlier chapters which concentrated on composition and performance and queried whether these were always so distinct as between oral and literate modes as often presumed, this chapter raises the same question in regard to modes of transmission: are there basic differences between oral and written traditions in this respect? Exploring this question has many ramifications. Some take us back to a more detailed critique of the general claims about the impact of literacy made in the strong technological determinist model presented in chapter 2, in the light of the arguments in chapters 3–5. Though universalizing Great Divide theories and generalized technological determinism are rejected, some recurrent patterns of oral and written transmission are explored which, once again, illustrate the continuum rather than divide between these two continuing communication technologies.

Transmission in oral and written traditions, togther with the corresponding nouns 'orality' and 'literacy', are terms which, like so many of those which deserve our serious interest, seem clear and unambiguous only until we try to apply them to specifics. In practice, as is now increasingly recognized, the terms bring a multitude of controversies and ambiguities. In this chapter I want to comment on some of these problems with two main themes in mind: first, that many of the commonly assumed associations of both 'orality' and 'literacy' that have been used to comment on the subject need to be re-assessed (building, that is, on the arguments of the earlier chapters here); and secondly, that, despite justified scepticism about the larger generalizations, certain recurring patterns of transmission, if of a more modest and specific kind, can be identified.

Transmission in 'oral' and 'written traditions' is obviously a huge and disparate topic. A natural first reaction is to wonder how to make any general comments on such a subject at all. A second reaction is likely to be the well-tried and accustomed one: to assert the need to narrow this down, say by concentrating on oral or written transmission in just one culture, period or group, or alternatively (and in more comparative spirit) by settling on just certain aspects of the central terms, maybe applying a simplifying model to identify central properties amidst the plethora of contingent historical and cultural variations.

I will start by looking at some comparatively-based approaches which have led to either explicit conclusions or (more often) implicit models about 'orality' and 'literacy' and which have underpinned some of the assumptions about oral and written traditions.

Polar typologies

This approach picks out 'essential' elements by setting up a 'pure' type of 'orality' and 'literacy' respectively. This arguably leads to greater understanding of the 'normal' associated properties and consequences of each and of their 'natural' settings; deviations can then be explained in terms of special conditions. Thus orality – and hence oral transmission – has been seen as characteristically and essentially found in cultures without writing and also, going back in history, without modern commerce or transport systems, resting on traditional and communal norms. Correspondingly, literacy has been associated with cultures characterized by the development of urban and bureaucratic systems and the rise of secular and scientific enquiry, patterns arguably further intensified with the advent of printing. In this view two very different types of culture are contrasted and the characteristics of oral and written traditions thus investigated in the framework of these essentially opposed settings.

This dichotomizing framework may sound extreme, but it has been extremely influential in comparative study. It is less popular nowadays than in the past – certainly in an explicit form – but the assumptions underlying it are still persistent. They surface from time to time in both general discussions and specific treatments of orality and literacy.

The approach is an attractive one. It appeals not only to the romantic in all of us, but to the desire to produce comparative generalizing theories to make sense of the complex phenomena that confront us. It seems highly rational to investigate orality and literacy from the concept of two opposing types: the one, the characteristic setting for oral tradition, typified as small-scale and face to face, rural and non-industrial, communal and conformist rather than individualist, and dominated by ascribed kinship, religion and revered traditions; the other – the locale for written transmission – typically industrial, urban and bureaucratic, characterized by a respect for rationality, individual achievement and impersonal norms, heterogeneous and secular.

Connecting the essence of orality and of literacy with these settings respectively seems to make sense, as well as to have the backing of the actual course of historical development. Further this juxtaposition, highlighting the contrasts between oral and written tradition, can help us to avoid ethnocentric value judgements since we can see each as valid and meaningful in its own natural context. Thus the textual variations in Yugoslav oral poetry (as in Lord 1968a) may seem like errors if judged against the canons for written texts. But when understood in an oral setting, with long poems composed in performance without the concept of a 'correct' text, then this *oral* mode can be recognized as fully authentic in its own terms. The contrasts remind us that the ways of other cultures can be valid too – indeed an expression of a many-sided and dignified form of life – rather than just deviations from the 'normal' ways of our own culture. Such contrasts can also lead to greater understanding of our own distinctive characteristics, feeding as these do on a tradition of written communication. Setting up contrasting ideal types of this kind is one standard basis for the kind of classification that forms an acceptable part of scientific procedure (not to speak of classic sociological theorizing), with the hope that through being able to assign the specific instances under study to one or other of these types we can then read off (or, for the future, predict) their associated characteristics.

With 'orality' and 'literacy', however, such a typology has serious drawbacks. Certainly, it helps us to make sense of complex data but at the cost of over-simplifying and so distorting. For how useful is this binary typology when it turns out that most known cultures don't fit? In practice a *mixture* of media (oral and written) is far more typical than a reliance on just one, with writing being used for some purposes, oral forms for others (and in recent cases electronic media playing a part too). This kind of mixture is and has been a common and ordinary feature of cultures throughout the centuries rather than the 'abnormal' case implied by the ideal types model.

The normality of mixed oral and written modes in human cultures is widely documented. Jack Goody sums this up effectively in his classic *Literacy in Traditional Societies*:

At least during the past 2,000 years, the vast majority of the peoples of the world (most of Eurasia and much of Africa) have lived . . . in cultures which were influenced in some degree by the circulation of the written word, by the presence of groups or individuals who could read and write . . . Even if one's attention is centred only upon village life, there are large areas of the world where the fact of writing and the existence of the book have to be taken into account, even in discussing 'traditional' societies. (Goody, 1968, pp. 4–5)

Even in areas outside this great span – in Australia, for example, the South Pacific or Amerindia – the main knowledge we have of these cultures is, almost by definition, for the period over the last few centuries when written as well as oral forms have (despite the romantic blindness which afflicts some observers) in practice *both* played a part. By now, at least, it would be hard to find actual examples of these supposedly mutually exclusive 'pure' types of culture; indeed, even for the past we very seldom encounter empirical evidence (rather than speculation) about communication in purely 'oral' societies; field research, for example, has often been in colonial – i.e. partly literate – settings (cf. Finnegan, 1974). It is the 'mixed' rather than the 'pure' type that provides the typical case and the available evidence for analysis.

The whole concept of opposed pure types of society is in any case now generally subject to criticism in the light of the many detailed studies of 'non-industrial' cultures. Binary typologies may be handy as a starting-off point for theorizing and are still influential, not least because of the continuing reverence within western higher education for the classic nineteenth-century sociological theorists. But the accumulating empirical evidence (some of it mentioned in earlier chapters) demonstrates that the postulated characteristics of each type simply do not always predictably follow. It is now clear, for example, that stress on achievement, individualism and secularization can occur in non-industrial as well as industrial cultures – the individualistic and competitive ethos of the Kapauku Papuans of New Guinea (Pospisil, 1963) or the Ibo of West Africa (Ottenberg, 1959) are often cited. And if the Yoruba of Nigeria are any guide, large-scale urbanism can develop without industrialization or mass literacy (Bascom, 1955; Mabogunje, 1968). Indeed contrasts among non-industrial cultures them-selves are as striking as those between industrial and non-industrial.

Once the assumption of some basic twofold division in human society is challenged it is no surprise to see the co-existence of oral and written modes not as something strange – representing, as it were, two radically different 'evolutionary stages' of human development – but as a normal and frequently occurring aspect of human cultures. It is true that differing cultures lay different emphases on, say, written learning and that the specific uses of oral media vary at different times and places – but this is something that demands detailed investigation rather than defining out of existence.

There is also the related idea that new media, once adopted, drive out older-established ones. Literacy is seen as replacing oral communication, or electronic media like television superseding the practice of reading and writing. Obviously there is sometimes some truth in this as earlier monopolies are challenged (the telegraph, say, by telephony, or printed books by electronic publishing) and a greater range of options thus opened up. But the assumption that there is something wholesale and irretrievable in such changes owes less to an examination of the detailed evidence than to the continuing influence of a great divide model implying some pre-set evolutionary progression through differing and mutually exclusive modes of communication. Exploiting both oral *and* written modes is in fact very common in the actual communication of written compositions, among them the publication of the classical works of Greek and Latin antiquity through public performances, modern poetry readings, radio stories and plays, hymn singing or lyrics on pop records. Similarly there is often interchange between oral and written modes in the transmission and circulation of many forms of so-called 'oral' literature, from Scottish and American ballads (both written down *and* sung from memory), Hausa and Swahili poetry, Maori legends, Irish national songs, Yoruba or American Negro sermons and European 'fairy tales', to the great Gesar epic in Tibet, Mongolia and China, the Indian Vedic literature, and Sumatran sung narratives (further references in Finnegan, 1976, pp. 137ff).

In setting up grand historical oppositions we can also misunderstand our *own* experience. In this dichotomizing approach the primary mode of communication and transmission in recent centuries in western Europe is often taken to be writing (and more especially printing), with perhaps a third 'new' phase of electronic communication now superseding the rest. But this model glosses over many complexities. One needs only mention the continuing significance of oral communication in the modern world, or the increasing distribution of books and newspapers, to give the lie to facile predictions that radio and television would inevitably bring the end of book reading. In practice people switch from oral to written to electronic communication and back and from personally generated to mass-media forms, without any sense that there is some radical change involved or that they are somehow thereby moving in different kinds of 'social space' (for some recent discussion of these interactions see, e.g. Tannen, 1982, 1984; Shuman, 1986). Once again, this kind of interaction only seems strange if we start from a model which presupposes that these forms of communication are essentially antipathetic modes.

The same point applies to the specific literary forms sometimes said to go with particular forms of society. Here again, a basic model of fundamentally opposed types of society often underlies these associations. Thus 'ballad communities' are claimed to be 'essentially medieval', 'homogeneous', 'unlettered, comparatively isolated and self-reliant, living and working co-operatively ... an oral culture would thrive in the communal environment, because the processes of oral transmission depend upon corporate activity' (Hodgart, 1950, p. 131; Housman, 1952, p. 43; Buchan, 1972, p. 26). Similarly epic has also sometimes been fitted into an evolutionist framework, in which it corresponds with a particular stage in society (the 'heroic' age), or is seen as an essential step in the progressive development of 'society' and 'literature' (e.g. Chadwick, 1926; Bowra, 1957; cf. Finnegan, 1977, pp. 246ff). Both theories draw at least some of their apparent attraction from the same implicit model of opposing ideal types of society –

for, aside from speculative assertion, there is really no evidence that either ballad or epic *are* only associated with societies of a certain type or that they form one necessary stage in socio-literary development.

A similar set of assumptions lends apparent credibility to the repeated claim often taken as so self-evidently true as to need no demonstration – that literacy is incompatible with oral creativity. As Kirk puts it 'literacy destroys the virtue of an oral singer . . . the acquisition of writing invariably destroys the powers of an oral poet' (Kirk, 1965, pp. 22, 30). This claim partly rests on the well-known work of Parry and Lord in Yugoslavia in the 1930s (in Parry and Lord, 1954; Lord, 1968a). This research demonstrated the oral process through which Yugoslav heroic singers improvised lengthy unwritten epic songs *in the act of performance*, texts which varied from performance to performance, in a way quite different from the fixed texts resulting from writing. Lord is clear about the contrast: 'The two techniques [oral and written] are contradictory and mutually exclusive. Once the oral technique is lost, it is never regained. The written technique . . . is not compatible with oral technique' (Lord, 1968a, p. 129). What is not so clear, however, is the *evidence* for his conclusion that once a singer came in contact with literate modes of composition he inevitably lost the power of true oral composition. Even among the singers Parry and Lord studied, the claim is scarcely proven, for it emerges elsewhere that a number of the poets they recorded (including those they classed as 'traditional') were literate (Parry and Lord, 1954, pp. 54ff) and most (or all?) had had at least indirect contact with writing.

But even if we accept Lord's interpretation of the Yugoslav case it does not follow that there is some *universally* found process of written modes of composition driving out oral. For many readers the real attraction of this theory must lie in its evocation of that same old binary model, for any examination of the detailed comparative evidence quickly turns up cases where not only do written and oral modes of composition co-exist in the same culture, but they can even be used by the same person. Opland, for example, describes how Zulu poets in South Africa use the traditional formulaic style of oral poetry even when composing in writing.

The Zulu poet B. W. Vilakazi writes of his poetry that he passed through a period of imitating European models, but subsequently returned to traditional forms. Having grown up in the Zulu tradition he expressed himself most easily in a manner that was part of his cultural identity. Colleagues of mine in the Department of African Languages at the University of Cape Town have written praise poems on the highway traffic, and on the Apollo moon landing. Their poetry conforms metrically and stylistically to the traditional praise poems sung by *imbongi* [traditional praise poets].
(Opland, 1971, p. 177)

And when I was teaching at the University of the South Pacific in Fiji it turned out that one of the third-year social science students was also a leading Fijian poet, composing in the traditional oral mode (see pp. 95ff above). This kind of interaction does not always happen and there doubtless are cases where one or the other form takes over as the main one for individual composers (not always in the direction of oral to written, perhaps). But to assume that one *always* drives out the other, or to use this assumption as the basis for speculative assertion in the absence of other data, is to let an initial theoretical model take us far beyond the actual evidence.

Yet these kinds of dichotomies still persist, pushed not only by the earlier but still influential classic social theorists or the technological determinism of more recent writers like McLuhan or Ong, but also answering to unconscious desires of our modern age. Roger Abrahams put his finger on some salient points when he wrote:

No area of poetics seems to produce quite so much hogwash as writings which involve generalizations on how oral (both preliterate and nonliterate) people put together, remember, and perform in display situations ... The radical discontinuity argument is commonly made for ideological rather than scientific reasons. Oral people are either regarded as backward and uncivilized, or at least under-developed – the position out of which the literacy campaigns for developing countries have developed – or they are innocent prelapsarians who have not yet entered into the alienating process of capitalistic production and exchange ...

The naive mechanistic evolutionism of this position simply does not bear up under any close scrutiny – that is, when a predominantly oral culture is observed, described and analyzed with regard to its expressive capabilities. Yet, a number of the most widely read social theorists have fallen into this Rousseauian trap, reinventing the idea of the nonliterate community which has maintained a kind of organic unity in the ways they act and interact. By this fiction they are able to project their own complicated structure of sentiments as it bears on the failures of modernity to maintain a sense of social centeredness. Not only does this potentially harmful fiction include those who have idealized the medieval monastic community, from the likes of William Morris to Ivan Ilych, but a great many of those who have been at the center of defining the 'logocentric' character of our social lives: Marshall McLuhan, Walter Benjamin, Jacques Derrida, and Michel Foucault are sacred cows who come to mind most immediately, but included in the list are all of those who posit an ancien regime or a folk society without exploring, in detail, specific societies. (Abrahams, 1985, pp. 555–6)

The binary opposition model can perhaps lead to some limited insights about possible contrasts both in social and in literary organization. But this, I suggest, does not outweigh its disadvantages: tempting us to generalize before we have the detailed evidence, over-simplifying situations in which complexity is not just an accidental distraction but an essential aspect of actual human activity and expression, and misleadingly implying that certain situations – 'pure oral' in particular – are somehow more 'natural' and unproblematic than others. The final result leads to a misunderstanding of *ourselves* as well as of the other historical or contemporary cultures we wish to study. This may seem too obvious to labour – for who now really believes in the existence of such opposed 'pure types' of society? But it *is* such an attractive model! However often you pitch it out, like nature it keeps coming back again when you're not looking. It is as well, in considering the central topic of this discussion, to be aware of its implications and power.

Some suggested characteristics of orality and literacy

A more modest approach to the study of orality–literacy looks more realistic: that is, not to search for opposing pure types of cultures as wholes, but rather for *specific* characteristics or consequences likely to be associated with orality and with literacy. Because of the complexities that I have been insisting on, this is scarcely a simple topic to research, but some interesting suggestions have been made which I will summarize and discuss here briefly (some of them have been evaluated in more detail in earlier chapters but are drawn together in a wider conspectus here).

As has frequently been pointed out (e.g. Innis, 1972; Goody, 1977; and the more detailed discussion and references in chapter 2 above), one of the great characteristics of written communication is that it is permanent. Written forms can be preserved through space, thus leading to the possibility of far-flung empires and enterprises, together with the development of impersonal norms and rational procedures – all difficult to conceive without writing. Writing can also be permanent through time – an equally significant quality. Once again, it is hard to picture large-scale administration and bureaucracy without permanent written records, from the running of a large-scale modern nation state to the administering of a city, a school, a factory, or the organization of national or international trade. Again, the practicability of directly comparing written accounts from different periods or areas, rather than having differences glossed over in face to face oral contexts, leads to the possibility of detachment, of scientific history, of science and of abstract reasoning. Similarly, objectivity and secularization may increase relative to supernatural and magical concepts, notably in the secular rationality sometimes regarded as the specific characteristic of recent western civilization.

Another aspect is the accumulation of information over time made possible with literacy. This applies even to a single individual who can keep notes or have access to written records on a far larger scale than could ever be kept in someone's head; how much more to whole generations and cultures. Without this accumulation of knowledge through writing it would be hard to conceive of the development of modern science and technology, or the kind of intellectual and literary cultures that we now take for granted. Following the same lines, it is easy to see how literacy and economic development may be connected, for written records facilitate formal accounting and systematic economic planning.

Yet other consequences of writing have also been postulated. Literacy has been seen as a precondition for democracy and freedom, for instance, or for the rise of individualism (e.g. Carothers, 1959; McLuhan, 1967, pp. 88ff). Again, the increase in urbanism is sometimes seen as dependent on writing (e.g. McLuhan, 1970, p. 14), together with a greater division of labour and generally increased heterogeneity in human society which in turn leads to greater opportunities of choice between differing philosophies. More speculatively there is Marshall McLuhan's suggestion that the advent of printing meant that visual modes of perception gained ascendancy over the previous acoustic or oral forms, an idea not unrelated to the radical oppositions between oral and written modes posited by Lord and Parry on the basis of their Yugoslav study. Indeed their work is singled out in the prologue to McLuhan's *Gutenberg Galaxy*: 'the enterprise which Milman Parry undertook with reference to the contrasted forms of oral and written poetry is here extended to the forms of thought and the organization of experience in society and politics' (McLuhan, 1962, p. 1).

Indeed the list of literacy effects sometimes seems endless. As Harvey Graff summed them up:

a truly daunting number of cognitive, affective, behavioral, and attitudinal effects. These characteristics usually include attitudes ranging from empathy, innovativeness, achievement-orientation, 'cosmopoliteness', information-and-media-awareness, national identification, technological acceptance, rationality, and commitment to democracy, to opportunism, linearity of thought and behavior, or urban residence. Literacy is sometimes conceived of as a skill, but more often as symbolic or representative of attitudes and mentalities. On other levels, literacy 'thresholds' are seen as requirements for economic development, 'take-offs', 'modernization', political development and stability, standards of living, fertility control and so on. (Graff, 1982, pp. 13–14)

So writing has apparently been held responsible for just about everything that is supposed to be characteristic of western civilization, not to speak of contemporary states everywhere else in the world too.

This may not be quite so extravagant as it seems. After all, one change goes with another, so that it would not be surprising if writing was part of a cluster of multi-faceted changes; all the different possible aspects of literacy that have been mentioned thus *could* well be valid, as connected implications even if not necessarily direct consequences. If the functionalist social scientists have taught us anything, it is that looking at one factor in isolation misconceives the dynamics of actual social processes. So perhaps writing is not something in isolation but part of a whole process of change – from face to face, oral, small-scale, heterogeneous and rural communities to the literate, urban, industrial and mechanical cultures we know now.

But here we are again with the radical divide model. This is the kind of approach which, as Talcott Parsons put it in the context of 'evolutionary universals', envisages writing as a 'watershed' in social evolution, 'the focus of the fateful development out of primitiveness' (Parsons, 1966, p. 26). It is a model which, as we have seen already, has only limited usefulness – and even that at the risk of substituting speculative generalizations for research into specifics. Perhaps, then, the way to test out those suggested associations of literacy is either to study the possible interaction of many factors in *specific* cultures and historical periods or, alternatively, to look more directly at some of these suggested associations one at a time. I want to follow the latter line here, not for full examination of the evidence (which would take several books) but to reinforce and draw together some of the earlier discussions (specially that in chapter 2) and suggest that the situation may be more problematic than it first appears.

First, *is* one of the consequences of literacy the rise of empires, bureaucracies, large-scale commerce? This certainly makes sense, and seems to fit with our understanding of the course of human history from the earliest times. As H. G. Wells put it in his *Short History of the World*, writing

put agreements, laws, commandments on record. It made the growth of states larger than the old city states possible. It made a continuous historical consciousness possible. The command of the priest or king and his seal could go far beyond his sight and voice and could survive his death. (Wells, 1946, quoted in Harris, 1986, p. 20)

It is hard to avoid seeing writing as a necessary condition for empires and monarchies in the past, as well as for more recent developments. Without written records, how could a modern state be administered, with its collection of taxes, administration of justice, publication and implementation of laws, public elections and appointments, or chain of command within government?

But we also have to be careful about pressing too far with this idea of writing as a precondition for bureaucratic organization. For one thing, there are *degrees* of reliance on literacy, and different kinds of writing. I presume that in, say, fifth-century Athens or the early Roman Empire different uses were made of written records and to a different degree, and that these were different yet again in, say, nineteenth-century Britain or, again, in earlier or in contemporary China. Nowadays, too, increasing use is made of the person-to-person telephone or other forms of telecommunications in some modern societies, so that this now carries messages which at different times or places might have been written. The situation is more complex and messy than can be summed up just by saying that writing is a precondition for bureaucratic large-scale organization, for the ways and the amount writing is used varies. The extent and the usage of written records in, say, ancient Mesopotamia must have been very different from that in contemporary Britain, and it would be hard to establish how far the social and political differences should be related to *writing*.

It is also tempting to start from an inevitably ethnocentric viewpoint and so assume that because in our own and familiar cultures writing does go with organized commerce, administration, etc., these are therefore *necessarily* impossible without it: that there is no other way these ends can be achieved. The increasing use of electronic media might make us pause, so too evidence about commerce or organizations relying on little or no use of written media. Consider, for example, the involved marketing and trading systems of traditional West Africa or Melanesia, or the ancient long-distance trading networks established by archaeological research. Or there is the more specific case studied in some detail by Abner Cohen, where the complex organization of credit in the Ibadan cattle market in Nigeria in the 1960s, involving the sale of some 75,000 cattle every year, functioned without writing. All sales were on credit and there was an outstanding total of about £100,000 current debt at any one time: 'no documents are signed and no resort is made to the services of banks or to the official courts . . . the whole organization . . . is entirely indigenous' (Cohen, 1965, pp. 8–9). As to the establishment of empires and large-scale administrative units, written communication and storage *may* be a necessary condition – but can we really be sure? We can guess, but in fact we do not really know how administration was organized in historical periods for which there are, by definition, no written records to inform us. Archaeological research is pushing the temporal bounds of large-scale organization back farther and farther (e.g. Hammond, 1986), but here again we cannot be sure just what role was played by writing.

The other side of the question is whether writing is a *sufficient* condition for bureaucratic administration or large-scale organization. At least in any obvious sense the answer here must clearly be in the negative. The existence of writing may facilitate large-scale political units and organization, but it is surely no guarantee of their development or continuance.

What about the qualities of rationality, objectivity and detachment? – all 'good' words, and ones that, in common with many reformers of the past and the present (themselves usually literate), we tend to associate with writing, above all with widespread literacy. And certainly in a culture in which a mastery of written knowledge and the arts of writing is often taken as the mark of detachment and formal learning, such an association seems incontrovertible. As with so many evaluative terms, however, the qualities clustering around the concept of 'rationality' and so on have manifold different meanings and are exceptionally hard to pin down. For this reason too it is tempting to let preconceptions that 'it must be so' take the place of hard evidence. It is illuminating to pick out some specific aspects often implied under the broad heading of 'rationality' to look at more closely.

One approach is to contrast cognitive processes such as abstraction with concrete and context-dependent verbalization or thinking, or of being able to argue with detachment as against immersion in the contingent and concrete present. Even just fastening on this aspect runs into a whole set of problems, though, which are a matter of current controversy in social psychology, linguistics and philosophy as well as sociology and social anthropology (see, e.g., Hollis and Lukes, 1982; Scribner and Cole, 1981; Johnson-Laird and Wason, 1977; Overing, 1985). But it is certainly fair to say that these questions are generally characterized by abstract analysis or by generalized or even speculative and rhetorical assertions more often than by incontrovertible demonstrations that there is a clear-cut and non-problematic association between *literacy* or *orality* on the one hand and specific cognitive processes on the other.

There have, it is true, been claims both by social anthropologists in cross-cultural studies and by social scientists working with 'deprived groups' in literate communities that lack of literate skills means less power of abstraction and detachment in the case both of individuals and of cultures as a whole. Patricia Greenfield, for example, concludes from her study of Wolof children in Senegal that those who relied on oral communication (the unschooled) were dependent on context and concrete activities, unlike the schooled children who were able to cultivate abstract habits of thought learnt 'through the training embodied in the written language' (1972, p. 174). She compares this to class differences in language use in America and England, where, she claims, the type of verbalization typical of lower-class speakers is '*totally dependent* on the concrete physical situation' (p. 171: italics in original), contrasted with the relatively abstract and context-free forms typical of those influenced by written forms: 'writing is practice in the use of linguistic contexts as independent of immediate reference' (p. 174). Again, Luria reports the relative lack of success of non-literate compared to literate subjects in Uzbekistan and Kirghizia in theoretical and logical thinking (1976, ch. 4), while Goody discusses the 'oral' method by which the LoDagaa of northern Ghana count cowries: 'an instance of the greater concreteness of procedures in non-literate societies' in contrast to the 'greater abstractness' that comes with literacy (Goody,

1973, pp. 7–8; other relevant research is summarized in Cole and Scribner, 1974).

Such instances are hard to interpret. As Cole and Scribner point out forcefully in their general discussion the design of cross-cultural research can be seriously flawed by 'experimental egocentrism' – taking theories developed within our own culture for granted through 'mistaking as universals the particular organizations of cognitive skills that have arisen in the historical circumstances of our own society, and interpreting their absence in other cultures as "deficiency"' (1974, p. 200). Similarly, doubt has been shed on the methodology used to establish different speech codes among 'deprived' groups: are enquiries carried out without regard to the local norms or idioms, or through an unfamiliar interviewer or linguistic code, really to be taken seriously? (for some discussion of such points see, e.g., Labov, 1973; Cole and Scribner, 1974; Fernandez, 1980; Agar, 1980). The trouble with such enquiries is the familiar one constantly (and rightly) raised about cross-cultural tests: are they really testing the powers of abstraction and concept handling, or just the culturally different socialization procedures into specific vocabularies and skills? If we define these terms narrowly enough to test directly, there is the difficulty that the tests may (tautologically) uncover nothing more than the presence or absence of our own cultural norms; if more widely, then can we be sure that, given present cultural differences, the tests definitively demonstrate writing as a *necessary* precondition for rational cognitive processes?

The evidence is thus not as clear-cut as one would guess from the many emotive references to the power of literacy in bringing rationality, lightening the darkness and so on: the kind of simplification that recalls the optimistic one-way developmental model, sometimes with the further implications of a vast evolutionary gap between those with and without the arts of writing. Indeed, we seem to be coming back yet again to the old models of 'primitive mentality' which most anthropologists would now repudiate. Certainly if we take cognitive processes in a *general* sense, the existence of rich classificatory systems, symbolism, traditions of judicial reasoning, highly developed languages and complex literature among many non-literate peoples (all amply demonstrated in anthropological research), make one dubious about the dependence of abstraction on literacy, while the more specific claims about particular logical skills and verbal manipulation are at best too controversial and elusive for any definitive conclusion to be asserted.

It is *possible* that there is indeed some necessary connection between literacy and the ability to conceptualize abstractly and argue rationally. My own prejudices suggest that there is – indeed this belief is built into my whole socialization and forms one rationale for my own career and those like it! H. A. Innis (1950, p. 8) pertinently quotes Mark Pattison's warning that 'writers with a professional tendency to magnify their office have always been given to exaggerate the effect of printed words'. It would be sensible to be extra-scrupulous in our scrutiny of evidence linking rationality to writing. And I have to concede that I have not actually been convinced by any hard cross-cultural evidence that this link *must* be there.

As for whether literacy can be seen as a *sufficient* condition for cognitive processes that lead to abstraction and detachment in any clear-cut and demonstrable sense – that is surely only too easily answered in the negative.

'Rationality' is also sometimes represented as the kind of scientific and objective approaches to the world often taken to be characteristic of western culture. Is writing a necessary condition for this? This is certainly plausible, especially when we also recall the importance of writing in the accumulation of information. One cannot help but be impressed by arguments put forward by, for example, Jack Goody and Ian Watt, that in literate societies people

are faced with permanently recorded versions of the past and its beliefs; and because the past is thus set apart from the present, historical enquiry becomes possible. This by turn encourages scepticism and scepticism, not only about the legendary past, but about received ideas about the universe as a whole. (Goody and Watt, 1968, pp. 67–8)

But of course this is not to say that everything in scientific processes depends only or even primarily on writing. As with any technology, the effectiveness of writing depends on how it is actually used and its interplay with other media (including the oral communication and personal interaction that continues to play a part in scientific discovery and communication). In any case literacy of itself does not always lead to objective and sceptical enquiry. Kathleen Gough's interesting comparison (1968) of literacy in traditional China and India reveals that in the former there was secular historical research, but in the latter not: *literacy* itself was not enough. It has to be faced too that writing can as easily be used to interfere with objective scientific or historical enquiry as to support it.

The same applies to the related topic of secularization and the sense of 'rationality' which implies the rejection of magical, mystical and supernatural modes of thought. Here again, writing can play a part, especially perhaps with mass literacy and/or the widespread use of printing which makes access to a *range* of books possible (more feasible in a print than a manuscript culture) and hence facilitates critical comparison between these (see, e.g., Eisenstein, 1968, pp. 7ff). But secular and utilitarian ways of approaching the world can also exist without the use of either writing or printing (let me refer again to the emphasis on secularism and the 'rationalistic and almost scientific view of the world' of the Kapauku Papuans as described in Pospisil, 1963). Correspondingly an emphasis on religious and mystical ideology can co-exist with – even be encouraged by – dissemination in writing. Thus the spread of printing in western society resulted not just in new forms of enlightenment but also in the print of 'a vast backlog of occult lore' and 'new forms of mystification' (Eisenstein, 1968, pp. 9–10). Indeed one of the aims of those encouraging literacy in early modern Europe was a religious one: 'the immediate evidence [is] that, in America as in Europe, in so far as literacy moved rapidly toward universality the prime motive force was the conservation of piety, which by all available measures appears to have succeeded' (Lockridge, 1974, p. 101, cf. pp. 84–6). Once again, it is not so much the technology that is significant, whether for secularization or science, but the actual use that is made of it; and a study of this is likely to lead quickly into research into historical and cultural complexities rather than just the simplified 'impact' of the technology of writing.

'Rationality' is also sometimes used to allude to the impersonal and objective procedures often held characteristic of bureaucracy – the form of administration held typical of the modern nation state. This is often specifically connected with writing, for example in the influential view which sees modern western institutions as depending on 'rationally established norms by enactment, decrees and regulations' (Weber, 1962, p. 25), where 'administrative acts, decisions and rules are formulated and recorded in writing' (Weber, 1964, p. 332). Once again, connecting the development of bureaucracy with literacy does indeed make sense – so long, that is, as we do not press the causal relationship too far or too universally. For of course the existence of writing does not necessarily lead to bureaucratization in exactly the nineteenth- or early twentieth-century form in western Europe described by Weber. Perhaps this form of bureaucracy is indeed dependent on writing (it is certainly hard to conceive it without) but this should not lead us to suppose that *all* forms of administration are necessarily of this sort or that there is something 'universal' about the particular institutions of recent western civilization. Nor should we fall into the trap of identifying so closely with the impersonal objective *ideals* set for western bureaucracy that because written regulations are theoretically paramount we therefore subsume *all* administrative action under that head: in practice personal views, individual decision-making, oral discussion and informal interaction play a far greater part than one would suppose from the normative ideals of how things are *supposed* to work in western administration.

'Rationality' may be a slippery and emotive set of concepts, but the idea of the accumulation of information implied by the use of writing seems more straightforward: the possibility of passing on information and discussion from one generation to another. This is not just factual data but, as Jack Goody explains, the establishment of 'a cumulative tradition of critical discussion' (Goody, 1977, p. 47). The spread of information from one culture to another is also possible through writing, from the dissemination of the great 'religions of the book' like Islam or Christianity which depend on the existence and circulation of 'a virtually indestructible document belonging to one of the great world (i.e. literate) religions' (Goody, 1968, p. 5), to the transmission and rediscovery of the accumulated knowledge of the classical world at the Renaissance, or of the rich culture of China by Japan in the eighth century. Through writing, the exploitation of the learning of literate people throughout the ages and areas of the world is in principle made possible through the resources of writing.

Note the 'in principle', though, for this process does not take place just through the existence of writing in itself. The mere physical presence of books and papers in libraries does not necessarily mean that these are *used*, and certainly does not tell us much about the purpose for which they are employed or the possible barriers of, say, language, prejudice or self-interest, to particular usages. In particular, one needs to balance the optimistic connotation of progress that often seems to accompany the idea of accumulating and developing knowledge by remembering that another use of writing is precisely to perpetuate tradition. Innovation may then mean breaking *away* from the written traditions – as with Afro-American music or some educationalists' pleas to play down reading in favour of less conservative media (e.g. Postman, 1973). The actual *use* of material accumulated through writing may also itself involve oral means, through, say, oral teaching, personal communication and conference attendances. So, as with the other possible consequences of literacy, the accumulation of information *may* sometimes be important – but the actual use made of writing in this respect, its interaction with other media, and the choices and barriers involved are necessarily complex processes for any given culture or historical period.

What about the 'restructuring of consciousness' said by some to be brought about by literacy, in particular, the postulated move from 'acoustic' to 'visual' perception? Ong, for example, describes how 'hearing-dominance' yields to 'sight-dominance' with the establishment of literacy, while McLuhan expresses it even more strongly:

Until WRITING was invented, we lived in acoustic space, where all backward peoples still live: boundless, directionless, horizonless. The clash of the mind, the world of emotion, primordial intuition, mafia-ridden . . . A goose quill put an end to talk, abolished mystery . . . It was the basic metaphor with which the cycle of CIVILIZATION began, the step from the dark into the light of the mind. (McLuhan, 1970, pp. 13–14; cf. Carpenter and McLuhan, 1960, pp. 65ff)

It is not in fact easy to know just how such statements could be tested out in any detail for earlier civilizations. For more recent examples, anthropological fieldwork might be supposed to provide the evidence, but does not appear to do so convincingly.

One of the most detailed recent examinations of this topic was in Steven Feld's analysis of the poetry and thought of a non-literate culture, where on the basis of ten years' study he goes deeply into the poetic and musical experience of a Papuan New Guinean people (the Kaluli). One of the questions he started from was precisely that of whether they were indeed more 'acoustic' and 'non-lineal' than literate cultures. He found that Kaluli spatial, temporal, visual and auditory concepts were complex and culture-specific, employing a logic which had to be studied empirically rather than predicted from first principles:

This logic is not given, cognitively or any other way, by the state of being oral rather than literate; in other words, the historical, environmental, and biocultural conditions which promote and lead to successful adaptation do not necessarily produce the same adaptive strategies in similar circumstances. Certain features of the Kaluli situation are unique, others can be generalized, but that ratio is complicated, and is not clarified by considering orality/literacy as the dependent variable in the evolution of consciousness . . .

In the Kaluli case there are many musical and performative features that bear either superficial or strong similarity to the typifications of oral/nonlineal/ear/acoustic space 'consciousness' as described by McLuhan, Carpenter, Ong and their associates. While these features are indeed real and meaningful for Kaluli, it only trivializes their significance to claim that they can be explained as consequences of 'orality'. These features, traits, and processes, and the contingent subtleties and contradictions that one inevitably uncovers in studying them, are products of local history – by which I mean products of invention, adaptation, response, and use. Some of these features cannot be found to characterize other oral tradition societies; some can be found in certain literate traditions. What is important, ultimately, is not the musical traits, but the socio-historical process through which they become meaningful . . . These meanings are far more complex than can be reduced to 'orality', ear dominance, nonlineality, acoustic space, and so forth. (Feld, 1987, pp. 12, 14–15)

His overall conclusion about the great divide dichotomies is that:

These confounding typologies of society, social organization, techno-economic complexity, and symbolic focus do little to explain the dynamics of oral and literate processes, but rather, simply blur or push aside social detail, historical accuracy, and the complexities of oral–literate interactions for the sake of sweeping generalizations that do not provide real evidence for the assertion that oral/literate are fundamentally different states of mind. (Feld, 1987, p. 5)

On the other possible implications of writing I only want to comment briefly. One is the importance sometimes attached to literacy as a precondition for development. This has been one of the optimistic tenets of various

UNESCO campaigns and government development plans: if mass literacy can be brought to 'Third World' countries, this will lead to social and economic development. Literacy is necessary 'to raise productivity and welfare in the underdeveloped world' (UNESCO, 1970, p. 10), and 'the best possible means for a developing nation to break the vicious circle of general backwardness and to make progress along the path of modernisation' (Roy and Kapoor, 1975, p. 1). Similarly it has been argued that printing, together with other changes in the mass media, leads to a situation in which change is more readily tolerated and people are progressively involved in 'modernization' (see, e.g., Lerner, 1964; Oxenham, 1980, pp. 51ff; Clammer, 1976, pp. 94ff).

Again, however, the evidence is not clear-cut, even assuming we can disentangle the consequences of printing, of writing in general, or of a certain level of literacy from other concurrent factors. Writing *as such* does not guarantee particular economic effects though it may, in certain conditions and given certain choices by particular groups, facilitate them. And there are circumstances when, as far as communication and organization are concerned, radio may well be a more suitable medium than the written word. In many of the archipelagos of the South Pacific, for instance, such as Kiribati, Vanuatu, Tuvalu or Fiji, made up of inhabited islands widely separated by still inhospitable seas and without regular sea or air transport, the oral medium of radio is both speedier and more effective than writing. As for 'modernization', writing, as mentioned earlier, *can* be used as a medium for new development – but it can equally be used to preserve traditional culture, even to give it a new lease of life (for some discussion of this process in the context of early modern Europe see Burke, 1978). Indeed much of what is called 'oral tradition' is known precisely because it has been recorded and circulated in *writing*. Once again, the technology is not the crux but how it is used.

Again, what about the importance of writing in leading to individualism, and, perhaps as a consequence, democratic ways of life? Again there are senses in which this optimistic equation is plausible. The art of reading is often seen as an essentially private and withdrawn process – though perhaps this is more properly the consequence of print accompanied by a convention of reading silently to oneself, for writing itself can equally be linked with a practice of reading aloud. McLuhan puts it more directly: 'Print created individualism . . . in the sixteenth century' (1970, p. 28). True, perhaps, but is the value of privacy and individuality never found in non-literate contexts? (Recent anthropological work throws doubt on this easy assumption, e.g. Lienhardt, 1980; Heelas and Lock, 1981; Carrithers, Collins and Lukes, 1985.) And does print never also encourage conformism, unthinking regurgitation and copying?

There is also the greater access to different viewpoints made possible in literate cultures with the resultant greater range of choices between differing viewpoints possible for individuals – 'open' as against 'closed' societies, with the latter arguably more characteristic of 'oral' contexts (see Horton, 1967). Again, fair enough up to a point, though how far writing is the most crucial variable here is debatable. But even this contrast is not self-evidently acceptable. Many anthropologists hold that the extent of choice and diversity in some non-industrial societies has been concealed by the functionalist framework of earlier ethnographic research (sometimes itself linked to the binary opposition model criticized earlier). And also, looking at it from the other end, many social scientists (especially Marxian ones) would argue that the amount of open-ness *actually* possible in modern society – literate or not – is in practice extremely circumscribed and that we are far less free in our choices than we believe. Indeed it can be argued that writing can be used precisely to *uphold* the current authority structure and prevent dissenting views: 'if you cannot read, you cannot be an obedient citizen . . . In order to be a good and loyal citizen, it is also necessary for you to believe in the myths and superstitions of your society. Therefore, a certain minimal reading skill is needed so that you can learn what these are, or have them reinforced' (Postman, 1973, p. 88).

The question of democratic participation and consensus is just the same: it cuts both ways. Certainly writing can provide a road to new forms of self-advancement or even perhaps to 'peace and understanding' as increased literacy spreads across the modern world (Jeffries, 1967, p. 14). But equally it can be used for *control* in the interests of those with power over writing and written resources. Innis (1964) points, for instance, to the power of the priests over the secrets of writing in ancient Egypt, or the church's control of copying and distribution of written documents in medieval Europe. In more recent times too the spread of literacy has been closely allied to the question of power. Furet's and Ozouf's conclusion from their historical study of the growth of literacy in modern France could no doubt be applied more widely: 'wherever we look, in every period, social stratification presides over the history of literacy' (1982, p. 303). Once again, the technological potential can be turned either way depending on the actual use and control of writing and written resources in a given culture.

One final question, more directly linked to the topic of transmission, is the particular form of literature and of literary composition associated with orality and literacy respectively. Parry's and Lord's so-called 'oral theory' is at the heart of this. As explained in chapter 5, this assumes that there is a special form of *oral* composition based on improvization from a stock of formulae during performance, and that this is fundamentally different from *written* composition (and written literature). The publications of Parry and

Lord were based primarily on their Yugoslav fieldwork on heroic poetry but already contained the implicit (sometimes explicit) claim that their findings could be generalized beyond Yugoslavia and possibly even beyond epic to oral composition and oral literature more generally. Many scholars have been inspired, consciously or not, by Lord's *The Singer of Tales* (1968a), so that it is now widely supposed of oral literature that, in contrast to written literature, it is always variable from performance to performance, never characterized by prior performance or exact memorization, and lacking the concept of a 'correct' or 'authentic' version. This model is sometimes taken as so well-established that it is assumed that if one element in this syndrome is present (e.g. a formulaic style) the rest must be there too, whether there is direct evidence for it or not.

But, as explained in chapter 5, comparative evidence has now thrown doubt on this wider application of the theory. For though oral composition-in-performance and oral variability are indeed often found, so too are *other* forms of oral composition. In particular, exact memorization of oral texts, oral composition divorced from the act of performance, and the concept of a correct oral text (all supposed impossible according to the accepted 'oral theory') have been found in a number of cultures. Examples have already been given of forms of sung poetry in South Pacific cultures, where inspired composition is transmitted through exact memorization (often by a group of assistants rather than the poet himself/herself), followed by an often lengthy series of rehearsals; only after this does the public performance take place, usually by a troupe of performers singing the exactly memorized text in unison. There are other instances too of exact memorization, specially with religious texts, and there is sometimes a separation between composition and performance, most obviously when composers and performers are different individuals (for instance the medieval Irish poets as distinct from reciters, the medieval European *trobador* (composers) as against *joglar* (performers) or the contrast between composers and performing bards in Ruanda (Finnegan, 1976 and 1977, pp. 73ff)).

The theory, then, that orality necessarily leads to only *one* kind of oral literature and oral composition is to some an unfalsifiable dogma: but in fact is mistaken. Following this, one must also be cautious about the related claims that all formulaic texts are orally composed, for written literature too can be composed in formulaic language (for some discussion of this debate see, e.g., Magoun, 1953; Lord, 1968a; Benson, 1966; Finnegan, 1977, pp. 69ff; Niles in Foley, 1985). More important perhaps than these somewhat mechanical points is the *nature* of oral as against written literature. As was argued in chapter 4, the assumptions that oral literature is necessarily communal and traditional and lacks detachment, careful aesthetic form or personal insight, turns out to be false when tested against the empirical evidence. Furthermore, as recent work (such as Cosentino, 1982; Okpewho, 1983; Bauman, 1986) has also demonstrated, the qualities of fancy and fantasy in human creativity which mould our perceptions of reality are found in oral, as in written, narrative.

It seems from the evidence, then, that there is in fact no one kind of literature or literary style that always follows from orality, nor is the effect of literacy on oral processes necessarily to bring about radical changes in either form of composition or literary style. For this, as for other postulated characteristics of literacy or of orality, generalized conclusions have been based on instances from only a limited number of situations and cannot be taken to be universal.

Must we follow a unidirectional and deterministic model?

So far I have been querying generalizations about human development which envisage the consequences of literacy in causal terms: literacy being seen as the sufficient or necessary condition for some further state of affairs. There are enough exceptions and qualifications to each of these popular generalizations to make them very doubtful as definitive explanations or predictions of social processes. Indeed it is only too likely that we have been misled by our own rhetoric – the constant chorus from academics, powerful educators, moral leaders or optimistic developers over the last few centuries – into believing that reading and writing necessarily bring about the effects we would like: a situation that has led at least one recent writer to speak of 'the literacy myth' (Graff, 1979). However, it is perhaps too easy just to pick holes in such models about human development. After all what interesting and suggestive model in the human sciences was ever free from possible counter-examples and qualifications in the light of cross-cultural comparison? So let me emphasize that the central point is not so much a negative one about exceptions to the supposed rule as the positive argument that these relationships are in fact more complex than can be summed up in simple causal attributions between literacy on the one hand and specific results on the other.

This complexity has two main aspects. First, literacy (or indeed orality) can be more fruitfully looked at not as an effective cause, but as an enabling factor: something which *can* facilitate particular forms of cognitive development, etc., but does not of itself bring them about (an idea put forward by, e.g., Gough, 1968; Graff, 1981b; Street, 1984; and at times by Jack Goody). As already discussed in chapter 2, this line is of course much less striking than the 'stronger' causal model. But it does fit much better with the realities of actual historical situations. It also has implications for further research, since a large number of *other* factors like the current political and economic conditions, social structure or local ideologies become as important to investigate as the technology of communication. The whole research enterprise into orality and literacy becomes much more complex than if we swallow the causally determined dichotomies.

The second aspect follows on from this. The framework of the 'stronger' model often implies a focus on the *technology* of communication as itself being the motive force rather than on the *uses* to which that technology is or can be put. Thus one has the implicit but influential technological determinism model of McLuhan and others which pictures human development as the result of the technology of writing (then later of printing or electronics) leading to specific social, literary and cognitive consequences. Lying behind this, and giving it extra plausibility, often lies the ethnocentric evolutionist view of development as basically uni-directional, moving onwards in natural progression from one stage to another – the stages in this case defined in terms of the technology of communication.

It is notable that these causal consequences are so often seen as those of *literacy* (and then, later, of printing and sometimes electronic media); and that they are presented as a one-way historical development, usually stated in western ethnocentric terms starting from the 'classic' civilization of the Greeks, working on towards the mass literacy and industrialization of the present. Of course this pattern of development *is* discernible in many cases – but that does not mean that specific communication usages only progress in one direction. Amidst all the speculation about consequences of literacy, why are there so few studies which investigate the consequences of orality, or of the loss of literacy, or of a choice to use one rather than another? What about the changing balance and possible consequences when people rely less on written communication and more on oral forms? What happens when telephones are increasingly used for communication rather than letters, or when an administration based on centrally-generated written forms (say, in a colonial situation) changes to more local, personal and oral forms in a newly independent nation? Or when written bureaucratic rules are found to be less appropriate in the administration of micro-states? If the implications of using different media of communication are indeed significant, then it is surely worth looking at the differing combinations and changes between them, rather than – as often in the implicit technological determinism model – just at apparently unidirectional and 'natural' progress based on 'ascending' technologies of communication.

The technological determinism model is in any case often a misleading guide in the study of orality and literacy because of its focus on the *medium*. This focus draws attention away from the way people in practice use technologies, make choices and select from (or ignore or even oppose) what is available to them. Certainly different media imply differing constraints and opportunities. But they would not be in use at all without the exercise of human choices and activities in the context of a large range of other factors – each of *them* doubtless with their own constraints and opportunities. It is within the context of actual *use* that the study of the different technologies of communication becomes most interesting.

Some uses of literacy

Focusing on the *uses* of literacy and orality means shifting attention away from the search for universals, ideal types or human development in general terms to more detailed investigation into actual choices in specific societies. Research into orality and literacy in this sense becomes more difficult and complex, because one cannot just pick out one technical variable – say, printed media – and draw consequences from that, but must also take into account the whole organization that lies behind this: the organization of writers or printers, say, the oppositions between those who control different media, the distribution and marketing, the constraints of using particular materials or of the different forms of writing (alphabetic as against non-alphabetic, for instance), the costs and benefits of new technological processes . . . Similarly there are questions to ask about the way print media are used by various sections of the community in particular places for various purposes at various times, or the interaction between, say, the use of printed books and papers and of other media such as music, sermons, public addresses, pictures or word of mouth communication. Against this kind of background, some of the simple generalizations about the effects of one medium look simplistic.

A number of studies illustrate the differing ways in which certain media can be used. This is especially striking in the case of writing where it turns out that its actual use is certainly *not* predictable from the widely assumed generalizations. One piece of research, for instance, compares the uses of recently acquired literacy in two different cultures in New Guinea (an area till lately totally non-literate). The first group, the coastal Melanesians, treated writing as something of ritual importance, imbued with mystical significance:

[They] displayed a curiously ritualised (yet practically understandable) attitude towards literacy. They took writing to be merely one more of those inherently ambiguous modes of communication with the supernatural with which they were already familiar. From this point of view, the virtue of writing lay in men's ability to manipulate it as an entity in a defined ritual fashion so that they could get a grip on the mission god and force from him his secrets. Indeed, writing soon came to be, in itself, an important symbol of the very goals of wealth and authority to which the people aspired . . . Writing was rarely treated as a straightforward technique of secular action. (Meggitt, 1968, p. 302)

The upland Papuans, however, took a different course. For them literacy was just another 'empirical tool to be added to hard work and the exercise of shrewdness in the struggle to get ahead in life' (Meggitt, 1968, p. 307). Writing was used not for ritual purposes but for such jobs as keeping accounts, recording transactions and writing letters – and letters which were 'prosaic and effective communications of information, giving facts, asking questions and offering advice' (p. 308). These opposing attitudes to writing and its use can perhaps be attributed to the differing religion and ethos in the two cultures – but whatever the explanation it is clear that it was something more than the mere adoption of writing in itself.

Similarly in traditional India, westerners have assumed that the obvious use of writing is for the kind of 'cognitive modernism' and 'rationality' expected in Goody (1977) and others. So no doubt it sometimes is, but as a recent cautious study by J. Parry has clearly shown, literacy is also used to evade the recording of individual innovations and, indeed, to provide a kind of immunity *against* scepticism. As Parry concludes, 'there is at least as much evidence to suggest that literacy promotes Sanskritization as secularization' (1985, p. 217).

The use of writing among the Vai of Liberia illustrates how complex the different uses of literacy can actually be, especially when several languages are involved. The Vai are of particular interest as having – exceptionally for Africa – developed their own indigenous script in the nineteenth century, which now co-exists with Arabic and Roman scripts. All three forms of writing are important in contemporary Vai culture but they are used for different purposes. The Vai script itself (in which three out of five Vai men over thirty are literate on a self-taught basis) is used for personal communication and personal record-keeping mainly in a rural context – but even Arabic scholars turn to this form for personal uses. The Arabic script and language, largely learnt in the context of Koranic schools, is the form used for religious topics, while English and Roman script are used primarily by those educated in western schools (also sometimes self-taught) for matters to do with big business, political hierarchy and administration. In the past Vai tended not to be literate in both English and Arabic (though often in Vai and Arabic, and sometimes in Vai and English) but recently tri-lingual literacy has been increasing, with people switching between one and the other according to situation and purpose (M. Smith, 1979; also Goody, Cole and Scribner, 1977).

Clanchy's account of changing patterns of writing in twelfth- and thirteenth-century England (Clanchy, 1979) also reveals a complex picture.

In the change-over 'from memory to written record' a number of different processes came in. Once again this involved switching between different languages (Latin, French, English and sometimes Hebrew) for different purposes. There were also the practices of dictating, reading aloud, translating between oral forms and writing, and between different languages even in the course of one lawcase, together with the reliance on seals and symbols which were often regarded as more reliable for proving rights than written documents (the latter liable to be forged and inaccurate). This was followed by a gradual move from the use of writing as a sacred script associated with monasticism and revered texts to literacy used for practical and administrative purposes. Social and political processes rather than literacy itself were the crucial factors.

The varying uses of printing too need to be seen in their social context rather than just as the automatic result of the technology. For printing can be – and has been – used for enlightenment *and* for mystification; for self-expression or rebellion *and* for repression; for systematic analysis and the development of knowledge on the one hand *and* for obfuscation, dogma and the propagation of prejudice and intolerance on the other. Nor does printing on its own necessarily bring about specific effects – these depend on how people actually use it and how it interacts with a large number of other factors in the current situation. Elizabeth Eisenstein (1979), for instance, while stressing the significance of printing has also demonstrated the complex relations involved in its uses in early modern Europe. A recent study too, by R. Scribner, has argued that the importance of printing in the Reformation must also be related to the uses of visual propaganda and of oral communication, and the spread of printing is result as well as cause of the Reformation (Scribner, 1981).

The wider spread of literacy beyond a narrow minority has also often been held responsible for a number of effects. But here again whether the potential of writing is actually exploited or not (and in what directions) is what makes the difference rather than the theories about what it ought to do if certain political or religious ideals were fulfilled. David Cressy concludes his analysis of the increase in literacy in sixteenth- and seventeenth-century England by suggesting that the ability to read and write in *practice* was used for a number of purposes, not all related to the grand ideals of the reformers.

Finally, we must ask what good literacy did for the people who possessed it. It is easy to be swayed by the rhetoric of moralists and reformers and agree that literacy was a liberating force which taught man his duty to God and improved his understanding of fellow man. Literacy is associated with independence, political alertness, superior information, rationality, modernity and a host of equally desirable accomplishments. We might pause, however, to consider whether the expansion of literacy brought about all that was promised.

First, it should be stressed that people were capable of rational action, of acquiring and digesting information, and of making well-founded political and religious decisions without being able to read or write. Illiteracy was not necessarily a bar to economic advancement nor did it stand in the way of common sense. Second, we should not assume that people were wiser or more in control of their environment just because they had become literate. The skill could be squandered, used to rot the mind as well as inform it . . . and might find no exercise beyond scanning an almanac or signing a receipt. Popular literacy expanded the audience for politics but it did not inexorably bring about an explosion in political participation. We must distinguish the liberating potential of popular literacy from its more mundane reality. (Cressy, 1980, p. 189)

This fits with the comparative evidence about the flexibility of writing and of printing: sometimes used for the establishment of science or of objective history, sometimes not (see Gough, 1968 on the contrast between India and China); sometimes for religious purposes and the conservation of piety, sometimes for practical reasons and for secularization; to challenge tradition and to uphold it; for personal and for inpersonal communication; for fixed, unchanging transmission or for abridgement, editing, and explicit or secret manipulation. And these differences, furthermore, are not just to be found between cultures, but also between differing groups in the same culture (those with control over the teaching and products of writing often laying particular emphasis on its value), and interacting in different situations and contexts.

Some uses of orality

What about the uses that can be made of orality? Enquiries into this are seldom pursued compared to the more 'obvious' question about the uses of literacy. It is also not an easy one to tackle. Few 'purely oral' cultures have been studied in detail, for the spread of literacy (or at any rate of the restricted literacy) has been wider and longer-established than often recognized. However, if we follow the general line that I have been suggesting and assume that it is sensible to look at particular *uses* of various media (oral and written) rather than 'pure' types, then it is possible to comment on the range of uses to which an emphasis on primarily oral communication can be put.

The list here (as with writing) could be almost endless, but I want just to stress a few points that are sometimes overlooked. First, oral media can be used not just to preserve the status quo (a role perhaps over-emphasized in functionalist ethnographies of non-literate societies) but *also* to challenge it. True, there are many authority-supporting oral myths and panegyrics, but so too are there effective oral rebel poems, party political songs and slogans, revivalist hymns and sermons, and political oratory (for some examples, see Finnegan, 1970, ch. 10, 1977, pp. 242–3): all means of communication which have at times troubled those in control and led to banning and censorship – the ultimate tribute to their effectiveness. Indeed, it has been suggested that in one sense change is easier in oral than in written contexts, owing to the way in which changes can be assimilated unnoticed when there are no written records to draw attention to them (cf. Goody and Watt, 1968, pp. 30ff; Clanchy, 1970; Bloch, 1961, p. 113).

Oral communication is indeed linked to the *context* in which it takes place, and thus tends to encourage pragmatic face to face interaction, close to the actual situation. But orality can also be used for reflection and detachment, and oral literature may involve the kind of insight and comment on the human condition that we associate with literary expression more generally. There are also, as mentioned earlier, various conventions by which oral literary forms can convey a sense of detachment, of standing back and, as it were, introducing a universalizing note. The kind of 'distancing' which in written literature is achieved partly through the convention of the written page may be performed by other devices in oral literature (varying with different cultures or different genres): through the existence of specialist and learned poets, a special poetic or musical language, the presentation of human foibles through the masking device of animal characters, or special conventions about time, place and mode of performance. This use of oral media for personal expression as well as for detached and reflective, even ironic, comment is in fact far more common than one might gather from many of the generalized comments about everyday concerns in 'oral societies' (further elaborated in chapter 4 above).

Abstraction too – at least of a kind – is another purpose to which oral media can be put. Of course, oral communication, like written, is often used to deal with the concrete particularities of everyday life (and here abstract only in the sense that any language inevitably involves a certain degree of abstraction). But despite some of the arguments rehearsed earlier, there are also ways in which speakers of non-written languages use oral media quite specifically to deal with abstract concepts. One example was discussed in chapter 3: the Limba reflective interest in their own speech, the concept of speaking, and the use of abstraction. On a much larger scale, there is widely accepted evidence that highly complex and articulate philosophies and cosmologies have been formulated by intellec- tuals in a number of non-literate societies working in an oral context. Examples range from the Dogon of West Africa (Calame-Griaule, 1965) or the massive arithmetical scheme of the 256 different permutations of the Ifa divination system among the Yoruba and their neighbours (summarized in Finnegan, 1970, pp. 191ff), to the complex Trukese navigation system in the South Pacific (Gladwin, 1970) or the Maori 'school of learning' (Best, 1923).

Again, oral media are especially suitable for flexible variation to suit the needs of the moment or the interests of those in power. There is also its use in the impressive oral-formulaic composition-in-performance of lengthy poetry. This well-documented use of orality is often contrasted with the fixity of written communication, which has led to the further impression that memorization and exact reproduction is not one of the options open in an oral context. This assumption is not justified, however. It has already been queried above (p. 158) and a counter-example discussed at more length in chapter 5 (poetry in the South Pacific). A further illustration can extend this further.

The example of the Somali of the Horn of Africa has already been mentioned. Here memorization together with the careful preservation of verbally fixed versions is one important use of orality. In the past, oral messages acted as a kind of 'postal system' among the scattered Somali and there was a strong obligation on the carrier to deliver a message once accepted and memorized. There were careful safeguards to ensure the accuracy of this orally memorized version. For example the messenger was asked to number the items ('first', 'second', etc.) to aid recall, or, if accuracy was especially important, 'to memorize the message word for word', using the alliteration and scansion patterns of Somali oral poetry 'as well-tried mnemonics' (Andrzejewski, 1979, p. 6). Even if the messenger did not understand the meaning he must still learn it as given him. Indeed sometimes a message was sent in code, understood only by sender and recipient, and the messenger would still be expected to deliver it exactly. Andrzejewski cites an example of a student's message to his father:

The college was very short of food, but Raage was embarrassed to disclose to the traveller that he was hungry since some measure of asceticism would be expected of theological students. In his message of general news and greetings, therefore, he included one seemingly pointless item: he said that the ablutions which he had performed for his early morning prayers were still valid for his evening prayers, and the traveller, who was not a particularly pious man, did not understand the real meaning of the words even though he memorized the message. In fact the obligatory ablutions before prayers in Islam are valid for subsequent prayers only if meanwhile the person has not incurred ritual pollution by defecating, urinating or copulation or by contact with unclean animals or objects. The father guessed immediately that his son was sometimes too hungry for the first kind of pollution to occur during a whole day, and sent him some supplies. (Andrzejewski, 1979, p. 7)

Memorization also plays an important part in Somali poetry. Poets compose certain genres of poetry prior to performance – a long and laborious activity in view of the complex alliterative skills expected of them – and their poems are then memorized word for word by reciters: 'unaided by writing they learn long poems by heart and some have repertoires which are too great to be exhausted even by several evenings of continuous recitation' (Andrzejewski and Lewis, 1964, p. 45).

The Somali emphasis on precise memorization is a striking and perhaps extreme one, but comments on the importance of memorization in oral contexts have been made, for instance, for literary forms in South Pacific cultures (see chapter 5 above), for specific genres in Zulu and Xhosa where there is a poetic tradition of *both* memorization *and* improvisation (Opland, 1971), and even for the famous Yugoslav epic tradition where it seems that, though Lord and Parry concentrated on the improvising poet, there is also a tradition of poets as memorizers (Opland, 1980, p. 10). Tape recorders have been enthusiastically taken up in a number of recently literate cultures, as if the option of preserving correct versions by *auditory* means is a congenial and useful one. Most of us have been brought up in a context in which prestige and high culture have been especially associated with the *written* word, and so are perhaps slow to recognize that exact transmission and the dissemination of multiple identical copies can be possible by oral as well as by written means.

Control over the public record and the means of communication may be as important in oral as in literate contexts. One or another group may try to retain a monopoly over the teaching and learning of certain oral skills, or insist on the central importance of oral forms. This is perhaps especially so when their position is threatened as new uses of writing, western education and increasing literacy appear to undermine those who control and value oral communication.

This reminds us yet again that even in the same culture and in the same historical period there are different uses and different media interacting together. Thus people grow up and learn to operate in a number of situations and can switch from one form of discourse to another as appropriate, whether these discourses are distinguished by different linguistic registers, differences between prose and verse, emphases on oral or written media, or a mixture of all these. This may seem obvious, but it is worth re-emphasizing in view of the common model of language which assumes that the primary and 'natural' mode is spoken language (and within that conversational prose) and that other forms, especially writing, are somehow secondary and derivative (for discussion see, e.g., Stubbs, 1980, ch. 2; Bauman, 1977, p. 17; Harris, 1986). But in practice all cultures recognize differing forms of discourse which people can manipulate and switch between for various purposes, no one any more 'natural' than the other. It should not seem surprising, therefore, that people can also use what at first sight seems a 'mixture' of media in a number of situations – written formulation of themes or texts, for example, which are also sometimes orally performed, or oral delivery of written texts. Which medium and which form of discourse is going to be used for what purpose and in what context cannot be predicted *a priori*.

This discussion has been able to illustrate only some of the many uses of orality and of literacy, and the mixed way in which many people use these. But enough has been said to show that actual uses are intertwined with complex social, religious, political and personal factors, and are far from the automatic results of particular technologies.

Once again what it comes down to is that many of the suggestions about the implications of the contrasting technologies of 'orality' and 'literacy' necessitate so many exceptions and qualifications that we need to be extremely cautious about accepting many current generalizations as proven. There are no short cuts starting from first principles as to the potential or – even more important – the *actual* uses of orality or of literacy.

Some comparative patterns in oral and written transmission

If neither general conclusions about the implications of 'orality' and 'literacy' nor a binary division between 'oral' and 'literate' cultures are altogether satisfactory can one only investigate transmission in oral and written tradition via case studies in specific cultures and historical periods, with no hope of comparative study? This would be to take the argument too far. Certainly there is no substitute for detailed, painstaking research into particularities and this must continue to form the foundation against which more general suggestions can be discussed. But this does not mean that there is no future in comparative analysis, nor that the only line left open if one rejects both the grand dichotomy and the technology model of human society is the kind of 'diffuse relativism' castigated by Jack Goody (1977, pp. 50, 151) which refuses to recognize differences and regards each culture as a thing on its own. Looking for recurrent patterns and differences can still be illuminating in the study of human societies even if one has to treat them with caution, and (as I would urge) avoid the idea of universally applicable causal mechanisms based on specific technologies.

I want therefore to conclude by pointing briefly to some of the recurrent patterns that it can be helpful to distinguish in the study of transmission in oral and written traditions – even though they *can never be assumed to apply in particular cases in advance of the detailed research*. I will concentrate just on certain limited aspects to do largely with verbal (and sometimes musical) formulations, rather than social processes more generally.

First, some possible patterns about *what* is transmitted. Because of our socialization into the western traditions of the last few centuries and sometimes also, more specifically, into a literary and academic ethos, it is easy for scholars to assume when they envisage 'transmission' that what is transmitted is a *text*: either a text in the sense of something which appears in a fixed documentary form, or as the product of an oral performance which is, at least in principle, 'writable'.

In some cases, this textual model *is* the appropriate one. It is normally correct to use it of written documents in literate cultures and (in comparable, if not identical, sense) of memorized versions in an oral context of the kind recorded for the Somali or for modern rock lyrics. The same is true for religious and other texts which are repeated with verbal accuracy (or near-accuracy) whether or not actually written down.

There are also the related, but rather different examples, in which a *particular* oral performance (unique in itself) is written down and published as a 'text' in its own right. Where such texts are generated through the process of composition-in-performance, and the performances themselves are variable, the resultant 'text' has a different status from one which started in a written form. From the scholar's point of view it *is* 'the text', disseminated and studied in written form. But what is transmitted locally is more a storehouse of known formulae and themes and the performer's skill and experience in using these in a particular performance rather than an abiding text as such. The amount of textual crystallization in particular literary genres varies between cultures (even between genres, and between performances in a single culture). This variation has now been documented in a number of studies. There is the contrast, for instance, between the increasing stabilization in Mandinka narrative poems according to the age and experience of the singers (Innes, 1973) and the variability in West Sumatran *sijobang* sung poetry in which as poets become more experienced they gradually 'rely less heavily than novices on memorization and word-for-word repetition, and instead exploit their ability to express the same meaning in varied form' (Phillips, 1981, pp. 169–70). This contrasts yet again with the higher degree of variability in much Yugoslav heroic poetry (Lord, 1968a) on the one hand and the relative fixity of Finnish oral epic on the other (Kiparsky, 1976).

Thus a piece of text on the page, once it has been recorded and published, may represent a number of different starting points: a fixed and memorized text, a unique and perhaps one-off performance never repeated in similar form, a version by an experienced specialist who, despite minor verbal variations, has gone through many similar performances often in his career, an experiment by a young poet still in his apprenticeship, or a gallant try by a willing but inexperienced non-specialist in response to a foreign researcher's proddings. We would do well not to assume from the similar-looking transcriptions on a published page that the kind of transmission that lies behind it was always of an already frozen text.

All these instances do involve at least some degree of verbal articulateness in the sense of belonging to a recognized literary genre in the local culture. But sometimes what we have on the page results from even less crystallized elements. In such cases, we misrepresent the reality if we assume that what we have – and what has been transmitted locally – is really a 'text' at all in the sense of something already explicitly formulated in the local culture. It can equally be the result of pressure from outside researchers or teachers, eager to record some 'text' which they expect or wish to be there. One striking example is the so-called Kaunitoni 'myth of Fijian origin', written down in response to a late nineteenth-century competition for a definitive version of legendary history following the historical speculations about Fijian origins taught in the mission schools (further details in chapter 6 above). We cannot be sure how many other of the 'myths' so confidently published in our collections of oral tradition had a similar origin. The collectors are only too often silent on their genesis but I surmise that a number of such 'texts' were, in fact, formulated in response to particular historical situations rather than representing already-articulated local genres or texts. They exist, of course, and often go on to have their own pedigree of written and sometimes oral distribution, so they cannot just be dismissed. But we do need to be circumspect in drawing conclusions about the transmission of such a 'text' in the local culture prior to the recording of a written version by outsiders.

Another pertinent case is the celebrated one of 'African epic', by some assumed to be characteristic of the oral cultures of that continent in a similar sense to the epic texts of ancient Greece or India. For some African cultures this may be a reasonable interpretation, especially with Mandinka heroic poetry in West Africa, where there does indeed seem to be a local performance tradition of (relatively) lengthy and crystallized poetic narratives. Some of the supposed instances in the Congo region, however, illustrate well how one can be misled by the presupposition that what is involved in oral transmission is necessarily a text, and, furthermore, that the full text, even if not actually realized in performance, is somehow really 'there' in the culture. Thus Biebuyck describes his discovery of the famous Mwindo epic of the Banyanga as the result of a long, unsuccessful search in which, though he was convinced of the existence of the epic, the potential informants he met were all 'too old and too confused ... or did not remember the complete text' or were 'simply unco-operative' (Biebuyck and Mateene, 1971, p. vi). At last he found a skilled and willing informant, said to be the greatest contemporary performer in Nyanga country. This poet repeatedly asserted that this was the first time he had ever performed the whole story in a continuous span of days – and even as it was it had to be spun out over twelve days, owing to the performer's exhaustion (Biebuyck and Mateene, 1971): scarcely an active performance tradition. Biebuyck himself is convinced that in some sense there *was* an existent text there, waiting to be discovered, even if the only manifestations were shorter pieces which he regards as 'fragments of larger epic wholes', some as yet unrecorded (Biebuyck, 1978, p. 337). But this is a text in a different sense from ones already crystallized in regular performance. Indeed, until Biebuyck and his assistants wrote it down, did the famous 'Mwindo epic' really exist as an epic text at all?

This idea, that a text is somehow 'there' and that *this* is what is involved in 'transmission in oral tradition', is a pervasive one. It has resulted in the publication of many texts that implicitly – sometimes even explicitly (e.g. Driberg, 1932; Boelaert, 1949) – represent a synthesis or even a new creation by the researcher rather than what was actually already transmitted in any textual form within the culture.

The point I want to emphasize, then, is that though in some cases the transmission *is* of texts, in others this is not so (or not so in the same sense). In such cases, of course, there may be the *potential* for formulating texts. That is, there may be the transmission of specific linguistic and musical skills and styles (either written or oral), or a tradition of trained experts, of themes and stories, or of conventional occasions for literary or artistic display. But all these are different from the transmission of texts as such. Thus in speaking of transmission, in particular of oral traditions, it is important to distinguish which of these patterns is involved. Otherwise it is only too easy for most of us to jump in our ethnocentric way to the conclusion that it is necessarily textual transmission, and when we think we are comparing like with like, sometimes to be doing nothing of the sort.

Second, are there recurrent patterns about *how* transmission takes place in oral and in written traditions? I have already stressed the enormous diversity involved, dependent on a whole set of cultural variables, and it would not be possible to give a comprehensive account of all possible processes. Nevertheless certain recurrent patterns of transmission can perhaps be roughly distinguished. This is worth doing if only because treating them as if they were all the same can mislead us as to what is really involved.

It is worth remembering here that when we speak of both 'orality' and 'literacy' one or more of three main aspects may be involved: composition, performance and transmission over time. These three do not always coincide. Thus it is possible for a work to be oral in performance but not in composition or transmission, or to have a written origin but non-written performances or transmission. These various combinations constitute a background to considering different patterns of transmission. As will be seen, the differing patterns do not coincide neatly with the distinction between oral and written traditions.

One form of written transmission is the actual physical preservation of records. Sometimes this is all that is intended when the term 'transmission' is used, but it is also sometimes extended to the copying and/or depositing of these written records. The process of written transmission can also be the reading of these written forms. Who they are read by, and how, can be crucial for their social significance. Reading is, in fact, a more problematic term than appears at first. It conceals a number of variants between silent individual reading, reading aloud in private or (a different situation) in public, or basing a full performance on a written text, sometimes accompanied by music or dance – all equally 'natural' processes by which written texts can be transmitted, and illustrating well the way written and oral processes can run into each other. Not so very different is the apparently somewhat more 'oral' process in which a performer starts from a written text but then uses this as a basis (more or less memorized) for declaiming or performance without necessarily using direct reference to the written text. Drama is a good example, or various lyrics and musical performances. Another pattern – again, partly linking with the previous one – is of transmission through the interaction or combination of the concurrent oral and written versions. This is in fact commonly found, perhaps especially in situations of 'restricted' literacy, but also in, for example, well-known hymns, songs and proverbs in western culture. Primarily auditory transmission occurs too, musical as well as verbal (it is easy but misleading to think of memorization and transmission as always cognitive or propositional). This can be found in remembered musical forms but also through radio and tape or cassette recorders – a form not so different, perhaps, from some of the processes of memorization found in non-literate cultures.

I began by mentioning patterns of transmission mainly to do with writing, but have now gradually moved towards the more oral side of the continuum. In this connection, more or less exact verbal memorization must certainly be mentioned as one pattern of transmission. This has been played down by scholars recently (understandably after its over-emphasis in earlier romantic interpretations), but it *is* one common pattern. The old idea of lengthy memorized transmission over centuries or even millennia may no longer be tenable, but over shorter time spans memorized transmission certainly takes place. It is perhaps particularly important in texts that have a definite religious value or function (a suggestion well discussed in Kiparsky, 1976), or have stylistic features that make memorizing essential, such as public performance by a unison group or the taxing alliterative requirements demanded of the Somali poet. In such a pattern the degree of verbal accuracy expected varies, no doubt, but some such concept and practice can certainly be found in oral transmission.

A further category is the well-known composition-in-performance pattern. This is a broad term, which can cover both transmission with relatively minor variations and the type described by Milman Parry and Albert Lord in which transmission is not of a text as such but of the skill of composing from a stock of 'ready-made' formulae and themes in the act of performance. In its extreme form, this is very different from the relatively fixed textual process of the memorized pattern, and is worth distinguishing from it (it sometimes shades into it, in that some oral poets gradually work up their live performances until they approach something not unlike a memorized and predictable version).

Different yet again is the transmission of *skills*. This may be the power of creating texts or musical works, perhaps by inspiration, perhaps through a long period of apprenticeship and hard work. These kinds of skills may, in certain historical circumstances, lead to the formulation and hence transmission of fixed texts, for they can form the basis for orally dictated or recorded versions. In some cases, like the Polynesian narratives discussed in chapter 6, texts of so-called 'oral tradition' are written by newly literate converts – sometimes followed by feedback (often as authoritative 'tribal myths') into oral forms. This process is also often spoken of as 'oral transmission' and as recorded 'from oral tradition', and is indeed a perfectly understandable and extremely common pattern. But it is in practice very different from some of the other patterns of oral transmission and needs to be distinguished from them.

This final pattern of newly created 'texts', leading to written versions, is not really very different from formulations by writers in literate cultures building on their own personal and literary experience and responding (at times) to new situations with writings which, in time, feed into the written record. Indeed this kind of similarity is a perfectly obvious one, once we stop being distracted by the romantic view of noble and natural primitives with their close-to-nature oral traditions and primeval myths. So we have come full circle back to written transmission again.

The various transmission processes mentioned are certainly not comprehensive, but they do represent recurrent patterns which, though partly overlapping, are *different* from each other. Researchers do not always make clear which pattern is involved when they publish their studies and their 'texts'. But distinguishing them would avoid many of the misunder-standings that arise when 'written transmission' or 'oral transmission' are spoken of in general terms. Being aware of these distinctions, too, makes it easier to sort out in particular cases exactly which form of transmission is used for what purpose (often several are at work in different ways in the same culture). As more detailed studies are made, it may well emerge that particular features tend to go with particular patterns (memorization, say, as against composition-in-performance) but I doubt whether such associations are ever likely to reach the status of generalizable causal explanations.

Reflecting on patterns of this kind, I suggest, gives some comparative perspective to the study of orality and literacy in specific cultures. This is less ambitious than investigating the *general* consequences of the various technologies of communication, let alone the unrealistic attempt to delineate the characteristics of two opposing types of society. But concentrating on local-level and limited patterns of transmission in this kind of comparative perspective can provide discriminating information about how certain forms of communication are actually transmitted in practice in specific situations, an aspect that is often missed when the focus is on grander questions about the technologies of print, writing or oral communication in general.

Conclusion

I would end therefore with a plea for middle-range comparison on a fairly modest set of topics, whether of the distribution and implications of transmission patterns or of the various uses to which different media have been put. This gives both a useful background against which more detailed specific studies can be set and a complement (or, I would claim, an antidote) to the higher-level analyses with their focus on binary dichotomies or the determined consequences of differing technologies. The technological model can certainly be an illuminating one (far more so, to my taste, than that of two opposed ideal types). It is especially attractive in those versions which abrogate the optimistic claims for any particular communication technology as the necessary or sufficient *cause* for specific effects and tend more towards the enabling or facilitating view. But even the latter version retains its attraction partly through the inevitable over-simplification of complex historical processes that follows from focusing on generalizable principles of such wide application. The final point, then, is that on the topics of oral and written transmission there are no simple and generalizable answers or even clear-cut definitions. Research into this subject is bound to continue to be complex and non-universifiable precisely because of the continuing creativity and complexity of human beings and the social processes they create, and the manifold ways in which they can turn both orality and literacy to their own uses.

9

Postscript

It may now be clear why I was hesitant to start out in chapter 1 with a crisp definition of 'orality' or 'literacy'. For the main burden of the discussion in this volume has been that 'orality' and 'literacy' are not two separate and independent things; nor (to put it more concretely) are oral and written modes two mutually exclusive and opposed processes for representing and communicating information. On the contrary they take diverse forms in differing cultures and periods, are used differently in different social contexts and, insofar as they can be distinguished at all as separate modes rather than a continuum, they mutually interact and affect each other, and the relations between them are problematic rather than self-evident.

The implication of this is that looking for clear-cut 'consequences' or 'impacts' from these traditional technologies is not likely to be very productive. Given that oral and written forms are diverse in their development and usage, so too will be their consequences – something it is also worth bearing in mind when assessing the often naive prognostications about the (apparently) automatic results expected from the new 'information technology revolution'.

One of the main themes then has been to query the simple model of the nature of, and relations between, 'orality' and 'literacy' which sees them as clear-cut and opposing technologies, leading to a series of inevitable or (at least) highly probable social and cognitive consequences, and perhaps even to different and revolutionary historic stages in human development or human thought and consciousness. Such views are still often stated as the conventional wisdom, but, it should now be obvious, are highly controversial. They are vulnerable from two directions, both touched on in this volume. First, many would now, like myself, challenge their theoretical assumptions: i.e. the implicit technological determinism that underlies them. And secondly, the accumulating empirical evidence from many different areas (only a selection of it presented here) increasingly throws doubt on many of the once taken-for-granted assumptions about unitary consequences from orality or literacy. Furthermore, if both the theoretical and empirical foundations of many of the generalized conclusions about these traditional information technologies turn out to be shaky, this also raises questions about similar views on more recent information technology, when, as often, they have implicitly built on the kinds of assumptions queried in this volume.

Must we remain content, then, with merely the negative conclusion that earlier generalizations, both optimist and pessimist, were unfounded and that all we can aim to do is to study *particular* contexts and systems, whether of oral or literate or electronic communication, eschewing all generalities? I believe we can be more positive than that. Combating mistaken conclusions about human culture and experience is, of course, in any case an advance, with implications for a better-informed understanding of ourselves as well as others. But beyond that, some more general lessons can perhaps be drawn from the analyses here.

It is, certainly, true that one main theme has been the central importance of taking account of the particular: the specific developments and uses of oral, written and electronic forms in particular historical conditions and by specific individuals, groups and cultures (or sub-cultures). These detailed studies remain essential, revealing as they do the specificities and contingencies, rather than the general laws, of human action. It is through such studies too that it becomes clear that the striking differences and similarities that exist among human cultures do not necessarily go along with some simple separation into 'oral' and 'literate'. Studies of this modest and particularistic kind, rather than yet more generalized speculation on the basis (often) of imaginations about the future and romanticized projections into the past, are what is needed to advance our empirical understanding of the uses and implications of our various information technologies.

But we can also go beyond this. If there are no general and determining ideas about the development and implications of information technologies as such, there are perhaps some common tendencies and syndromes which are worth reflecting on – the kinds of patterns which in our human and historical experience seem likely to recur. These are to be found not primarily in the technologies themselves, but in the way these technologies are liable to be controlled and used. The crucial questions are to do with power, access, national and international inequalities, and people's values and ideas about themselves and about the nature of human destiny. What is involved, in other words, are not primarily technical questions but those same age-old tendencies that have formed the constant subject of social, historical and literary studies.

Thus the implications of specific information technologies in particular cultural contexts are likely, for example, to be closely connected to who has power to control them, for what purposes and in what contexts. Similarly the extent of their distribution among all or particular categories of people is likely to be crucial for their specific import, together with the *kind* of access people have: those individuals and groups, for example, who can merely *read* the written texts or *receive* electronic messages are liable to have fewer opportunities for control and choice than those able to organize the formulation and sending of communications through their mastery of writing or higher-level computing and telecommunications skills. Similarly it is likely to be not so much the technical capacity provided by the various information technologies that affects how they are developed and interpreted or how people think about (or through) them, as the culturally-generated *values* placed on their mastery and/or the particular purposes for which they are to be used, buttressed no doubt by the local educational and ranking system. So too with the various forms of literature or oral artistry and the modes by which they are created and transmitted: which of the recurrent syndromes discussed in earlier chapters are taken up in particular cultures or situations depends not on some abstract 'orality' or 'literacy' but on the specific genres, occasions and skills valued in particular contexts.

This is a different view, then, from that which sees human history as punctuated by vast historic discontinuities, shaped ultimately by changes in the technology of communication. Rather, historical development is viewed here as characterized not just by change (certainly), but also by continuities and even in a sense by repetitions. For the crucial questions about the control, access and actual (not idealized) usage of communication technologies remain essentially the same now as they always were. They constitute social, political and economic, not primarily technical, patterns of human action.

The same is true in the cultural sphere. Despite all the detailed changes over the ages there is not some radical change in cultural consciousness with the adoption of writing. Instead we find the continuing repetition in varying forms of people's search for ways to locate themselves in the universe and clothe their insights in beautiful or fantastic or riddling verbal and/or musical formulations. These find expression, among other forms, in the recurrent syndromes of oral and written composing and performing described earlier (composition-in-performance, prior composition transmitted through repeated oral and written media, and prior-composition-through-practice followed by repetition, described particularly in chapters 4, 5 and 7), as well as the various patterns of transmission in oral and written traditions, some more 'textual' and 'crystallized' than others, discussed in chapter 8. So too we find repeated processes of interaction between oral and written media, whatever the exact mix, with one feeding on, and in turn influencing, the other, a pattern described for a particular case in chapter 6 but with many wider applications. In the end, the repeated cycles of how knowledge and artistry are valued, interpreted and manifested in human action may be more important and more recurrent than the particular medium chosen from time to time over history to represent this.

And now too, just as so often in the past, changes are prefigured as the token of some magnificent and radically different coming age. The great new future to result from electronic media, as prophesied (say) by Carpenter and McLuhan in 1960 or by the earlier proponents of the telephone in the nineteenth century (Pool, 1977 and 1983a), but still not with us, recalls the pursuit of the millennium among the medieval mystical anarchists or modern cargo cults – the millennium which never comes but still goes on being heralded. So too people still continue the cycle of prophecies about the imminent wonderful (or cataclysmic) revolution about to arrive from our latest technology.

In thus stressing the social and cultural shaping of information technologies, I am not intending to deny that particular technologies (just like, say, particular educational systems) offer particular constraints and opportunities, and are liable, according to their nature, to either facilitate or hinder particular social developments. These indeed form a proper subject of study, one that is perhaps rightly attracting increasing interest today as people realize the need to concern themselves not just with technical and scientific discovery as such but with such aspects as 'user-friendliness', 'the human–technology interface', the needs of users, or the likely social implications of installing particular technological systems. But, in the light of the comparative perspective taken here, how such opportunities and constraints are dealt with is, once again, likely to be the result not of 'blind technology' but of social arrangements and human choices. The technology cannot tell us if print is to be used for censorship or for democratic expression, whether new opportunities for computer networking will bring greater Big Brother surveillance or increased personal support, whether artificial intelligence will be used to enhance human freedom or, as Weizenbaum (1984) among others has warned, to undermine rightful human responsibility. These are a matter for social and ethical, not for technical, choices.

The discussions in this volume have focused only on certain forms of communication technology: those summarized in the terms 'orality' and 'literacy'. As I have argued, these terms dissolve on analysis and perhaps now need to be discarded as *generalized* comparative concepts, the more so that recent work across a wide range of disciplines from history and anthropology to education and socio-linguistics has come together in emphasizing that these technologies are not self-standing but are always and everywhere dependent on social context for their meaning and use.

But if the terms 'orality' and 'literacy' turn out not to refer to clear and independent entities, they do still focus our attention on certain forms of representing and processing information rather than others. In conclusion, then, I want just to point briefly to some of the important aspects that a focus on 'orality' and 'literacy' leaves out. It is easy, brought up as we have been in what Roy Harris rightly terms the 'scriptist bias' of western educational systems (1986, p. 46), to assume that information – indeed human experience generally – is 'naturally' to be subsumed under the headings of writing and print. Speech is allowed to come in as the text's precurser and counterpart, and (nowadays) we also recognize the additional medium of computing-plus-telecommunication, building on oral and written media – but the model of literacy is still subconsciously dominant.

Up to a point that is correct. But it is also worth reminding ourselves that to think of script and speech as the only technologies for representing information, even in the past, is misleading. *Words*, written or spoken, and in particular words envisaged on the model of alphabetic writing, are not the only stuff of human communication, easy though this is to assume in the cognitively biased outlook of western academic study and conventional wisdom. Take just two examples. Musical and auditory forms, whether expressed in notated or, as in the Far East, through other graphic forms (see Tokumaru, 1986), or somehow stored and transmitted through audio media, have only been touched on briefly in this volume (chapters 5 and 7). But these comprise one whole realm of human experience for which information technologies may be potentially as important as for 'words' and 'propositional information'. The same can be said for visual art and expression. In some cultures, memory and historical awareness are transmitted and represented not through words but through the reflective preservation of particular plastic art forms, well developed in some Melanesian societies in Papua New Guinea and the South Pacific (see, e.g., Küchler, 1987). This is an aspect of communication which is seldom explicitly considered in the context of the representation of information and experience but which may be of greater importance even in our own culture than is sometimes realized.

Maybe here we have after all come on one important consequence of modern forms of information technology: not that they *in themselves* do anything, far less bring about the kind of automatic social impacts envisaged by many of their advocates, but that they provide an opportunity and a challenge for us to re-assess our own consciousness of the problematics of human communication and information representation. 'Oral' and 'written' media have perhaps held the centre of the stage too long. This is not just because (as described here) their 'impacts' as technologies have been exaggerated or misunderstood, but because they have also given us too narrow a vision of what is involved in human experience and communication.

Alphabetic writing has perhaps indeed had profound effects on our consciousness and organization in the west over the last few centuries, not because writing in itself brings effects but because of the way we have chosen to use and regard it, sanctioned by a whole series of educational, economic and political institutions. 'Modern IT', through its potential for new ways of representing musical, graphic, mathematical and visual information, among them moving pictures and auditory forms, can perhaps be used as the occasion for re-awakening us to the manifold forms of human expression and understanding through the world and through the ages which we may have omitted in our own culture to make as much of as we might, owing to our narrow focus on alphabetic literacy and a view of speech modelled on this. If so, and if we can take the opportunity to re-notice some relatively submerged but still existent forms of human experience, then this reaction to modern information technology could indeed have important consequences for the human spirit.

The final conclusion, then, must be a positive not a negative one. That is, that just as speech, writing and print have not determined human existence but have been formed and exploited by human beings so as to provide opportunities for development in particular directions, so too with the opportunities offered by modern communication technologies. As ever, the choices are not purely technical ones, but social, artistic, intellectual and ethical.

References

Abraham, W. E. (1962) *The mind of Africa*, Chicago University Press, Chicago.
Abrahams, R. D. (1977) 'Toward an enactment-centred theory of folklore', in Bascom, 1977.
Abrahams, R. D. (1985) Review of Opland, 1983, *Poetics Today*, 6.
Agar, M. H. (1980) *The professional stranger: an informal introduction to ethnography*, Academic Press, New York.
Agir, David (1977) Personal communication.
Alexandre, P. (1967) *Langues et langage en Afrique noire*, Paris.
Alpers, A. (1970) *Legends of the south seas, the world of the Polynesians seen through their myths and legends, poetry and art*, Murray, London.
Anderson, C. A. and Bowman, M. J. (eds) (1966) *Education and economic development*, Cass, London.
Andrzejewski, B. W. (1963) 'Poetry in Somali society', *New Society*, 1, 25, 21 March.
Andrzejewski, B. W. (1979) 'Traditional media of communication in Somalia', paper to the African Studies Conference, Los Angeles.
Andrzejewski, B. W. and Lewis, I. M. (1964) *Somali poetry. An introduction*, Clarendon Press, Oxford.
Aristotle (1962) *Politics*, trans. C. A. Sinclair, Penguin, Harmondsworth.
Austin, J. L. (1962), *How to do things with words*, Clarendon Press, Oxford.
Babalola, S. A. (1966) *The content and form of Yoruba ijala*, Clarendon Press, Oxford.
Bagdikian, B. H. (1971) *The information machines. Their impact on men and the media*, Harper & Row, New York.
Baldwin, B. (1950) 'Kaduguwai. Songs of the Trobriand sunset isles', *Oceania*, 20.
Barrère, D. B. (1967) 'Revisions and adulterations in Polynesian creation myths', in G. A. Highland et al. (eds), *Polynesian culture history. Essays in honor of Kenneth P. Emory*, Bishop Museum Press, Honolulu.
Bascom, W. R. (1955) 'Urbanization among the Yoruba', *American Journal of Sociology*, 60.
Bascom, W. R. (ed.) (1977) *Frontiers of folklore*, AAAS, Selected Symposium, 5, Westview Press, Boulder, Colorado.
Basso, K. H. (1974) 'The ethnography of writing', in Bauman and Sherzer, 1974.
Bastide, R. (1968) 'Religions africaines et structures de civilisation', *Présence africaine*, 66.
Bauman, R. (1977) *Verbal art as performance*, Newbury House, Rowley, Mass.

Bauman, R. (1986) *Story, performance, and event*, Cambridge Studies in Oral and Literate Culture, 10, Cambridge University Press, Cambridge.

Bauman, R. and Sherzer, J. (eds) (1974) *Explorations in the ethnography of speaking*, Cambridge University Press, London.

Bäuml, F. H. and Spielman, E. (1975) 'From illiteracy to literacy: prolegomena to a study of the Nibenlungenlied', in Duggan, 1975.

Beaton, R. (1980) *Folk poetry of modern Greece*, Cambridge University Press, Cambridge.

Becker, H. S. (1982) *Art worlds*, University of California Press, Berkeley, Los Angeles and London.

Beckwith, M. (1919) 'The Hawaiian romance of Laieikawai', *Bureau of American Ethnology*, 33rd Annual Report.

Beier, U. (ed.) (1967) *Introduction to African literature*, Longman, London.

Ben-Amos, D. and Goldstein, K. S. (eds) (1975) *Folklore: performance and communication*, Mouton, The Hague and Paris.

Benedict, R. (1935) *Zuni mythology*, 2 vols, Columbia University Press, New York.

Benson, L. D. (1966) 'The literary character of Anglo-Saxon formulaic poetry', *Publications of the Modern Language Association*, 81.

Berry, J. (1958) 'Nominal classes in Hu-Limba', *Sierra Leone Studies*, n.s., 11.

Berry, J. (1960) 'A note on voice and aspect in Hu-Limba', *Sierra Leone Studies*, n.s., 13.

Best, E. (1923) *The Maori school of learning*, Dominion Museum Monograph 6, Wellington.

Best, E. (1925) *Games and pastimes of the Maori*, Whitcombe and Tombs, Wellington.

Best, E. (1934) *The Maori as he was*, Dominion Museum, Wellington.

Biebuyck, D. (1978) 'The African heroic epic', in F. J. Oinas (ed.), *Heroic epic and saga*, Indiana University Press, Bloomington.

Biebuyck, D. and Mateene, K. C. (eds) (1971) *The Mwindo epic from the Banyanga*, University of California Press, Berkeley and Los Angeles.

Biggs, B. (1964) 'The oral literature of the Polynesians', *Te Ao Hou*, 49.

Bloch, M. (1961) *Feudal society*, trans. L. A. Manyon, Routledge & Kegan Paul, London.

Bloch, M. (ed.) (1975) *Political language and oratory in traditional society*, Academic Press, London.

Boelaert, E. (1949) 'Nsong'a Lianja. L'épopée nationale des Nkundo', *Aequatoria*, 12.

Bohannan, L. (1952) 'A genealogical charter', *Africa*, 22.

Bowra, C. M. (1952) *Heroic poetry*, Macmillan, London.

Bowra, C. M. (1957) *The meaning of a heroic age*, Earl Grey Memorial Lecture 37, Andrew Reid & Co., Newcastle upon Tyne.

Bowra, C. M. (1962) *Primitive song*, Weidenfeld & Nicolson, London.

Breach, R. W. and Hartwell, R. M. (eds) (1972) *British economy and society, 1870–1970*, Oxford University Press, London.

Buchan, D. (1972) *The ballad and the folk*, Routledge & Kegan Paul, London.

Burke, P. (1978) *Popular culture in early modern Europe*, Temple Smith, London.

Burns, A. (ed.) (1984) *New information technology*, Horwood, Chichester.

Burridge, K. O. L. (1960) *Mambu. A Melanesian millennium*, Methuen, London.

Burridge, K. O. L. (1969) *Tangu traditions*, Clarendon Press, Oxford.

Burrows, E. G. (1945) 'Songs of Uvea and Futuna', *Bernice P Bishop Museum Bulletin*, 183.

Burrows, E. G. (1963) *Flower in my ear: arts and ethos of Ifaluk Atoll*, University of Washington Press, Seattle.

Calame-Griaule, C. (1965) *Ethnologie et langage: la parole chez les Dogon*, Gallimard, Paris.

Campbell, R. (1971) *La herencia musical de Rapanui. Etnomusicologia de la Isla de Pascua*, Ed. Andrés Bello, Santiago.

Carey, J. W. (1967) 'Harold Adams Innis and Marshall McLuhan', *The Antioch Review*, 27.

Carothers, J. C. (1959) 'Culture, psychiatry, and the written word', *Psychiatry*, 22.

Carpenter, E. and McLuhan, M. (eds) (1960) *Explorations in communications*, Beacon Press, Boston.

Carrithers, M., Collins, M., and Lukes, S. (eds) (1985) *The category of the person*, Cambridge University Press, Cambridge.

Carter, T. F. (1925) *The invention of printing in China and its spread westward*, Columbia University Press, New York.

Cassirer, E. (1953) *The philosophy of symbolic forms.* vol. 1, *Language* (English translation), Yale University Press, New Haven.

Chadwick, H. M. (1926) *The heroic age*, Cambridge University Press, Cambridge.

Chadwick, H. M. and N. K. (1932–40) *The growth of literature*, 3 vols, Cambridge University Press, London.

Chadwick, N. K. (1939) 'The distribution of oral literature in the Old World. A preliminary survey', *Journal of the Royal Anthropological Institute*, 69.

Chadwick, N. K. and Zhirmunsky, V. (1969) *Oral epics of Central Asia*, Cambridge University Press, London.

Chaytor, H. J. (1945) *From script to print*, Heffer, Cambridge.

Cherry, C. (1971) *World communication: threat or promise? A socio-technical approach*, Wiley-Interscience, London.

Chinnery, E. W. P. and Haddon, A. C. (1917) 'Five new religious cults in British New Guinea', *Hibbert Journal*, 15.

Cipolla, C. M. (1969) *Literacy and development in the west*, Penguin, Harmondsworth.

Clammer, J. R. (1976) *Literacy and social change. A case study of Fiji*, Brill, Leiden.

Clanchy, M. T. (1970) 'Remembering the past and the good old law', *History*, 55.

Clanchy, M. T. (1979) *From memory to written record: England 1066–1307*, Arnold, London.

Clarke, A. C. (1968) 'Prediction, realization and forecast', in UNESCO (1968) *Communication in the space age*, Paris.

Cohen, A. (1965) 'The social organization of credit in a West African cattle market', *Africa*, 35.

Cole, M. and Scribner, S. (1974) *Culture and thought, a psychological introduction*, Wiley, New York.

Colenso, W. (1880) 'Contributions towards a better knowledge of the Maori race', *Transactions and proceedings of the New Zealand Institute*, 13, Wellington.

Collocott, E. E. V. (1928) 'Tales and Poems of Tonga', *Bernice P Bishop Museum Bulletin*, 46.

Cook-Gumperz, J. (ed.) (1986) *The social construction of literacy*, Cambridge University Press, Cambridge.

Cope, T. (1968) *Izibongo. Zulu praise-poems*, Clarendon Press, Oxford.

Cosentino, D. (1982) *Defiant maids and stubborn farmers: tradition and invention in Mende story performance*, Cambridge Studies in Oral and Literate Culture, 4, Cambridge University Press, Cambridge.

Craig, D. (1973) 'Song as common property', *Times Higher Education Supplement*, 95, 10 August.

Cressy, D. (1980) *Literacy and the social order: reading and writing in Tudor and Stuart England*, Cambridge University Press, Cambridge.

Crosby, R. (1936) 'Oral delivery in the Middle Ages', *Speculum*, 11.

Culley, R. C. (1967) *Oral formulaic language in the Biblical psalms*, Toronto University Press, Toronto.

Curshmann, M. E. (1967) 'Oral Poetry in mediaeval English, French and German literature: some notes on recent research', *Speculum*, 42.

Dalby, D. (1965) 'The Mel languages: a re-classification of Southern "West Atlantic"', *African Language Studies*, 6.

Delargy, J. F. (1945) 'The Gaelic story-teller', *Proceedings of the British Academy*, 31.

Dillon, M. (1948) *Early Irish literature*, Chicago University Press, Chicago.

Dillon, M. (ed.) (1954) *Early Irish society*, Radio Éireann, Dublin.

Dizard, W. P. (1985) *The coming information age*, Longman, New York, 2nd edition.

Dorson, R. M. (1960) 'Oral styles of American folk narrators' in T. A. Sebeok (ed.), *Style in language*, Wiley, New York.

Driberg, J. H. (1932) *Initiation. Translations from poems of the Didinga and Lango tribes*, Golden Cockerel Press, Waltham St. Lawrence.

Duggan, J. J. (1973) *The Song of Roland: formulaic style and poetic craft*, University of California Press, Berkeley.

Duggan, J. J. (ed.) (1975) *Oral literature. Seven essays*, Scottish Academic Press, Edinburgh.

Einarsson, S. (1957) *A history of Icelandic literature*, Johns Hopkins Press, New York.

Eisenstein, E. L. (1968) 'Some conjectures about the impact of printing on western society and thought: a preliminary report', *Journal of Modern History*, 40.

Eisenstein, E. L. (1979) *The printing press as an agent of change: communications and cultural transformations in early modern Europe*, Cambridge University Press, Cambridge.

Elbert, S. H. and Monberg, T. (1965) *From the two canoes. Oral traditions of Rennel and Bellona Islands*, University of Hawaii Press and The Danish National Museum, Honolulu and Copenhagen.

Ellis, W. (1829) *Polynesian researches*, 2 vols., Fischer, Son, & Jackson, London.

Entwhistle, W. J. (1939) *European balladry*, Clarendon Press, Oxford.

Evans-Pritchard, E. E. (1967) *The Zande trickster*, Clarendon Press, Oxford.

Feld, S. (1982) *Sound and sentiment: birds, weeping, poetics, and song in Kaluli expression*, University of Pennsylvania Press, Philadelphia.

Feld, S. (1987) 'Orality and consciousness', public lecture at International Council of Traditional Music Conference 'The oral and literate in music', published in Tokumara and Yamaguti, 1986.

Fernandez, J. (1980) 'Edification by puzzlement', in I. Karp and C. S. Bird (eds), *Explorations in African systems of thought*, Indiana University Press, Bloomington.

Finnegan, R. (1960) 'Early Irish kingship', unpublished B.Litt. thesis, University of Oxford.

Finnegan, R. (1967) *Limba stories and story-telling*, Clarendon Press, Oxford.

Finnegan, R. (1969a) 'Attitudes to speech and language among the Limba of Sierra Leone', *Odu*, n.s., 2 (chapter 3 in this volume).

Finnegan, R. (1969b) 'Attitudes to the study of oral literature', *Man*, n.s., 4.

Finnegan, R. (1970) *Oral literature in Africa*, Clarendon Press, Oxford.

Finnegan, R. (1973) 'Literacy versus non-literacy: the great divide?' in Horton and Finnegan, 1973 (chapter 4 in this volume).

Finnegan, R. (1974) 'How oral is oral literature?', *Bulletin of the School of Oriental and African Studies*, 37.

Finnegan, R. (1976) 'What is oral literature anyway? Comments in the light of some African and other comparative evidence', in Stolz and Shannon, 1976.

Finnegan, R. (1977) *Oral poetry: its nature, significance and social context*, Cambridge University Press, Cambridge.

Finnegan, R. (1981) *Short time to stay: comments on time, literature and oral performance* (Hans Wolff Lecture), African Studies Program, Indiana University Press, Bloomington.

Finnegan, R. (1985) 'Oral composition and oral literature in the Pacific', in Gentili and Paione, 1985 (chapter 5 in this volume).

Finnegan, R. (forthcoming) *The practice of music: a study of local music making in a modern English town*, Cambridge University Press, Cambridge.

Finnegan, R. and Pillai, R. (eds) (1978) *Essays on Pacific literature*, Fiji Museum, Oral Tradition Series, 2, Suva.

Firth, R. (1936) *We the Tikopia: a sociological study of kinship in primitive Polynesia*, Allen & Unwin, London.

Fischer, J. L. and A. M. (1970) *The Eastern Carolines*, Human Relations Area Files Press, New Haven.

Foley, J. M. (ed.) (1981) *Oral traditional literature: a Festschrift for Albert Bates Lord*, Slavica Publishers, Columbus, Ohio.

Foley, J. M. (1985) *Oral-formulaic theory and research: an introduction and annotated bibliography*, Garland Publishing, New York and London.

Forester, T. (ed.) (1980) *The microelectronics revolution*, Blackwell, Oxford.

Forester, T. (ed.) (1985) *The information technology revolution*, Blackwell, Oxford.

Fornander, A. (1916–20) 'Fornander Collection of Hawaiian antiquities and folklore', *Bernice P Bishop Museum Bulletins*, 4, 5, 6 (reprinted 1973).

Fortune, R. F. (1932) *Sorcerers of Dobu*, Routledge & Kegan Paul, London.

France, P. (1966) 'The Kaunitoni migration. Notes on the genesis of a Fijian tradition', *Journal of Pacific History*, 1.

Freeman, J. D. (1959) 'The Joe Gimlet or Siovili cult', in J. D. Freeman and W. R. Geddes (eds), *Anthropology in the South Seas*, Avery, New Plymouth.

Freuchen, P. (1962) *Book of the Eskimos*, Arthur Barker, London.

Furet, F. and Ozouf, J. (1982) *Reading and writing: literacy in France from Calvin to Jules Ferry*, Cambridge Studies in Oral and Literate Culture, 5, Cambridge University Press, Cambridge and Editions de la Maison des Sciences de l'Homme, Paris.

Gentili, B. and Paioni, G. (eds) (1985) *Oralità: cultura, letteratura, discorso*, Edizioni dell' Ateneo, Rome.

Gifford, E. W. (1924) 'Tongan myths and tales', *Bernice P Bishop Museum Bulletin*, 8.

Gill, W. W. (1894) *From darkness to light in Polynesia, with illustrative clan songs*, Religious Tract Society, London.

Gladwin, T. (1970) *East is a big bird*, Harvard University Press, Cambridge, Mass.

Goldsmith, E., Allen, R., Allaby, M., Darroll, J. and Lawrence, S. (1972) 'A blue-print for survival', *The Ecologist*, January.

Goody, J. (ed.) (1968) *Literacy in traditional societies*, Cambridge University Press, London.

Goody, J. (1973) 'Evolution and communication: the domestication of the savage mind', *British Journal of Sociology*, 24.

Goody, J. (1977) *The domestication of the savage mind*, Cambridge University Press, Cambridge.

Goody, J. (1987) *The logic of writing and the organization of society*, Cambridge University Press, Cambridge.

Goody, J. and Watt, I. (1968) 'The consequences of literacy', in Goody, 1968.

Goody, J., Cole, M. and Scribner, S. (1977) 'Writing and formal operations: a case study among the Vai', *Africa*, 47.

Gough, K. (1968) 'Implications of literacy in traditional China and India', in Goody, 1968.

Graff, H. J. (1979) *The literacy myth: literacy and social structure in the nineteenth century city*, Academic Press, New York.

Graff, H. J. (1981a) *Literacy in history: an interdisciplinary research bibliography*, Garland, New York and London.

Graff, H. J. (ed.) (1981b) *Literacy and social development in the west*, Cambridge Studies in Oral and Literate Culture, 3, Cambridge University Press, Cambridge.

Graff, H. J. (1982) 'The legacies of literacy', *Journal of Communication*, 32.

Greenfield, P. M. (1972) 'Oral or written language: the consequences for cognitive development in Africa, the United States, and England', *Language and Speech*, 15.

Grey, G. (1854) *Nga mahinga a nga tupuna Maori*, London.

Grey, G. (1855) *Polynesian mythology*, London.

Grimble, A. (1957) *Return to the islands*, Murray, London.

Gunn, W. (1914) *The Gospel in Futuna*, Hodder & Stoughton, London.

Hall, S. (1973) 'The "structured communication" of events', paper to Obstacles to Communication Symposium, UNESCO, Division of Philosophy, Paris.

Hammond, N. (1986) 'New light on the most ancient Maya', *Man*, 21.

Handy, E. S. C. and Winne, J. L. (1925) 'Music in the Marquesas Islands', *Bernice P Bishop Museum Bulletin*, 17.

Harris, R. (1986) *The origin of writing*, Duckworth, London.

Havelock, E. A. (1982) *The literate revolution in ancient Greece and its cultural consequences*, Princeton University Press, Princeton.

Havelock, E. A. and Hershbell, J. P. (1978) *Communication arts in the ancient world*, Hastings House, New York.

Haymes, E. R. (1973) *A bibliography of studies related to Parry's and Lord's oral theory*, Harvard University Press, Cambridge, Mass.

Heath, S. B. (1980) 'The functions and uses of literacy', *Journal of Communication*, 30.

Heelas, P. and Lock, A. (eds) (1981) *Indigenous psychologies*, Academic Press, London.

Henige, D. P. (1974) *The chronology of oral tradition*, Clarendon Press, Oxford.

Henry, T. (1928) 'Ancient Tahiti', *Bernice P Bishop Museum Bulletin*, 48.

Herbert, D. (1972) *Urban geography*, David & Charles, Newton Abbot.

Hochstetter, F. (1867) *New Zealand, its physical geography, geology and natural history*, Stuttgart.

Hodgart, M. J. C. (1950) *The ballads*, Hutchinson, London.

Hollis, M. and Lukes, S. (eds) (1982) *Rationality and relativism*, Blackwell, Oxford.

Holmes, L. D. (1969) 'Samoan oratory', *Journal of American Folklore*, 82.

Horton, R. (1963) 'The Kalabari *Ekine* society: a borderland of religion and art', *Africa*, 33.

Horton, R. (1967) 'African traditional thought and western science', *Africa*, 37.

Horton, R. and Finnegan, R. (eds) (1973) *Modes of thought: essays on thinking in western and non-western societies*, Faber, London.

Housman, J. E. (ed.) (1952) *British popular ballads*, Harrap, London.

Hughes, H. G. A. (1957) 'Origin of the Ruoia and the Kainikam'aen', *Journal of the Polynesian Society*, 66.

Hymes, D. (1964) (ed.) *Language in culture and society*, Harper & Row, New York.

Hymes, D. (1981) *'In vain I tried to tell you': essays in native American ethnopoetics*, University of Pennsylvania Press, Philadelphia.

Innes, G. (1973) 'Stability and change in griots' narrations', *African Language Studies*, 14.

Innis, H. A. (1950) *Empire and communications*, Clarendon Press, Oxford; revised edition (1972) University of Toronto Press, Toronto and Buffalo.

Innis, H. A. (1964) *The bias of communication*, University of Toronto Press, Toronto and Buffalo.

Jahn, J. (1961) *Muntu: an outline of neo-African culture* (English translation), Faber, London.

Jarrett, D. (1982) *The electronic office: a management guide to the office of the future*, Gower with Philips Business Systems, Aldershot.

Jeffries, C. (1967) *Illiteracy: a world problem*, Pall Mall, London.

Jochelson, W. (1928) *Peoples of Asiatic Russia*, American Museum of History, New York.

Johnson, J. W. (1974) *Heellooy Heelleellooy: the development of the genre heello in modern Somali poetry*, Indiana University Press, Bloomington.

Johnson-Laird, P. N. and Wason, R. C. (eds) (1977) *Thinking: readings in cognitive science*, Cambridge University Press, Cambridge.

Jones, J. H. (1961) 'Commonplace and memorization in the oral tradition of English and Scottish popular ballads', *Journal of American Folklore*, 74.

188   *References*

Kaeppler, A. L. (1976) 'Dance and the interpretation of Pacific traditional literature', in A. L. Kaeppler and H. A. Nimmo (eds), *Directions in Pacific traditional literature*, Bishop Museum Press, Honolulu.

Kagame, A. (1951) *La poésie dynastique au Rwanda*, Institut Royal Colonial Belge, Brussels.

Kailasapathy, K. (1968) *Tamil heroic poetry*, Clarendon Press, Oxford.

Karoua, Nanimatang (1977) Personal communication.

Kaunda, K. D. (1966) *A humanist in Africa*, Longman, London.

Keddie, N. (ed.) (1973) *Tinker, Tailor . . . the myth of cultural deprivation*, Penguin, Harmondsworth.

Kelly, L. G. (1940) 'Some problems in the study of Maori genealogies', *Journal of the Polynesian Society*, 49.

Kenny, R. W. (1956) *New Zealand journal, 1842–4 of John B Williams*, Peabody Museum, Salem.

King, A. (1984) *The coming information society*, The British Library, London.

Kiparsky, P. (1976) 'Oral poetry: some linguistic and typological considerations', in Stolz and Shannon, 1976.

Kirk, G. S. (ed.) (1964) *The language and background of Homer*, Heffer, Cambridge.

Kirk, G. S. (1965) *Homer and the epic*, Cambridge University Press, London.

Kishibe, S. (1980) 'Japan. I, General', in S. Sadie (ed.), *The new Grove dictionary of music and musicians*, vol. 9, Macmillan, London.

Knott, E. (1957) *Irish classical poetry*, Colm Ó Lochlainn, Dublin.

Kubuabola, S., Seniloli, A. and Vatucawaga, L. (1978) 'Poetry in Fiji: a general introduction', in Finnegan and Pillai, 1978.

Küchler, S. (1987) 'Malangan: art and memory in a Melanesian society', *Man*, n.s., 22.

Labov, W. (1973) 'The logic of non-standard English', in Keddie, 1973.

Landtman, G. (1927) *The Kiwai Papuans of British New Guinea*, Macmillan, London.

Laxton, P. B. (1953) 'A Gilbertese song', *Journal of the Polynesian Society*, 62.

Layard, J. W. (1944) 'Song and dance in Malekula', *Man*, 44.

Leach, MacE. (ed.) (1955) *The ballad book*, Yoseloff, London.

Lerner, D. (1964) *The passing of traditional society. Modernizing the Middle East*, The Free Press, New York.

Levine, K. (1986) *The social context of literacy*, Routledge & Kegan Paul, London.

Lienhardt, G. (1980) 'Self: public and private. Some African representations', *Journal of the Anthropological Society of Oxford*, 11.

Lockridge, K. A. (1974) *Literacy in colonial New England*, Norton, New York.

Loeb, M. E. (1926) 'History and traditions of Niue', *Bernice P Bishop Museum Bulletin*, 32.

Longley, D. and Shain, M. (1985) *Macmillan dictionary of information technology*, Macmillan, London, 2nd edition.

Lord, A. B. (1965) 'Oral poetry', in A. Preminger (ed.), *Encyclopedia of poetry and poetics*, Princeton University Press, Princeton.

Lord, A. B. (1968a) *The singer of tales*, Atheneum, New York (first published 1960).

Lord, A. B. (1968b) 'Homer as an oral poet', *Harvard Studies in Classical Philology*, 72.

Lord, A. B. (1975) 'Perspectives on recent work on oral literature', in Duggan, 1975.
Love, J. (1977) Personal communication.
Luetkemeyer, J., Van Antwerp, C. and Kindell, G. (1984) 'An annotated bibliography of spoken and written language' in Tannen, 1984.
Luomala, K. (1949) 'Maui-of-a-thousand-tricks: his Oceanic and European biographers', *Bernice P Bishop Museum Bulletin*, 198.
Luomala, K. (1950) 'Melanesian mythology', 'Micronesian mythology', 'Polynesian mythology', in M. Leach (ed.), *Funk and Wagnalls standard dictionary of folklore, mythology and legend*, II, Funk & Wagnalls, New York.
Luomala, K. (1955) *Voices on the wind. Polynesian myths and chants*, Bishop Museum Press, Honolulu.
Luria, A. R. (1976) *Cognitive development; its cultural and social foundations* (English translation), Harvard University Press, Cambridge, Mass.
Mabogunje, A. (1968) *Urbanization in Nigeria*, University of London Press, London.
McLean, M. (1964) 'Can Maori chant survive?', *Te Ao Hou*, 47.
McLuhan, M. (1962) *The Gutenberg galaxy: the making of typographic man*, Routledge & Kegan Paul, London.
McLuhan, M. (1967) *Understanding media, the extensions of man*, Sphere Books, London.
McLuhan, M. (1970) *Counterblast*, Rapp & Whiting, London.
McNeill, I. (1963) 'The meter of the Hittite epic', *Journal of Anatolian Studies*, 13.
McQuail, D. (1969) *Towards a sociology of mass communications*, Collier-Macmillan, London.
Maddison, J. (1983) *Education in the microelectronics era*, Open University Press, Milton Keynes.
Maddox, B. (1972) *Beyond Babel. New directions in communication*, André Deutsch, London.
Magoun, F. P. (1953) 'The oral-formulaic character of Ango-Saxon poetry', *Speculum*, 28.
Mbiti, J. S. (1966) *Akamba stories*, Clarendon Press, Oxford.
Meeker, M. E. (1979) *Literature and violence in North Arabia*, Cambridge University Press, Cambridge.
Megarry, J. (1985) *Inside information: computers, communications and people*, BBC, London.
Meggitt, M. (1968) 'Uses of literacy in New Guinea and Melanesia', in Goody, 1968.
Mera, G. (1977) Personal communication.
Merriam, A. P. (1964) *The anthropology of music*, North Western University Press, Evanston.
Mitcalfe, B. (1961) *Poetry of the Maori*, Paul's Book Arcade, Hamilton, Auckland.
Mitcalfe, B. (1974) *Maori poetry. The singing word*, Price Milburn for Victoria University Press, Wellington.
Monberg, T. (1956) 'Ta' aroa in the creation of myths of the Society Islands', *Journal of the Polynesian Society*, 65.
Murray, David (1977) Personal communication.
Newbury, C. W. (1967) 'Te hau pahu rahi; Pomare II and the concept of inter-island government in Eastern Polynesia', *Journal of the Polynesian Society*, 76.

References

Ngata, A. T. (1959) *Nga Moteatea. The songs. Scattered pieces from many canoe areas*, Part 1, Polynesian Society, Wellington; revised edition (1972).

Ngata, A. T. and Hurinui, P. T. (1961, 1970) *Nga Moteatea. The songs. Scattered pieces from many canoe areas*, Parts 2 and 3, Polynesian Society, Wellington.

Nichols, S. G. (1961) *Formulaic diction and thematic composition in the Chanson de Roland*, Studies in the Romance Languages and Literature, 36, University of North Carolina Press, Chapel Hill.

Nketia, K. (1958) 'Akan poetry', *Black Orpheus*, 3.

Norris, H. T. (1968) *Shinqiti folk literature and song*, Clarendon Press, Oxford.

Notopoulos, J. A. (1964) 'Studies in early Greek oral poetry', *Harvard Studies in Classical Philology*, 68.

Okpewho, I. (1983) *Myth in Africa*, Cambridge University Press, Cambridge.

Olson, D. R., Torrance, N. and Hildyard, A. (eds) (1985) *Literacy, language, and learning*, Cambridge University Press, Cambridge.

Ong, W. J. (1967) *The presence of the word*, Yale University Press, New Haven and London.

Ong, W. J. (1971) *Rhetoric, romance, and technology*, Cornell University Press, Ithaca and London.

Ong, W. J. (1974) 'Is literacy passé?', in Potter and Sarre, 1974.

Ong, W. J. (1977) *Interfaces of the word*, Cornell University Press, Ithaca and London.

Ong, W. J. (1982) *Orality and literacy: the technologizing of the word*, Methuen, London and New York.

Opland, J. (1971) '"Scop" and "imbongi" – Anglo-Saxon and Bantu oral poets', *English Studies in Africa*, 14.

Opland, J. (1980) *Anglo-Saxon oral poetry, a study of the traditions*, Yale University Press, New Haven.

Opland, J. (1983) *Xhosa oral poetry: aspects of a black South African tradition*, Cambridge Studies in Oral and Literate Culture, 7, Cambridge University Press, Cambridge.

Opland, J. (1986) 'World epic: on heroic and epic traditions in oral and written literature', in E. S. Shaffer (ed.), *Comparative criticism*, 8, Cambridge University Press, Cambridge.

O'Rahilly, T. F. (1922) 'Irish poets, historians and judges', *Proceedings of the Royal Irish Academy*, 36.

Ottenberg, S. (1959) 'Ibo receptivity to change' in W. R. Bascom and M. J. Herskovits (eds), *Continuity and change in African cultures*, University of Chicago Press, Chicago.

Overing, J. (ed.) (1985) *Reason and morality*, Tavistock, London and New York.

Oxenham, J. (1980) *Literacy: writing, reading and social organization*, Routledge & Kegan Paul, London.

Paredes, A. and Bauman, R. (eds) (1972) *Toward new perspectives in folklore*, American Folklore Society, University of Texas Press, Austin and London.

Parr, C. J. (1963) 'Maori literacy, 1843–1867', *Journal of Polynesian Society*, 72.

Parry, J. (1985) 'The Brahmanical tradition and the technology of the intellect', in Overing, 1985.

Parry, M. and Lord, A. B. (1954) *Serbocroation heroic songs. I, Novi Pazar* (English translations), Harvard University Press and Serbian Academy of Sciences, Cambridge Mass. and Belgrade.

Parsons, T. (1966) *Societies. Evolutionary and comparative perspectives*, Prentice-Hall, Englewood Cliffs.

Parsonson, G. S. (1967) 'The literate revolution in Polynesia', *Journal of Pacific History*, 2.

Phillips, N. (1981) *Sijobang: sung narrative poetry of West Sumatra*, Cambridge Studies in Oral and Literate Culture, 1, Cambridge University Press, Cambridge.

Phillpotts, B. (1931) *Edda and saga*, Thornton Butterworth, London.

Pool, I. de S. (ed.) (1977) *The social impact of the telephone*, MIT Press, Cambridge, Mass.

Pool, I. de S. (1983a) *Forecasting the telephone: a restrospective technology assessment*, Ablex, Norwood, N.J.

Pool, I. de S. (1983b) *Technologies of freedom*, Belknap Press, Cambridge, Mass.

Pospisil, L. (1963) *The Kapauku Papuans of West New Guinea*, Holt, Rinehart & Winston, New York.

Postman, N. (1973) 'The politics of reading', in Keddie, 1973.

Potter, D. and Sarre, P. (eds) (1974) *Dimensions of society: a reader*, University of London Press in association with Open University Press, London.

Pound, L. (1921) *Poetic origins and the ballad*, Macmillan, New York.

Propp, V. (1958) *Morphology of the folktale*, trans. L. Scott, Indiana University Press, Bloomington.

Pukui, M. K. (1949) 'Songs (meles) of Old Ka'u, Hawaii', *Journal of American Folklore*, 62.

Quain, B. H. (1942) *The flight of the chiefs. Epic poetry of Fiji*, Augustin, New York.

Radin, P. (1956) *The trickster, A study in American Indian mythology*, Routledge & Kegan Paul, London.

Radin, P. (1957) *Primitive man as philosopher*, Dover Publications, New York, revised edition.

Radlov, V. V. (1866–1904) *Proben der Volksliteratur der türkischen Stämme und der dsungarischen Steppe*, St Petersburg.

Rasmussen, K. (1931) *The Netsilik Eskimos. Social life and spiritual culture*, Gyldendalske Boghandel, Copenhagen.

Robinson, F. N. (1912) 'Satirists and enchanters in early Irish literature', in *Studies in the history of religion presented to C. H. Toy*, Macmillan, New York.

Rosenberg, B. A. (1970) 'The formulaic quality of spontaneous sermons', *Journal of American Folklore*, 83.

Ross, J. (1959) 'Formulaic composition in Gaelic oral poetry', *Modern Philology*, 57.

Roy, P. and Kapoor, J. M. (1975) *The retention of literacy*, Macmillan, Delhi.

Salmond, A. (1975a) *Hui. A study of Maori ceremonial gatherings*, Reed, Wellington.

Salmond, A. (1975b) 'Mana makes the man: a look at Maori oratory and politics', in Bloch, 1975.

Sapir, E. (1949) *Language. An introduction to the study of speech*, Harcourt, Brace, New York.

192   *References*

Sapir, E. (1960) *Culture, language and personality, selected essays*, University of California Press, Berkeley and Los Angeles.
Schiller, D. (1982) *Telematics and government*, Ablex, Norwood, N.J.
Scholderer, V. (1963) *Johann Gutenberg. The inventor of printing*, British Museum, London.
Scribner, R. W. (1981) *For the sake of simple folk: popular propaganda for the German Reformation*, Cambridge Studies in Oral and Literate Culture, 2, Cambridge University Press, Cambridge.
Scribner, S. and Cole, M. (1981) *The psychology of literacy*, Harvard University Press, Cambridge, Mass. and London.
Scupham, J. (1970) *The revolution in communications*, Holt, Rinehart & Winston, London.
Senghor, L. S. (1961) *Nation et voie africaine du socialisme*, Présence africaine, Paris.
Seniloli, A. (1976) Personal communication.
Seymour-Smith, M. (1986) *Guide to modern world literature*, Macmillan, London, 3rd edition.
Sherzer, J. (1985) 'Tellings, retellings, and tellings within tellings. The structuring and organisation of narrative in Cuna Indian discourse', in Gentili and Paioni, 1985.
Shuman, A. (1986) *Storytelling rights: the uses of oral and written texts by urban adolescents*, Cambridge Studies in Oral and Literate Culture, 11, Cambridge University Press, Cambridge.
Simmons, D. C. (1960) 'Tonal rhyme in Efik poetry', *Anthropological Linguistics*, 2.
Simmons, D. R. (1966) 'The sources of Sir George Grey's *Nga Mahi a Nga Tupuna*', *Journal of the Polynesian Society*, 75.
Singer, C., Holmyard, E. J. and Donaldson, J. M. (eds) (1954, 1958) *A history of technology*, vols 1 and 4, Clarendon Press, Oxford.
Slack, J. D. (1984) 'Surveying the impacts of communication technologies', in B. Dervin and M. J. Voigt (eds), *Progress in communication sciences*, 5, Ablex, Norwood. N.J.
Smith, J. D. (1977) 'The singer or the song. A reassessment of Lord's "oral theory"', *Man*, n.s., 12.
Smith, M. (1979) 'Changing patterns of literacy and literate education among the Vai', paper at Sierra Leone Studies Symposium, Birmingham.
Smith, M. G. (1957) 'The social functions and meaning of Hausa praise-singing', *Africa*, 27.
Sommerville, I. (1983) *Information unlimited: the applications and implications of information technology*, Addison-Wesley, London.
Sorrenson, M. P. K. (1979) *Maori origins and migrations*, Auckland University Press.
Sparkes, J. (1973) 'Telecommunication and urban development' in Open University Course DT201, *Urban development*, Unit 18, The Open University Press, Milton Keynes.
Spinden, H. J. (1933) *Songs of the Tewa: preceded by an essay on American Indian poetry*, The Exposition of Indian Tribal Arts, Inc., New York.
Stolz, B. A. and Shannon, R. S. (eds) (1976) *Oral literature and the formula*, Center for the Coördination of Ancient and Modern Studies, University of Michigan, Ann Arbor.

Street, B. V. (1984) *Literacy in theory and in practice*, Cambridge Studies in Oral and Literate Culture, 9, Cambridge University Press, Cambridge.

Street, B. V. (1986) 'Literacy – comparative perspectives: "autonomous" and "ideological" models of "computer literacy"', in K. S. Gill (ed.), *Artificial intelligence for society*, Wiley, Chichester.

Stubbs, M. (1980) *Language and literacy: the social linguistics of reading and writing*, Routledge & Kegan Paul, London.

Tannen, D. (ed.) (1981) *Analyzing discourse: text and talk*, Georgetown University Round Table on Language and Linguistics, Georgetown University Press, Washington D.C.

Tannen, D. (ed.) (1982) *Spoken and written language: exploring orality and literacy*, Ablex, Norwood, N.J.

Tannen, D. (ed.) (1984) *Coherence in spoken and written discourse*, Ablex, Norwood, N.J.

Taylor, N. M. (ed.) (1966) *The journal of Ensign Best, 1837–1843*, Government Printer, Wellington.

Tedlock, D. (1977) 'Toward an oral poetics', *New Literary History*, 8.

Tedlock, D. (1983) *The spoken word and the work of interpretation*, University of Pennsylvania Press, Philadelphia.

Tedlock, D. (1985) 'Phonography and the problem of time in oral narrative events', in Gentili and Paioni, 1985.

Thurnwald, R. C. (1936) 'Profane Literature in Buin, Solomon Islands', *Yale Publications in Anthropology*, 8.

Tokumaru Yosihiko and Yamaguti Osamu (eds) (1986), *The oral and the literate in music*, Academia Music, Tokyo.

Tongia, M. (1976–7) Personal communications.

Tongia, M. (1977) 'Rarotonga songs and their functions', unpublished research paper (SE300), University of the South Pacific, Suua.

Tongia, M. (1978) 'Cook Islands songs and their functions', in Finnegan and Pillai, 1978.

Trask, W. R. (1969) *The unwritten song. Poetry of the primitive and traditional peoples of the world*, 2 vols, Jonathan Cape, London.

Treitler, L. (1986) 'Orality and literacy in transmission of medieval European music', paper at International Council of Traditional Music Conference, 'The oral and literate in music', Tokyo, published in Tokumaru and Yamaguti, 1986.

Trenaman, J. and McQuail, D. (1961) *Television and the political image. A study of the impact of television on the 1959 General Election*, Methuen, London.

UNESCO (1966a) *Provisional guide for the evaluation of experimental literacy projects*, Paris.

UNESCO (1966b) *World congress of Ministers of Education on the eradication of illiteracy (Teheran 1965): speeches and messages*, Paris.

UNESCO (1970) *Educational planning: a world survey of problems and prospects*, HMSO, London.

Waldron, R. A. (1957) 'Oral-formulaic technique and Middle English alliterative poetry', *Speculum*, 32.

Wardhaugh, R. (1986) *An introduction to sociolinguistics*, Blackwell, Oxford.

Watts, A. C. (1969) *The lyre and the harp. A comparative reconsideration of oral tradition in Homer and Old English epic poetry*, Yale University Press, New Haven.

Wauthier, C. (1966) *The literature and thought of modern Africa: a survey* (English translation), Pall Mall Press, London.

Weber, M. (1946) *Essays in sociology*, trans. H. H. Gerth and C. W. Mills, Oxford University Press, New York.

Weber, M. (1958) *The rational and social foundations of music* (English translation), Southern Illinois University Press, Carbondale.

Weber, M. (1962) *The Protestant ethic and the spirit of capitalism*, Allen & Unwin, London.

Weber, M. (1964) *The theory of social and economic organization*, Free Press, New York.

Weizenbaum, J. (1984) *Computer power and human reason*, Penguin, Harmondsworth.

Wells, H. G. (1946) *A short history of the world*, revised edition, Penguin, Harmondsworth.

Westermann, D. and Bryan, M. A. (1952) *Languages of West Africa*, International African Institute and Oxford University Press, London.

Whallon, W. (1969) *Formula, character and context. Studies in Homeric, Old English, and Old Testament poetry*, Harvard University Press, Cambridge, Mass.

Wheeler, G. C. (1926) *Mono-Alu Folklore (Bougainville Strait, Western Solomon Islands)*, Routledge and Sons, London.

Whiteman, M. F. (ed.) (1981) *Variation in writing*, Erlbaum, Hillsdale, N.J.

Winks, R. W. (1953) 'The doctrine of Hau-Hauism', *Journal of the Polynesian Society*, 62.

Xavier, Sister Frances (1976) 'Dancing and singing in the Gilbert Islands', *Mana Review*, 1.

Zorkoczy, P. (1985) *Information technology: an introduction*, Pitman, London, 2nd edition.

Index

Index by Barbara Hird